WRONG

WRONG

*Nine Economic Policy Disasters
and What We Can Learn
from Them*

Richard S. Grossman

OXFORD
UNIVERSITY PRESS

OXFORD
UNIVERSITY PRESS

Oxford University Press is a department of the University of Oxford.
It furthers the University's objective of excellence in research, scholarship,
and education by publishing worldwide.

Oxford   New York
Auckland   Cape Town   Dar es Salaam   Hong Kong   Karachi
Kuala Lumpur   Madrid   Melbourne   Mexico City   Nairobi
New Delhi   Shanghai   Taipei   Toronto

With offices in
Argentina   Austria   Brazil   Chile   Czech Republic   France   Greece
Guatemala   Hungary   Italy   Japan   Poland   Portugal   Singapore
South Korea   Switzerland   Thailand   Turkey   Ukraine   Vietnam

Oxford is a registered trademark of Oxford University Press
in the UK and certain other countries.

Published in the United States of America by
Oxford University Press
198 Madison Avenue, New York, NY 10016

Library of Congress Cataloging-in-Publication Data
Grossman, Richard S.
Wrong : nine economic policy disasters and what we can learn from them /
Richard S. Grossman.
p. cm.
Includes bibliographical references and index.
ISBN 978–0–19–932219–0 (alk. paper)
1. Financial crises—Case studies.   2. Economic policy—Case studies.   I. Title.
HB3722.G76 2013
339.509′04—dc23

1 3 5 7 9 8 6 4 2
Printed in the United States of America
on acid-free paper

For Ruth, with love

Du, meine Freundin, mein Zuhaus,

Mein Weg zurück, mein Blick voraus,

Mein Jetzt, mein Damals, mein Inzwischen.

Mein Aufbruch, meine Wiederkehr,

Du, mein Wohin und mein Woher...

Reinhard Mey

The problem with any ideology is it gives the answer before you look at the evidence. So you have to mold the evidence to get the answer that you've already decided that you've got to have. It doesn't work that way.

BILL CLINTON, *September 20, 2012*

CONTENTS

PREFACE

This book is about failure. Specifically, it is about economic policy mistakes which, combined with bad luck, led to some pretty awful outcomes: a lost decade that humbled an economic superpower; an economic depression that was the worst the industrialized world has ever seen; and a devastating famine that led to emigration, misery, and death. Not exactly a tour through history's lighter moments.

Given the depressing subject matter, a reader might conclude that the author is obsessed with bad choices and bad luck—in short, failure. Nothing could be further from the truth. While writing this book, colleagues, friends, and family have served as a constant reminder of the very good fortune that I enjoy every day. I am grateful to Jorge Arroyo, Teo Dagi, Barry Eichengreen, Jeff Frieden, Ruth Grossman, Tim Guinnane, Masami Imai, and several anonymous referees for their helpful comments on the manuscript. They bear no responsibility for the mistakes that no doubt remain.

I thank the Federal Reserve Bank of New York for permission to quote from the Benjamin Strong papers and the UK Public Records Office for access to Crown copyright materials cited in this book. I offer an especially heartfelt thanks to Reinhard Mey for permission to quote his lyrics in the dedication.

I am grateful to my agent, Peter Bernstein, for his wise counsel on many aspects of this book. I thank my editors at Oxford University Press, Terry Vaughn and Scott Parris, for their enthusiasm and patience, and their editorial assistant, Cathryn Vaulman, for insuring that *WRONG* turned out right. I am grateful to copy editor Ginny Faber and production editor Kendra Millis for the care they took with the manuscript, and to Maria Coughlin for creating the index.

Our children Dina, Joshua, Yonatan, and Yael are truly the four best pieces of good fortune in our lives. They are kind, loving, and curious. Being able to watch them grow is life's greatest privilege.

If there is the opposite of a mistake in my life, my wife Ruth is it. Her love and support mean everything: ואת עלית על כלנה

Newton Centre, Massachusetts
April 2013

PROLOGUE

[T]he ideas of economists and political philosophers, both when they are right and when they are wrong, are more powerful than is commonly understood. Indeed, the world is ruled by little else. Practical men, who believe themselves to be quite exempt from any intellectual influences, are usually the slaves of some defunct economist.

JOHN MAYNARD KEYNES
The General Theory

In the early hours of September 15, 2008, Lehman Brothers filed for bankruptcy. The 158-year-old company was one of Wall Street's oldest and most distinguished firms—and one of its most important. At the time that it failed, Lehman had more than 25,000 employees around the world and was the fourth-largest investment bank in the United States. With some $600 billion in assets and more than $1 trillion in liabilities, it was America's largest bankruptcy ever.

The failure of Lehman Brothers was a turning point in the subprime crisis. Following Lehman's collapse, virtually every aspect of America's already existing financial and housing market troubles intensified. Stock prices tumbled: the Dow Jones Industrial Average fell by 4.4 percent on the day Lehman filed for bankruptcy; within

six months, stocks had fallen by 40 percent. The failure accelerated the ongoing downturn in the housing market. Mortgage
defaults and delinquencies increased dramatically and the value of
mortgage-backed securities plummeted in the weeks following the
failure. The day after Lehman's bankruptcy, the Federal Reserve
opened an $85 billion credit on behalf of insurance giant American
International Group (AIG), which had insured a large amount of
these mortgage-backed securities, allowing AIG to avoid Lehman's
fate. Less than three weeks later, President George W. Bush signed
legislation establishing the Troubled Asset Relief Program (TARP),
which authorized the Treasury to buy or insure up to $700 billion of
these now-toxic mortgage-backed securities in hopes of preventing
a full-scale meltdown of the financial system.

The effect on the broader economy was similarly severe. The
unemployment rate, which had been just above 6 percent before the
Lehman failure, rose continuously during the subsequent months,
reaching 10 percent in October 2009. Bank failures and bankruptcy
filings continued their upward march. And, six weeks after the
Lehman failure, the National Bureau of Economic Research con-
firmed what everyone already knew by declaring that the US economy was in recession. The disastrous state of the economy in the
months following the Lehman collapse led policy makers, journalists, and academics alike to label the crisis "the worst since the Great
Depression."

One year and 5000 miles removed from the Lehman disaster,
another financial crisis was brewing. Shortly following the country's
October 2009 election, Greece's new finance minister announced
that the previous government's estimate of the budget deficit—at
6.7 percent of gross domestic product (GDP), already quite large by
developed-country standards—had been severely understated. The
new estimate was a staggering 12.7 percent of GDP. Some portion
of the deficit can be blamed on the economic slowdown that followed the American subprime meltdown; however, a much larger
share was due to irresponsible fiscal management. The previous

government had increased spending and reduced tax collections to curry favor with voters in the run-up to elections for the European and then the national parliament, while tax evasion—always popular in Greece—had become even more rampant than usual.

When the magnitude of the country's fiscal problems became widely known, creditors began to doubt Greece's ability to make payments on its dangerously large public debt. Because of these fears, Greece's credit rating was downgraded to the lowest level of any eurozone country. Further, the Greek government found it necessary to pay investors who *were* prepared to buy their debt increasingly high interest rates to compensate them for the now all-too-real possibility that Greece would default. The yield on Greek 10-year bonds, which had been in the 4 percent to 6 percent range throughout 2009, exceeded 10 percent at the end of October 2010, 20 percent in the autumn of 2011, and was briefly above 35 percent in March 2012. By contrast, the yield on 10-year bonds issued by the more fiscally responsible German government rarely topped 3.5 percent, and was frequently much lower, during 2009–2012.

With bankruptcy looming, the Greek government approached other European Union (EU) governments and the International Monetary Fund (IMF) in search of loans to pay off their maturing debt. Because Greece had adopted the euro a decade earlier—which had made it easier for them to borrow from foreigners who might have been nervous about being repaid in Greek drachma—the government did not have the option of printing more money to pay off the debt. The Greeks needed more than 100 million euros—and soon—to stave off default. The EU and the IMF agreed to lend Greece the money, but the loans came with strings. Greece would have to cut government spending dramatically, laying off public sector employees, cutting subsidies, and privatizing state-owned companies. The combined effect of these cuts was an intensification of the economic downturn already underway and an overall contraction of the Greek economy. The unemployment rate exceeded 25 percent by the summer of 2012. The political situation was no more stable.

Parliamentary elections held in May 2012 left no party capable of forming a government, making a second set of elections necessary six weeks later. A consequence of Greece's economic and political instability was that in both elections candidates from a neo-Nazi party—never before successful in a Greek election—found themselves seated in parliament.

Suspicion soon fell upon other highly indebted European countries, notably Ireland, Italy, Portugal, and Spain, later to be joined by Cyprus. As in Greece, the adoption of the euro had made borrowing abroad easier for these countries: prospective lenders had been emboldened to lend since they would be repaid in what was expected would be a relatively stable euro, rather than the shakier Irish pound, Italian lira, Portuguese escudo, or Spanish peseta. Like the United States, Ireland and Spain experienced property booms following 2000. As real estate prices rose, financial institutions extended ever-increasing amounts of credit to finance purchases. When the property booms collapsed, many borrowers found themselves owners of real estate worth only a fraction of what they had paid—and borrowed to pay—for it. Portugal and Italy grew slowly during the decade, but spent money and piled up private and government debt so rapidly that serious doubts emerged about their ability to repay. With no signs of high consumption slowing in Portugal or of Italy reforming its hopelessly inefficient government institutions, investors became nervous about the sustainability of Portuguese and Italian debts and, more importantly, the prospects for repayment.

As the debt problem grew, European leaders and the IMF struggled to find both a consensus and adequate rescue funds. Bailouts were patched together in a series of all-night summit meetings. The global economic slowdown, however, combined with the fiscal austerity prescribed in an effort to cut debt burdens, reduced governments' ability to attack the recession with expansionary fiscal policy. And although membership in the euro had allowed countries easier access to foreign lending, it also prevented them from pursuing expansionary monetary policy and devaluation as an avenue toward recovery. As of the time of this writing, there is no easy solution to Europe's woes on the horizon, nor any expectation that the continent is likely to return to robust economic growth anytime soon.

The subprime and European sovereign debt crises described above are two of the most difficult economic challenges faced by the industrialized world during the past hundred years. These episodes have several elements in common. They both came about when overindebted economies became unable to service their obligations in the face of declining economic growth. Both crises took off following landmark events—the Lehman failure and revelations about Greek finances—that shook the confidence of the markets. And both crises were due, in large part, to irresponsible actions by governments and the private sector.

Most importantly, both crises were the result of bad economic policy. And not just minor errors in implementing sound economic strategies during the weeks and months leading up to the crises, but seriously deficient economic policies that had been pursued for years. Furthermore, these policy mistakes had a crucial element in common: they were based on ideology rather than sound economic analysis.

What does it mean to say that policy is based on ideology? Ideologically based policy comes about when decision makers grab hold of a key idea and use it as their one and only guide to economic policy. The idea might, in fact, be a good one but perhaps not appropriate under all circumstances. Consider the free market. The second half of the twentieth century provides ample evidence that the free market economies of the West did a far better job of providing consumer goods and services to their publics than the centrally planned economies of the old Soviet bloc. Believing in the superiority of the free market, however, does not mean that the state should never intervene in the market. If there is only one producer of a particular good or service—a monopoly—public welfare can be improved by government intervention. If consumers do not have access to accurate information about the products they buy, government-mandated labeling can improve economic efficiency. And in highly complex markets with trillions of dollars at stake—such as the derivatives markets that were at the heart of the subprime crisis—a commitment to completely free markets is madness. Thus, a slavish devotion to the idea of "free markets," can take a sensible idea and turn it into a policy nightmare.

It is also possible that the key idea at the center of an ideologically driven policy may have been reasonable at some point in the past, but has outlived its usefulness. For example, price controls and rationing might make sense in time of war to ensure that resources are available for war-related production and that during a period of national emergency wartime stringencies are shared by all sectors of society. During peacetime, however, such restrictive measures will retard economic development. The gold standard, to mention another example, worked well during the late nineteenth and early twentieth centuries but was an unmitigated disaster during the years between the two world wars. Not knowing when to abandon a familiar—even comfortable—conventional wisdom after it has become an outdated policy idea can buy a one-way ticket to economic disaster.

Finally, policy makers' key idea it might be something that isn't sensible at all but makes a good election slogan. The best example of this in recent years is the long line of American politicians who have pledged not to raise taxes. Under any circumstances. Not now. Or ever. Politicians—and economists—certainly can differ over their preferred level of taxation. Some might favor higher taxes so that the government can spend more to provide things like infrastructure and education; others might argue that lower taxes do a better job of encouraging private savings and investment. Both of these are legitimate points of view. However, any politician who signs a pledge—as all but a handful of the Republican members of the 112th Congress did—to oppose tax increases under any and all circumstances is no longer a serious policy maker, but an ideologue. And ideologues, as we will see throughout this book, are hazardous to our economic health.

Although the fallout from the subprime crisis was unusually severe, its origins were far from unique. In fact, the subprime crisis followed a boom-bust pattern that has been a common feature of financial crises for more than 200 years. Boom-bust crises occur when business cycles—the periodic, normally moderate swings in economic activity—become exaggerated, leading to an excessive economic expansion followed by a dramatic collapse. During the boom phase of the cycle, profit opportunities rise, giving firms and individuals incentives to borrow money to pour into new ventures. After all, if you can invest $100 of your own savings and earn a profit of $50, why shouldn't you borrow $1000 to invest and earn $500? Following a period of heightened investment activity, returns will begin to fall, and firms and individuals may find themselves with debts that exceed the returns from the previously profitable investments. This lands them—and those who loaned them money— in trouble, exacerbating the downturn. This is the bust phase of the cycle.

The economic boom that preceded the subprime crisis was fueled by wrongheaded economic policy, in particular fiscal and monetary expansion. Fiscal expansion came in the form of three tax cuts enacted during the first three years of the administration of President George W Bush. Accepting the nomination for president at the Republican's 2000 convention in Philadelphia, Bush made it clear that the budget surplus built up during the Clinton years should be returned to the people as a matter of principle, saying to enormous applause: "The surplus is not the government's money; the surplus is the people's money." The federal government had run deficits for 30 consecutive years before it achieved a balanced budget in the late 1990s; nonetheless, the notion of maintaining a small government surplus in case of emergency was taboo in Bush's ideology. The fiscal stimulus was further strengthened by increased government spending on overseas wars in Afghanistan and Iraq. On principle—or, was it for the sake of ideology?—the Administration gave no consideration to repealing any part of the previous tax cuts to pay for these wars.

The second major impetus for the boom came from expansionary monetary policy adopted by Alan Greenspan and his colleagues at the Federal Reserve from 2001 through 2004. Greenspan, an avowedly pro-free-market Republican who had chaired Gerald Ford's Council of Economic Advisors in the 1970s, had encouraged austerity under Democrat Bill Clinton but was an early supporter of Bush's call for tax reduction. Despite standard rule-of-thumb policy models that prescribed monetary tightening, Greenspan maintained expansionary monetary policy for a longer period than was advisable. It is unclear whether this expansionary monetary stance was an attempt to bring down unemployment or to offer a political boost to President Bush in the months before his reelection campaign; nonetheless, monetary policy remained looser than purely economic reasoning would have mandated.

The European sovereign debt crisis was similarly the result of a poorly conceived economic policy choice made for a distinctly ideological reason: the adoption of the euro. The euro came into existence as an accounting unit in 1999 and as currency notes and coins in 2002; however, the drive to establish a single European currency as a way of cementing European unity was much older. Given Europe's long history of warfare, particularly the two world wars, increasing the economic interdependence of European countries was—and is—an appealing prospect. Nonetheless, hardheaded economic analysis indicated that establishing a single currency for countries as diverse as Greece and Germany, Spain and Finland, and Portugal and the Netherlands could pose insurmountable problems. It is difficult to imagine a situation in which identical monetary policies, the only option under a monetary union, would be appropriate for all these countries. Further, in the absence of a single currency, an uncompetitive, highly indebted country such as Greece could have printed more money and devalued the drachma in order to increase exports and repay its debt with cheaper currency. Because of the overriding ideological goal of European unity, the more pragmatic problems of the single currency were swept under the rug.

This book considers nine of the worst economic policy mistakes of the past 200 years. The results of these mistakes have ranged from appalling to tragic. America's fear of centralized monetary authority caused it to reject two central banks, condemning the United States to three-quarters of a century punctuated by frequent financial crises. Britain's commitment to free markets, rather than to assisting the starving in Ireland, led to one of the nineteenth century's worst humanitarian tragedies, the Irish famine. Britain's re-establishment of the gold standard after World War I, fueled by a desire to recapture its prewar economic and military preeminence, helped to turn what would otherwise have been an ordinary recession into the Great Depression, the most severe economic crisis the industrial world has ever known. And a variety of ideologically based policies resulted in the American subprime crisis and European sovereign debt crisis.

These policy mistakes led to some of the worst economic disasters on record. It would be an oversimplification to say that each and every crisis discussed in the following pages had just one cause, and in each and every case that cause was an ideologically based economic policy. Many factors contributed to the poor policy choices and bad economic outcomes including, on some occasions, bad luck. Nonetheless, in the cases considered in the chapters that follow, the main culprits were policy makers who were guided by ideology rather than economics.

WRONG

Chapter 1

Introduction

This is the excellent foppery of the world, that when we are sick in
fortune—often the surfeit of our own behavior—we make guilty
of our disasters the sun, the moon, and the stars, as if we were
villains on necessity, fools by heavenly compulsion, knaves, thieves,
and treachers by spherical pre-dominance; drunkards, liars, and
adulterers by an enforc'd obedience of planetary influence; and all
that we are evil in, by a divine thrusting on.

KING LEAR (I, ii)

This book is about economic policy. Bad economic policy. Really bad
economic policy. More than two centuries of it. Specifically, it examines nine of the worst economic policy mistakes made during the
last 200 years.

Why write about *bad* economic policy? Surely *good* policy makes
more enlightening, not to mention more uplifting, reading. As
someone who has made a career out of writing about contemporary
and historical financial crises, I am periodically accused by my colleagues of being the economist's answer to an ambulance chaser: a
ghoulish soul who profits from the misfortunes of others. I prefer to
think of the study of panics, crises, and other economic disasters in
therapeutic terms. Hospitals large and small routinely conduct morbidity and mortality conferences in order to understand bad medical and surgical outcomes and to learn from their mistakes. This is
something that students of public policy *should* do; however, a survey of the curricula of a half dozen leading American public policy
schools suggests that they do not. Another good medical analogy is

1

pathology, where the profession's motto is variously given as "the living learn from the dead" or "the dead teach the living." Until our policy makers start to carry malpractice insurance that will compensate *us* for *their* mistakes, we need to understand historical policy blunders to avoid repeating them.

A second reason for focusing on policy mistakes is that they may be easier to spot than policy successes. During the past two centuries, the developed countries—the focus of this book—have grown consistently more prosperous: real gross domestic product (the total value of goods and services produced) per capita in these countries—a rough gauge of the average standard of living—has risen in 70 percent to 80 percent of the years for which data are available. Although countries may grow wealthy in the absence of good policy or less wealthy without the detrimental effects of bad policy, given the long-term upward trend in prosperity, the negative effects of bad policy are more likely to stand out than the positive effects of good policy.

Third, bad policy presents an opportunity to examine economic policy making under a microscope. Is bad policy the result of a flawed policy-making process? Does it occur because the political system, including the electorate, fails to weed out poor policy makers and promote good ones? Does it arise from a commitment to an outdated or somehow mistaken economic ideology? Or does it occur when individuals or groups are somehow able steer the policy-making process toward their private interests, which may come at the expense of the public good?

Finally, and here I might admit to being guilty of the ambulance-chaser charge, bad policy is fascinating. Some people slow down to watch accidents on the highway. Other people like to watch fires consume buildings. I immerse myself in the details of past episodes of failed economic policy. Perhaps this is a character flaw. Like someone having a bad dream, as I see the policy unfold I want to intervene: to shout something about lowering tariffs when they are being mistakenly raised; to urge the adoption of more sensible monetary, fiscal, or regulatory policies when the policy makers are headed in the wrong direction. Of course, just like in a bad dream, I can't affect the outcome because the episodes discussed here have already taken place. But perhaps this morbid fascination with rehashing old policy mistakes will come in handy when we find ourselves in similar situations in the future.

As long as the book focuses on bad policy, why include historical examples of poor economic policy? Surely the modern world provides enough examples of botched economic policy. Consider the recent subprime crisis, skyrocketing costs of education and health care, absence of a coherent energy strategy, and lack of effective environmental policies, just to name a few. Further, since government influence over the economy has become markedly larger in the years since World War II, modern economic policy mistakes must be even more costly—and therefore more worthy of study—than those of earlier eras.

Although several of the chapters that follow *do* focus on more recent episodes of bad policy, this book has an unabashedly historical outlook. There are two reasons for this. First, history provides a valuable perspective. Given enough chronological distance we can make educated judgments about the long-term consequences of a particular mistake in ways we cannot for more recent episodes. For example, it is much harder to discern the long-term consequences of the subprime crisis, which are still unfolding, than those of the financial crisis of 1907. This is not to say that the 1907 crisis is an open book to modern scholars: even today there are aspects of this episode that are not completely understood. Nonetheless, despite the relatively poor quality of the economic data from the early twentieth century, many of the long-term consequences of the crisis—for example, the establishment of the Federal Reserve System—are clear with the benefit of hindsight. At the time of this writing, the long-term consequences of the subprime crisis are still shrouded in mystery and are likely to remain so for some time.

Second, having spent the past 20 years writing and teaching about the economic history of the developed world, I am firmly convinced that there are few economic phenomena—either good or bad—that are wholly new. Take financial crises. The subprime crisis that marked the end of the first decade of the twenty-first century was in many ways a replica of the boom-bust crises that have plagued the developed world for the past two centuries. This pattern was already more than a half-century old over 150 years ago, when the British financial journalist D. Morier Evans observed:

> Within the last sixty years, at comparatively short intervals, the commercial world has been disturbed by a succession of those terrible convulsions that are now but too familiar to every ear by the expressive name "panic." Each separate panic has its own distinctive features, but all have resembled each other in occurring immediately after a period of apparent prosperity, the hollowness of which it has exposed. So uniform is this sequence, that whenever we find ourselves under circumstances that enable the acquisition of rapid fortunes, otherwise than by the road of plodding industry, we may almost be justified in arguing that the time for panic is at hand.

Certainly, the subprime crisis introduced some new elements and terminology, including collateralized debt obligations, credit default swaps, and a whole alphabet soup of derivative securities. These new—and ultimately dangerous—financial instruments had their antecedents in earlier crises as investors were similarly carried away on waves of enthusiasm over assets as diverse as real estate, railroad stocks, agricultural commodities, shares of limited liability companies, and Latin American debt securities. Fundamentally, however, the combination of an overindebted economy with a boom-bust economic cycle was as surely responsible for the subprime crisis as it was for countless others financial crises during the nineteenth and twentieth centuries.

None of the above is meant to suggest that our present—not to mention future—economic ups and down are merely reruns of the past over which policy makers have no control. Although current economic developments frequently resemble those of earlier eras, the predictive power of history is dubious at best. Nobel laureate Paul Samuelson famously derided the usefulness of stock prices as a tool for economic forecasting by saying that they have "correctly predicted nine out of the last five recessions." Each generation of policy makers confronts its own problems and has an opportunity to make policy anew. There are no forces—sinister or otherwise—that force us to repeat the same mistakes. Nonetheless, policy makers are often faced with dilemmas similar to those of their predecessors: weighing the benefits of international economic cooperation against domestic demands for more isolationist policies; balancing the benefits of tighter regulation to protect consumers with those of a looser regulatory stance that might benefit business and promote economic growth. And the incentives guiding the choices faced by policy makers today are frequently similar to those that faced their predecessors. Mark Twain's observation "History doesn't repeat itself, but it does rhyme" is particularly apt in this context.

The central conclusion of this book is that economic policy should be based on cold, hard economic analysis, rather than a commitment to a particular ideology. Ideologies become entrenched among policy makers for a variety of reasons. Sometimes it is the result of long-established practice combined with old-fashioned laziness. If it has "always been done this way," policy makers may be disinclined to go out on a limb to challenge conventional wisdom. Even if a particular ideology has served the public well, changing circumstances may render the old ways of doing business obsolete. Other times, ideologically based policy is implemented because policy makers—and perhaps the public that directly or indirectly chooses them—are true believers with an unwavering devotion to a particular idea. The episodes discussed here demonstrate that economic policy should never be subservient to ideology.

Another common thread among the policy mistakes examined here is the outsized, and often harmful, influence of "private" interests. Although policy makers are supposed to—and often do—operate with the best interests of the public at heart, many groups within the economy have interests that are not aligned with those of the public. Particular regions or industry groups frequently have a great deal to gain (or lose) from government policy, which gives them a strong incentive to lobby for policies that are favorable to their interests and against those that are harmful to them. Lobbying the government to enact favorable policies is, of course, an important right in democratic countries. However, when lobbying unduly influences the course of economic policy, the public interest may suffer. Hence, another important conclusion is that the policy-making process should be as transparent as possible, so that a vigilant citizenry can help prevent private interests from overwhelming the public interest.

Several of the policy blunders considered here resulted from what can be termed "nationalistic interest." If private interests involve shifting policy in favor of a few vocal, or otherwise influential actors, then the nationalistic interest involves shifting costs from the domestic population onto foreigners. Nationalistically inclined policies, such as imposing tariffs on foreign goods, may well be popular with the electorate and may even generate some benefits for the domestic economy in the short-run. In the longer run, however, they are likely to be costly.

A final important conclusion is that delay is costly. The policy mistakes discussed here were frequently compounded by excessive delays—either in the implementation of a beneficial policy or, more often, in the reversal of a policy mistake. No one, especially politicians, likes to admit that they have made a mistake. And nothing shouts "I made a mistake" quite as loudly as trying to reverse a policy that you previously championed. Nonetheless, the inability to recognize and reverse poor policy choices in a timely manner has been a major source of the policy disasters considered in this book.

The main part of this book consists of nine chapters, each of which tells the story of a significant economic policy blunder, including why the policy was adopted, how it was implemented, and its short- and long-term consequences. The episodes examined are diverse, both in terms of the types of policies and the eras in which they occurred. I focus on economically advanced countries because less developed countries have their own specialized set of problems and a subfield of economics, development economics, devoted to them. Chronologically, the chapters cover the period from the later 1700s until the present day. Given this great span of both time and space, it is reasonable to ask how suitable policy failures were chosen. After all, historical and contemporary eras present many examples of poor economic policy. How was it possible to narrow down the choices?

Before choosing policy failures, it makes sense to construct a working definition of economic policy. This is more difficult than it might appear.

On the one hand, a definition might seem obvious. Economic policy is implemented any time the government spends money, assesses taxes, alters interest rates, or adjusts regulations that affect how firms conduct business or change how individuals manage their spending patterns. A broader definition might include political corruption, in which government officials use the economic levers of the state to enrich themselves at the cost of the taxpayer. It might also include diplomatic and military policies, which have been intertwined with economic objectives for centuries. The decision to go to war, for example, has often been motivated by the desire to acquire territory or other resources. And since war is certainly one of mankind's most destructive activities, it would be easy to compile a catalog of wars and other conflicts that have imposed huge costs on society with little or no offsetting improvement in public welfare. That definition seems too broad, however, and so this book adopts a narrower focus, considering only policies that were distinctly economic, and were construed to be so at the time. Hence, war and political corruption are excluded from the book's coverage.

Even the narrower definition raises difficult questions. Must economic policy be the result of legislation? Clearly not, since a great many—perhaps the majority—of economic policies are set by administrators acting in accord with general principles laid down by legislatures, rather than by statute. Central bankers undertake important economic policy on a daily basis without direct input from lawmakers. Courts may rule particular aspects of regulation unconstitutional. A national executive may be empowered to raise or lower tariffs in response to actions by other countries without requiring specific legislation.

Despite the fact that the preponderance of economic policies emanate from administrative bodies rather than legislatures, this book will emphasize legislation-based policy. The main reason for this is that laws are more easily identifiable—both contemporaneously and in hindsight—than policies carried out by administrators. Administratively set policies are likely to be incremental and less dramatic, adopted with less fanfare, and more easily and quietly reversed than those enacted by legislatures. Consider monetary policy. Before World War II, most central banks were private institutions, operating largely behind the scenes. This trend has changed in recent years, however. The president of the European Central Bank and, more recently, the chairman of the Federal Reserve routinely hold press conferences after important policy meetings, an innovation that would have been unthinkable a generation ago. The chapters that follow will not completely ignore administrative policies; however, they will emphasize policies that can be tied to identifiable legislative enactments.

In order to analyze bad policies, we must undertake what economic historians call "counterfactual analysis." Simply put, this means conjuring up a world that never existed, a sort of alternative reality, for comparative purposes. For example, to assess the consequences for North American colonists of being part of the British Empire during the eighteenth century, we need to compare those costs and benefits with the costs and benefits of living outside the empire. But what would living outside the British Empire have entailed? Being part of the French Empire, with all that means for trade relations and economic development, not to mention cuisine? Or the Spanish Empire? Perhaps the appropriate counterfactual is a country that became independent of all empires? In short, we cannot study the consequence of a particular policy without making some calculated guesses about would have happened in the absence of that policy. Counterfactual analysis is a tricky business, however, since analyzing a world that never existed requires a great deal of conjecture.

This book is concerned with sins of commission rather than those of omission. That is, it focuses on the consequences of enacting bad policies rather than those of failing to enact good policies. Can we analyze sins of omission using counterfactual analysis? This exercise is even more fraught with difficulty than analyzing sins of commission because instead of calculating the consequences of *not* doing something that was actually done, we would need to design a policy from scratch and ask what would have happened if that policy *had* been implemented. The problem with this approach is that the policies we design in hindsight might not have been politically or technologically feasible—or even considered—at the time. It is a bit like asking if widespread use of penicillin would have reduced deaths from syphilis in the eighteenth century. The answer is, of course "yes," but since penicillin was not mass produced until the twentieth century, it is not a particularly useful or realistic counterfactual. Similarly, dreaming up more effective economic policies with the benefit of hindsight is easy—rescuing the banking system during the Great Depression, for example—however, if those policies were not under serious consideration at the time, we will not spend time analyzing them. This asks too much of counterfactual analysis.

The use of counterfactual analysis poses a serious challenge, namely, that it is an exercise in Monday-morning quarterbacking. How can we judge policy makers—especially those living in the distant past—when they did not have access to the hindsight, not to mention the theoretical tools and the data available to modern economists? The short answer is that often we cannot. The goal of this book is to explain the origins of poor economic policy choices. Not having the knowledge base sufficient to make better policy choices provides a partial explanation in several cases. In many other cases, however, failures resulted from policy makers' unwillingness or inability to use information that was available to them.

There are many different ways of categorizing economic policy. Economists frequently classify policies by the area of the economy that they affect. Fiscal policy includes government taxing and spending decisions; monetary policy generally consists of central bank intervention to affect interest rates, the money supply, and credit conditions; international policy involves altering tariffs and quotas and managing exchange rates; and regulatory policies include a host of rules that affect everything from consumer protection to the environment to public utilities. These policies are not necessarily completely distinct: monetary and exchange rate policies often have overlapping effects, as do fiscal and monetary policies. This book will touch upon all four of these policy areas.

Another way of classifying economic policies is by their consequences for the economic pie. Economic policies have two main types of consequences. First, they can affect aggregate economic welfare. In simpler terms, they can either make the pie bigger or smaller. Second, they can also affect how the pie is distributed. Some policies benefit the wealthier (or poorer) members of society; others may benefit those who pay interest on home mortgages, or dairy farmers, or oil company executives, or any one of a number of sectors of society. Using this pie analogy, policies fall into four groups: those that affect both the size and distribution of the pie, those that affect neither, those that primarily affect size, and those that primarily affect distribution.

The majority of economic policies have negligible effects on the size and distribution of the pie. Governments throughout the developed world constantly issue rules and regulations on matters great and trivial. The *Federal Register* in the United States and *Official Journal* in the European Union run to thousands of pages every year—and they contain only a fraction of the economic rules and regulations issued by local, regional, national, international, multinational, and supranational authorities in Europe and the United States. Some of these rules have more than trivial consequences for the size of the pie; even more of them have substantial distributional consequences, since any rule or regulation that affects a narrow enough slice of the economy will either help or hurt it relative to other segments. By and large, however, these policies are neither the most controversial nor the most consequential in terms of the pie's size or distribution. For the most part, they are ignored in this book.

The second category consists of policies that have substantial consequences for the size of the pie; the third consists of policies that have consequences for both the size and distribution. Excessively expansionary or contractionary monetary or fiscal policies, for example, may generate large economic fluctuations—booms and busts—in the short-term, making the pie larger at first, then smaller. Other economic policies, such as those governing tariffs, the monetary standard, or regulatory policies, may have profound effects on the size of the pie in the longer run. These policies almost always also have substantial distributional effects too, since short-term macroeconomic fluctuations and sustained changes in long-term economic growth rarely affect all sectors of the economy equally. These policies constitute the main focus of this book.

The fourth category consists of policies that substantially redistribute the pie, even though their effect on the size of the pie is not large. Any time the government taxes or subsidizes a particular economic activity or protects it with tariffs or price supports, there are distributional consequences. And because some sectors of the economy directly benefit from such policies, the beneficiary firms and individuals often lobby or otherwise try to exert influence to protect or extend their privileged position. This type of lobbying is a recurring theme in this book. With the exception of chapter 2, which describes a policy that had a relatively small aggregate but substantial distributional component and contributed to a major event in world history, this book does not focus on these events. Nonetheless, policies with distinct distributional consequences are ever present and a constant source of complaint—typically, but not exclusively, by those whom the policy hurts. Hence, a few words about them are in order.

I had a close personal encounter with such a policy just months into my very first job as a newly trained economist working in a small economic policy group in the Bureau of Economics and Business Affairs within the United States Department of State. I was sent by my boss to attend a meeting of staffers from several divisions within the Economics and Latin American bureaus that had been called because the International Coffee Agreement (ICA), to which the United States was a signatory, was about to expire. Our goal was to secure a last-minute extension to the agreement. The panic I encountered at that first meeting was palpable. The situation was dire. Fortunately, a new kid, armed with a PhD in economics was on the job.

I soon learned that the ICA and the organization it had created, the International Coffee Organization (ICO), operated a little like the Organization of Petroleum Exporting Countries (OPEC). To maintain higher prices, exporting countries limited their production of coffee. Unlike the oil market, however, in which the United States is more than happy to allow domestic firms to buy from non-OPEC member countries, such as Canada, Mexico, and Norway, as well as amounts produced by OPEC countries in violation of their OPEC-imposed production quotas, coffee-consuming countries that were signatories to the ICA agreed not to buy from non-ICA countries and not to buy coffee produced by ICA countries in excess of their production quotas. In other words, the US government was helping to enforce a cartel that raised the price of coffee faced by American consumers. The ICA was OPEC on steroids—or, more accurately, OPEC on caffeine!

The economist in me was outraged. Had I been a coffee drinker, the coffee drinker in me would have been even more outraged. "Why is the United States a member of an organization whose main objective appears to be to stick it to the American coffee consumer?" I asked (I may have used slightly more colorful language). After a stunned silence, I was told that the ICA *had* to be saved because of its vital role in supporting the democratic coffee-exporting nations of Latin America. I pointed out that Cuba and several other non-democratic Latin American nations were also being supported by the ICA and that it would be more cost effective for the government of the United States to just write a check to our friends than to have American coffee drinkers support both friend and foe alike. My arguments fell on deaf ears. I made the same argument at several successive meetings, typically concluding with, "This is a bad agreement. We should let it die." This was my impersonation of Cato the Elder, a senator in ancient Rome who began and ended every speech with the tagline "Carthage must be destroyed." Eventually, I stopped being invited to the taskforce meetings, and the rescue work went ahead at full speed without me. In the end, the ICA was extended. Because negotiators were not able to resolve the sticky issues surrounding the costly quota and price-control features, they were not included in the extension. Sadly, I cannot take any credit for this result.

Any policy involving taxes, tariffs, quotas, subsidies, or similar support for—or discouragement of—an economic activity brings with it what economists call "deadweight loss," which is just another way of saying that it introduces economic inefficiency. For example, if the government imposes a tax on bread, it (1) brings tax revenue into the government, (2) raises the price of bread that consumers face and therefore reduces the amount of bread they buy, and (3) reduces the money that bakers earn on each loaf and therefore the number loaves that can be sold. Thus, the tax unambiguously makes both producers and consumers of bread worse off. Sometimes such dead-weight losses are outweighed by the benefits of discouraging harmful activities or promoting activities that benefit society. If taxing cigarettes reduces the incidence of smoking, particularly among the young, then the reduction in smoking-related diseases such as lung cancer and emphysema may well be worth the deadweight loss imposed by such a tax. Similarly, if a gasoline tax reduces the use of polluting fossil fuels, reduces our dependence on imported oil, and encourages the use of nonpolluting renewable energy sources, the gains to society may well exceed the deadweight loss that this tax imposes.

Although it is possible for taxes and subsidies to bring about societal good, we should not underestimate their aggregate cost—or their potential to encourage mischief. Consider American agriculture. The 2008 farm bill (Public Law 110-246) provided more than $284 billion in financial support to US agriculture in 2008–12, a sizeable amount of money but less than 3 percent of the federal government's annual budget. It could be argued that subsidies to maintain the nation's food supply—particularly when that supply is subject to a host of unpredictable shocks (e.g., weather, pests) that might cause farmers to abandon farming for less risky enterprises—is important for economic and national security reasons. Others might counter that America's vast productive capacity in agriculture renders agricultural support unnecessary. Regardless of the advisability of subsidizing farming, the farm bill resulted in more than a trivial amount of agricultural support money being spent in places that lawmakers probably had not intended. Speaking about the 2008 farm bill, Senator Amy Klobuchar (D-Minnesota) said:

> When you look at what happened in the last few years, there are scandals. There are people that shouldn't have gotten this

[subsidy] money. There's an art collector in San Francisco. There's [a] real estate developer in Florida.

When you look at where the money went, I think there's not a lot of farms in, say, the District of Columbia, where we stand today, Mr. President. $3.1 million in farm payments went to the District of Columbia. $4.2 million has gone to people living in Manhattan. And $1 billion of taxpayer money for farm payments has gone to Beverly Hills 90210. Last time I checked, not a lot of farmland in those areas.

The worst parts of the ICA have passed away, but virtually every economic law, rule, or regulation enacted before or since has had distributional consequences. The important question is not whether distributional consequences exist—they do—but how large are they?

Rather than harp on the economic policy disasters of one time or place, this book looks across a number of regions and eras. Hence, it includes episodes from the three wealthiest and most productive regions of the developed world: the United States, Europe, and Japan. The period covered spans two centuries, including three episodes from each of three epochs: before World War I, the period between the world wars, and since World War II.

The most sparsely populated time period is the pre–World War I period, from which only three events are culled from more than a century of historical experience. In some sense, this period is the hardest to pin down: government policy was not as intrusive as it would later become, and although there were many policy blunders and costly economic collapses, the consequences of the policy failures were typically neither as severe nor widespread as those of later periods. Disasters from this period include Britain's Navigation Acts (chapter 2), the dissolution of the Bank of the United States (chapter 3), and the Irish Famine (chapter 4).

The interwar period is by far the most densely covered period. This is not surprising, since the Great Depression, the key economic event of the interwar period, constituted the greatest economic disaster that the industrialized world has ever known. The Great Recession that followed the collapse of the subprime crisis has inspired commentators all over the world to compare it with the Great Depression, but this more recent episode has been tame by comparison. If you were an American with a bank account before the onset of the Great Depression, there was a one in four chance that your bank would not be there by the Depression's end. The policy failures from the interwar period discussed in this book include the punitive reparations imposed by the allies on Germany after World War I (chapter 5), the British decision to return to the gold standard in 1925 (chapter 6), and the imposition of the Smoot-Hawley tariff by the United States in 1930 (chapter 7).

The post–World War II period is not as short as the interwar period, but includes three policy failures nearly as tightly spaced. It is perhaps not surprising that the modern period would yield a rich vein of economic policy mistakes since government policies have been far more active in peacetime economic affairs than at any other time in modern history. The failures from this period include Japan's lost decade of the 1990s (chapter 8), the subprime crisis (chapter 9), and the euro (chapter 10).

As bad as the policy disasters explored here are, this book does not argue that they were the worst ever to be perpetrated. Nor does it contend that the episodes explored represent all the important types of policy failures. Ultimately, the episodes were chosen because they spanned a number of countries, time periods, and areas of economic policy, because the consequences were severe, and because the stories are worth telling.

It is not the contention of this book that economic policy is bound to fail. Economic policy can be a powerful force for the improvement of mankind's well-being. On the international level, the General Agreement on Tariffs and Trade (and its successor, the World Trade Organization) has encouraged the elimination of trade barriers for more than 60 years and has made an important contribution to world prosperity. Similarly, the World Bank has undertaken projects that have helped to alleviate poverty in the developing world. Neither of these organizations has a perfect record, but both have improved the lives of millions. On the national level, the fiscal stimulus and prompt action by the Federal Reserve following the sub-prime crisis and the social safety net enacted in the aftermath of the Great Depression staved off disaster when the economy was on the verge of a total meltdown. There is plenty to criticize in these programs; however, on balance they have brought enormous benefits. Despite the notable successes of economic policy, it is not the task of this book to bask in our accomplishments. It is instead simply to recount some of our greatest failures and to see if we can learn something from them.

Chapter 2

How to Lose an Empire without Really Trying

British Imperial Policy in North America

From the time they get up in the morning and flush the toilet, they're taxed. When they go get a coffee, they're taxed. When they get in their car, they're taxed. When they go to the gas station, they're taxed. When they go to lunch, they're taxed. This goes on all day long. Tax. Tax. Tax. Tax. Tax.

ARNOLD SCHWARZENEGGER, 2003

Empire building is one of mankind's oldest preoccupations. This is not especially surprising since ruling an empire has several distinct advantages. First, as an empire you get to control more territory and govern more people than you would otherwise; this can give you a military edge over your rivals. Genghis Khan, son of a Mongolian tribal chieftain, and his successors during the thirteenth and fourteenth centuries conquered lands stretching from Europe to the Pacific, ruling an empire that at its height included more than 100 million people. Second, your influence may persist long after your empire has expired, providing a sort of immortality. No better example of this exists than the Roman Empire. According to one writer:

> The enduring Roman influence is reflected pervasively in contemporary language, literature, legal codes, government, architecture, engineering, medicine, sports, arts, etc. Much

of it is so deeply embedded that we barely notice our debt to ancient Rome. Consider language, for example. Fewer and fewer people today claim to know Latin—and yet, go back to the first sentence in this paragraph. If we removed all the words drawn directly from Latin, that sentence would read: "The."

Although history provides many examples of these and other reasons for empire building, no motive is more compelling than the economic one. Historically, imperial spoils were secured via expropriation, taxation, and enslavement, among other techniques. One of the most brutal examples of colonial exploitation was provided by the Belgian King Leopold II, who ruled over the Congo Free State between 1885 and 1908. During Leopold's rule, millions were murdered and maimed in the pursuit of rubber, copper, and other natural resources. Not all colonial regimes were as vicious as Leopold's, of course. Nonetheless, no matter how benign the rule, common sense dictates that in the struggle for economic advantage, the imperial power—as the better-armed party—will win, and the colony will lose.

In matters of economic policy, common sense is not always a reliable guide.

Consider North America. For the four western European powers that made determined efforts to colonize it—Britain, France, Spain, and the Netherlands—North America must have seemed an enormous prize. The land mass of North America was 15 times the size of all four countries combined and nearly 90 times that of Britain alone. The natural resources Europeans encountered were similarly staggering. When Europeans first arrived, there were an estimated 950 million acres of woodland providing an abundance of timber with which to build and furnish houses, keep them warm, and cook food. The soil and climate were conducive to the cultivation of a number of crops, including tobacco and a variety of grains. Rivers and coastal waterways teemed with fish, and the forests and plains were well stocked with animals that could provide both meat and fur. The mineral endowment was similarly great, although its full extent was certainly not known during colonial times. By the outbreak of World War I, the United States was the leading producer of almost every one of the major industrial minerals of that era. In short, North America was well endowed with natural resources, a veritable treasure for whatever colonial power could claim it.

With all this bounty, one would have thought that the colonial powers would have been anxious to transfer as much of it as they could to the home country, leaving the colonists as little as possible. Somehow, the British did not get that memo. During their rule of the colonies that would eventually become the United States of America, British imperial policy—including but not limited to the Navigation Acts—actually placed a very small net burden on the American colonies. True, the British did manage to profit from American natural resources; however, after accounting for the benefits that England provided the colonists—primarily defense, but also subsidies—the net return to the mother country was woefully small. To add insult to injury, Britain's imperial policy, as mild as it was, was perceived as being so detrimental to colonial interests that it fanned the flames of revolution and contributed to the establishment of the United States in 1776. Given the failure of Britain's policy in North America, it is amazing that the sun did not set on the British Empire for another 150 years.

To understand British imperial policy toward North America, we need to say a bit about the prevailing economic ideology of the day—a sort of economic nationalism that has come to be known as "mercantilism." Mercantilism was characterized by a high degree of state intervention in the economy, particularly in international trade, and had its origins in the second half of the Middle Ages (1000–1500 CE). Although the origins of mercantilism are diverse and complicated, two important trends that contributed to it stand out.

The first of these was the fall of the Roman Empire in the year 476 CE, which left the control of much of Europe in the hands of local rulers. Although these feudal lords often owed allegiance to a king, in practice they enjoyed substantial autonomy. In an attempt to consolidate their realms, kings undertook a number of measures aimed at centralizing—and strengthening—their authority and established economic rules to both enrich themselves and solidify their hold on power. Such rules included standardizing weights and measures and limiting trade in certain goods to particular times and places, which made commerce easier to monitor, regulate, and, most importantly, tax. Monarchs eliminated many of the tolls that divided their kingdoms. They also standardized the local coinage. This fostered trade since it reduced the need for buyers and sellers to assess the values of the many different types of coins in circulation. Because the king had a monopoly on producing these coins, anyone who wanted to conduct commerce had to bring their gold and silver to the royal mint. Naturally, the king charged a fee for minting coins, so monetary standardization also earned the crown a tidy profit. Rulers often granted (more precisely, sold) the right to hold a monopoly on certain types of economic activity. In England, such monopolies included gunpowder, salt, pepper, and mineral extraction, among others. Taxes would have been equally effective at raising money; however, collecting taxes was complicated by two factors. First, the king often shared taxing power—and hence tax revenues—with Parliament. Second, taxes were costly to collect—since the revenue also had to be shared with tax collectors—and often easy to avoid. Selling monopolies for a periodic fixed fee was a practical, and more certain, way to augment rulers' wealth and power. Hence, one characteristic of mercantilism was a high degree of state involvement in the economy.

The second trend contributing to the rise of mercantilism was the growth of colonial empires. After the 1450s, the Ottoman Empire's dominance of the trade in the eastern Mediterranean forced European countries to seek trade routes in the Atlantic and, eventually, further afield. This led to the establishment of colonial empires, first by Spain and Portugal, and later by the Netherlands, England, and France. Imperial governments managed these colonies with an eye to extracting raw materials from the colony, promoting domestic manufactures, and enriching the mother country.

Mercantilism was the prevailing economic ideology during the seventeenth and eighteenth centuries. A central pillar of this doctrine was that a nation's wealth and well-being were directly related to its holdings of gold and silver. Hence, government policies were directed toward promoting a surplus in the balance of trade, that is, an excess of exports over imports. Since international payments were made in gold and silver, a trade surplus would generate an inflow of precious metal. Because of this, trade policy often consisted of high tariffs (i.e., taxes on imports), which could exceed— sometimes by a substantial amount—the cost of the imported item, rendering it unattractive to potential consumers.

Imperial governments further required that many trade-related functions, such as shipping, finance, and insurance, be undertaken by agents from the mother country. Among the most common methods of fully exploiting the colonial trade was to establish companies with monopolies over all trade between the mother country and particular colonies or regions. For example, England, France, the Netherlands, Portugal, and Sweden all at one time or another chartered a firm called the East India Company. These state and quasi-state companies were sometimes made responsible for tax collection and other government functions in the colonies; some even had their own military to enforce the company's rule. In one instance, the British East India Company brutally put down a rebellion of its Indian soldiers in 1857, which led to the company's administration of India being taken over by the British government.

Mercantilism's influence was evident in other areas of statecraft as well. For example, the 1703 Methuen Treaty between England and Portugal granted Portuguese wines preferential access to the English market and English woolens preferential access to the

Portuguese market. England's goal in seeking the treaty was to gain greater access to gold and silver from Portugal's colonies in the New World. The eighteenth-century British economist and philosopher David Hume harshly criticized the treaty: "But what have we gained by the bargain? We have lost the French market for our woolen manufacturers, and transferred the commerce of wine to Spain and Portugal, where we buy worse liquor at a higher price." Hume's distain for mercantilism's heavy-handed government intervention in trade and other aspects of economic life, shared by modern economists, would not become the consensus view of policy makers until the nineteenth century.

From the perspective of the North American colonists, the most important pieces of England's mercantilist legislation were the Navigation Acts. These "Acts of Trade and Navigation," the first of which were enacted in the mid-seventeenth century, were the result of a variety of domestic and international developments. England had been commercially successful during the 1620s and 1630s; however, several factors dimmed her prospects during the subsequent two decades. These included England's bloody civil war (1642–51), which shook the foundations of the state, and the Venetian-Turkish war (1645–69), which disrupted trade in the eastern Mediterranean. Even more important was the Treaty of Münster (1647–48), which ended the Eighty Years' War between the Netherlands and Spain and recognized Dutch independence from Spain. The cessation of hostilities ended Spain's long-standing efforts to undermine Dutch maritime commerce via embargoes on ships, goods, and assets throughout the Iberian Peninsula and in Spanish-controlled parts of Italy, and by raids against Dutch fisheries and shipping. The treaty helped propel the Dutch Empire into a leading role in world commerce.

The Anglo-Dutch rivalry for commercial supremacy led to, among other things, three wars between England and Holland during 1652–75. It also encouraged the English to introduce the Navigation Acts, the first of which was enacted under Oliver Cromwell in 1651; subsequent versions were enacted after the restoration of Charles II, in 1660 and 1663. Although some of these were completely new, others had antecedents dating back to medieval times. The laws remained on the books until the repeal of the Corn Laws almost 200 years later (discussed in chapter 7), although the stringency of their enforcement—and the feasibility of doing so—varied over time. When enacted, the laws applied to all English colonies, although England's colonial empire at the time was largely confined to North America and the Caribbean. The Navigation Acts encompassed several different types of regulations. Some of these were to the detriment of the colonists, others were to their benefit, and still others had more ambiguous effects.

The Navigation Acts mandated that the owners and three-quarters of the crews of vessels in which colonial goods were shipped be English, excluding Dutch and other foreign-owned merchant vessels from the colonial trade. Irish and Americans were considered English for purposes of this law; however, before the 1707 Act of Union, Scotland was treated as a foreign country. Scotland's attempts to retaliate in kind were largely ineffective, since they lacked a colonial empire. Because freight accounted for as much as much as 20 percent of the cost of an international shipment, this provision ensured that a substantial portion of the revenue from commerce remained within the empire. In theory, this regulation should have benefited American shipbuilders and shipowners, since American ships had the same legal standing as English, although in practice it tipped the scales toward the English: under the Navigation Acts, approximately 80 percent of shipping between North America and England took place on English vessels; after the American Revolution, the proportion fell to 20 percent.

The Navigation Acts restricted the destinations to which certain colonial goods could be shipped, forcing most products to be shipped to the mother country before they could be sent elsewhere. This imposed substantial costs on colonial exporters. A Virginia planter sending tobacco to Hamburg would be forced to ship the cargo to first England, where it would be unloaded, hauled, ware-housed, hauled, and reloaded into another ship destined for the tobacco's final destination—accompanied by costly paperwork at every step of the way. Transshipping £100's worth of tobacco via England added as much as £40 to the freight cost, severely cutting in to the planter's profits.

Tobacco was only one of a long list of designated—known as "enumerated"—goods that were subject to export restrictions. The original list included sugar, indigo, cotton wool, ginger, and dyewoods. The list was later expanded to include lumber and other products used in shipbuilding, rice, molasses, hides, furs, silk, hemp, potash, copper ore, and coffee, among other goods, although tobacco, rice, lumber, and indigo were the most impor-tant North American exports. Goods that would have competed with those produced in England (e.g., meats and grains), were per-mitted to be exported directly anywhere—except to England. The treatment of enumerated goods varied considerably over time. For example, the geographic restriction on the direct export of rice from North America was eased in 1730 and again in 1764. The pro-portion of trade between North America and England affected by the Navigation Acts was substantial: more than three-quarters of US exports to Great Britain consisted of enumerated goods, and of these, more than 85 percent were subsequently re-exported to northern Europe. Hence, a large proportion of American exporters were affected by the Navigation Acts.

The Navigation Acts also mandated that the colonists purchase their European and East Indian goods in England. For example, Dutch goods bound for North America would have had to be shipped from Holland first to an English port, and then from England to North America, on a vessel that was owned and crewed by English or colonial personnel. North American colonists who bought slaves were required to buy them from English slave traders, and colonists were required to rely upon English agents to provide credit. British law also prohibited colonists from economic undertakings that might compete with those of England or, in some circumstances, those of her other colonies; tariffs and duties were set so as to enhance these prohibitions. The Molasses Act of 1733, for example, taxed molasses from non-British colonies entering England's North American colonies, targeting molasses imported from the French West Indies, in order to support molasses producers in the British West Indies.

The philosophy behind England's imperial policy was that the colonies should provide the mother country with raw materials at a reasonable price and buy finished products in return, bolstering manufacturing in England and retarding it in the colonies. The British statesman William Pitt the Elder went so far as to declare that "if the Americans should manufacture a lock of wool or a horse shoe," he would "fill their ports with ships and their towns with troops." And, in fact, examples of large-scale American manufacturing during the colonial period are rare. Output of iron, glass, and pottery—which there is evidence that pre-Revolutionary America had the capacity to produce—was either severely retarded or nonexistent.

The Navigation Acts had bizarre—and to the American colonists, no doubt infuriating—consequences. Colonists who wanted to consume snuff made from American tobacco and beaver hats made from American pelts had to import them from England. Well-to-do colonists ordered manufactured goods from agents in England who arranged for both purchase and shipping. Because of the difficulty in supervising agents—and lack of alternatives— colonial orders were often filled with less desirable but nonetheless expensive merchandise. "Good enough for America" became a catchphrase of English manufacturing. One prominent customer, a certain George Washington of Virginia, complained to his London agent that many of the products supplied "were mean in quality but not in price, for in this they excel indeed, far above any I have ever had."

The news for the North American colonists was not all bad. The Navigation Acts also enacted rules and regulations that gave favorable treatment to the colonists in certain economic spheres. Colonial products were often subject to lower tariffs than those coming from countries outside the empire, which reduced the cost of exporting them to the mother country. And certain economic activities which were seen as the prerogative of the colonists were prohibited in the mother country. For example, the Acts forbade the planting and cultivation of tobacco in England. And the government instituted a complicated system of rebates and drawbacks to allow the colonists to recover some of the tariff they paid on cargoes sent to England when they were transshipped to a third country. Further, England paid a "bounty" (i.e., subsidy) to encourage the production of some commodities. The most notable example was indigo, a plant used in the making of blue dye. The bounty must have been substantial, since the production of indigo in the United States ceased after independence.

Just how damaging were the Navigation Acts? The colonists complained bitterly about them, going so far as to put a clause in the Declaration of Independence citing them among their grievances against King George III:

> HE has combined with others to subject us to a Jurisdiction foreign to our Constitution, and unacknowledged by our Laws; giving his Assent to their Acts of pretended Legislation:
> . . .
> FOR cutting off our Trade with all Parts of the World:
> FOR imposing Taxes on us without our Consent:

Scholars have long debated the consequences of British imperial policy on the American colonies. The nineteenth-century historian and statesman George Bancroft wrote that "American independence, like the great rivers of the country, had many sources, but the headspring which colored all the stream was the Navigation

Act." Bancroft's *History of the United States*, the first volume of which appeared in 1834, was the first, and for many years the only, large-scale history of the United States and may have had an out-sized influence on American thinking on the subject for much of the nineteenth century. Writing eight decades later, the historian George Beer argued that British colonial policy was unremarkable for its time and that the colonists were fairly compensated for the costs of imperial policy by the benefits reaped from membership in the British Empire. Among the benefits was military defense, including escort by the Royal Navy of the convoys carrying com-merce to and from England. Oliver Dickerson concurred, writ-ing: "No case can be made out for the Navigation Acts as a cause of the Revolution on the grounds that such laws were economically oppressive and were steadily reducing the Americans to a condition of hopeless poverty."

Writing at about the same time as Dickerson, Curtis Nettels argued that during the 75 years prior to the end of the French and Indian War in 1763, the Navigation Acts had not been especially burdensome. Those years had been marked by military conflict and brought much-needed British resources to the North America col-onists. Following the war, the easy money that had flowed to the colonies dried up; instead, the colonists were called upon to sup-port the postwar defense establishment that was to be maintained in America. Summing up, Nettels concludes that "In its total effect, British policy as it affected the colonies after 1763 was restrictive, injurious, negative." This view was supported by Lawrence Harper, who assembled a vast amount of data on the goods enumerated in the Navigation Acts, including information on the duties, boun-ties, and taxes on each item, as well as on the quantities imported, exported, and re-exported via Britain. From this detailed account-ing, Harper found that the "basic provisions [of the Navigation Acts] concerning the trans-Atlantic trade placed a heavy burden upon the colonies." Specifically, based on calculations for 1773, he estimated that the net burden of the Navigation Acts was between two and seven million dollars per year. The lower of these two estimates would have come close to meeting all the operating expenses of the national government during Washington's administration. The higher estimate, over the course of 1790–1801, would have been sufficient to pay off both the domestic and foreign debt incurred by the United States during the Revolutionary War.

The debate over the consequences of the Navigation Acts was taken up by a new generation of scholars in the 1960s, working with somewhat better data, different counterfactuals, and more formal economic models. Robert Paul Thomas completed the first of these new studies. His results suggest that the net cost to the colonists over the alternative of an independent United States was less than two million dollars, or somewhat below Harper's lower bound estimate, concluding that they were not, in fact, especially high. The ensuing decade and a half saw an outpouring of rigorous quantitative studies and a robust debate over the methods of analysis employed, with the majority concluding that the Navigation Acts themselves were not especially burdensome for the American colonists. And, in fact, that remains the consensus view among a broad sample of modern scholars: a recent study concluded that nearly 90 percent of the economists and historians surveyed agreed with the proposition that "[t]he costs imposed on the colonists by the trade restrictions of the Navigation Acts were small."

If the burden of the Navigation Acts was so slight—no more than 1 percent of GDP, according to Thomas's calculation—why did the Americans make such a fuss over it? The short answer is that although the burden to the American colonies as a whole was low, it did not fall evenly across the entire economy: some sectors and regions suffered disproportionately, while others were barely affected. Those that suffered the most from the Navigation Acts tended to be the strongest supporters of the Revolution.

American merchants involved in Atlantic commerce were among the hardest hit by imperial policy. During the three decades prior to the Revolution, the volume of English exports to the North American colonies expanded dramatically. This surge was accompanied by qualitative changes in Anglo-American commerce. Previously, English exporters had worked primarily through American merchant houses; from the mid-1700s onward, British exporters bypassed their American counterparts and sold directly to shopkeepers via auctions and through networks of correspondents—including as many as 150 in one city alone. The effect on American merchants was pronounced, particularly in the port cities (and distribution centers) of Boston, New York, Philadelphia, Charleston, and Baltimore, and led to several organized boycotts of British goods. Combined with the constraints placed on American trade, it is perhaps not surprising that that about a quarter of the signers of the Declaration, including such notables as John Hancock and Robert Morris, were prominent merchants. Urban artisans and domestic manufacturers who faced competition from British imports, including colonists like Paul Revere and Benjamin Franklin, also suffered under the Navigation Acts and were among the stronger supporters of the Revolution.

Virginia tobacco planters, such as Washington and Jefferson, as well those from North Carolina and Maryland, also bore the brunt of the Navigation Acts. The Acts granted a monopoly on the profitable tobacco trade to British merchants. They also required that all exports be shipped to Britain initially, no matter what their final destination, further cutting into the planters' profits. The Acts also gave British merchants a monopoly on the financing of the tobacco trade; as the indebtedness of tobacco farmers grew, so did their revolutionary zeal.

In contrast to tobacco farmers, rice producers were less encumbered by the Navigation Acts and, as a result, were less hostile to British rule. Although a lot of colonial rice was shipped to England (both for local consumption and re-export), in 1731, rice was permitted to be shipped directly to southern Europe without a stopover in England; in 1763, direct rice exports to the French West Indies were allowed; and in 1764, South America was added to the list of permitted export destinations. Rice exports to the British Caribbean had never been restricted; other shipments, exported via the northern colonies, had also escaped the Navigation Acts. Because of these exceptions, the burdens of the Navigation Acts were proportionately lower on rice growers than on tobacco growers. This helps to explain why the more heavily burdened Chesapeake tobacco farmers were enthusiastic revolutionaries while Carolina rice growers were more content with British rule.

A back-of-the envelope calculation of the distribution of the burdens of the Navigation Acts helps to illustrate the point. Assume that the cost of the Navigation Acts fell disproportionately on merchants and tobacco farmers, and much less on other segments of the economy. Assume further that the entire urban population of the colonies, about 5 percent of the colonies' nearly 4 million population, was engaged in the transatlantic trade (this certainly overstates the number). Also assume that the entire population of Virginia, about 19 percent of the population, was engaged in tobacco cultivation. This assumption is also an overstatement, but since parts of Maryland and North Carolina were also involved in tobacco cultivation, it can serve as a rough approximation.

Combining these admittedly sketchy estimates suggests that the main burden of the Navigation Acts affected slightly less than 25 percent of the population. If the aggregate cost of the Navigation Acts, about 1 percent of GDP, fell on one quarter of the economy, the burden on the affected sectors would have been about 4 percent. To the extent that the sum of the population of urban areas and Virginia overstates the portion of the economy affected by the Navigation Acts, the proportionate burden would be even higher. If the affected sectors constituted only 20 percent of the economy, the burden would have been 5 percent.

Recall the question posed earlier: if the burden of the Navigation Acts was so slight why did the Americans make such a fuss over it? They fussed because although the aggregate burden of the acts was small, less than 1 percent, it fell more heavily—four to five times more heavily—on certain sectors of the economy, particularly merchants, artisans, manufacturers, and tobacco planters. Not coincidentally, those making their living in these more heavily burdened sectors were the most enthusiastic revolutionaries.

The British Empire was the largest the world has ever known: at its height, it spanned approximately one-quarter of the world's land mass and ruled about an equal proportion of its population. The empire's earliest colonial outposts were in the Caribbean and North America. The Western Hemisphere was also the site of the first important exit from the empire. In 1776, the United States famously declared its independence from Britain. In 1781, the United States won the last major battle of the Revolutionary War when the British surrendered at Yorktown. American independence was formally recognized by the British under the 1783 Treaty of Paris.

The loss of the American colonies did not constitute the end of the British Empire, although it did signal the beginning of a new phase—one in which African and Asian colonies became its most important component. Prior to World War II, it could truly be said that the sun did not set on the British Empire; after the war, exodus from the empire became something of a stampede. The British left India/Pakistan and the Palestine Mandate in the 1940s. During the 1950s and 1960s, decolonization reached Britain's African colonies, as well as those in the Caribbean. By the mid-1980s, the remaining ties between Britain and its former colonies were largely ceremonial. The age of empire was over.

Did the Navigation Acts cause the American Revolution? No. The Acts were not so oppressive that they reduced the Americans "to a condition of hopeless poverty." In fact, the aggregate burden of the Navigation Acts was relatively light. That burden, however, was not spread equally across the population, but was concentrated among a relatively few economic sectors. Those who earned their living in the affected sectors became the most fervent supporters of the Revolution. In the years leading up to the Revolution, several observers—including the French foreign minister—speculated that the American colonies would soon be ripe for independence. America had grown too populous, too wealthy, and too sophisticated to remain a colony. In the absence of a substantial modification of the terms of the relationship between Britain and its North American colonies, it is likely that independence would eventually have come anyway. The Navigation Acts did not lead to the Revolution, but they sped up the process.

The Navigation Acts were a colossal policy failure. Enacted in the belief that they would enrich England at the expense of its colonies, they returned relatively little to England. To add insult to injury, they enraged key segments of the American population. Although the Navigation Acts were tinkered with frequently during the eighteenth century, there was never any serious thought given to repealing them. In part, this may have been because repeal would have been seen as weakness and encouraged other imperial policies to be challenged. More importantly, the Acts were maintained because the ideology of mercantilism was so deeply ingrained in the economic thought of the day that it was easier for policy makers to accept business as usual than to be swayed by the arguments of antimercantilists such as David Hume. England's commitment to an outdated ideology cost her dearly.

Chapter 3

Establish, Disestablish, Repeat

The First and Second Banks of the United States

Richard: Dar'st thou resolve to kill a friend of mine?
Tyrrel: Please you;
But I had rather kill two enemies.

RICHARD III (IV, ii)

If you want to start your own country, you should have, at a minimum, a flag, an anthem, and a currency. The flag should be bold, the anthem inspiring, and the currency should bear your portrait—or, at least, the portrait of one of your ancestors. For a flag, you'll need a graphic designer and someone who can sew. For an anthem, you'll need a composer and, possibly, a lyricist. To create a currency, you should first establish a central bank.

Virtually every country in the world has a central bank—and almost all have had them for a very long time. The central banks of the advanced industrial countries are among the world's most venerable financial institutions. The Swedish Riksbank, the world's oldest central bank, was established in 1668. The Bank of England is only slightly younger, having been established in 1694, but it was by 1781 so well ensconced in public life that the prime minister, Lord North, already spoke of it as being "from long habit and usage of many years...a part of the constitution." The central banks of Austria (established 1816), Belgium (1850), Denmark (1818), Finland (1811), France (1800), Germany (1846), Italy (1893), Japan (1882), the Netherlands (1814), Norway (1816), Portugal (1846), and Spain (1856) each originated with institutions that have histories stretching back well over one hundred years—in some cases more than two hundred.

The most notable exception to this near-universal pattern is the United States, which both established and dismantled a central bank—not once, but twice—during the late eighteenth and early nineteenth centuries. From the demise of the second of these institutions in 1836 until the outbreak of World War I, the United States remained—practically alone among industrialized countries—without a central bank. This cost America dearly: during the next 75 years, the United States suffered financial crises about once every decade, more often than any other developed country during this period and more frequently than the United States had experienced before—or has since. And the crises during this period were severe, with those of 1873, 1893, and 1907 ranking among the worst in US history. The 1907 crisis was so devastating that policy makers were spurred into establishing the United State's third central bank, the Federal Reserve System, which, unlike its predecessors, has endured. Had either of the first two central banks survived, America's financially turbulent nineteenth century would have been far calmer.

Before discussing the circumstances surrounding the unique central banking history of the United States, it is important to understand what a central bank is and what it does. Central banks today undertake a variety of tasks. They are often the government's banker, receiving payments, holding deposits, and making payments on its behalf. Historically, central banks were often established for the purpose of lending money to the government, so acting as the government's banker was not much of a stretch. For example, the Bank of England was granted a charter in 1694 in return for a £1.2 million loan to the government, which was used prosecute war with France. As one nineteenth-century observer noted, the bank was not created for some high-minded purpose of public policy but "as a device for getting an unpopular king out of a financial hole."

When it was established, the Bank of England, like other central banks of the time and completely at odds with modern central banks, had no mandate to operate in the public interest. The bank was, in fact, a wholly private institution, albeit one with official responsibilities and government-granted privileges. Those responsibilities and privileges were the subject of frequent negotiations between the bank and the government, since the Bank of England's initial charter did not establish the bank permanently but guaranteed it a life of 11 years. After that time, with one year's notice, the British government could repay the loan and cancel the bank's charter. In fact, the government did not do so but instead renewed the charter nine times during the next 150 years. Charter renewals frequently took place when the government was fiscally strapped—usually because it was fighting a war—when it offered to extend the bank's charter in return for a fresh loan and additional privileges.

Many modern central banks are also often involved in the supervision and regulation of the domestic commercial banking system, either alone or in combination with other government agencies. The founders of the earliest central banks would not have envisioned them as banking supervisors for two reasons. First, these banks were often the first chartered commercial bank of any sort in the country and often remained so for decades—for more than a century in the case of England and Sweden. It is therefore extremely unlikely that the founders would have been foresighted enough to imagine a situation in which there would be a banking "system" to supervise. Second, since the early central banks were private, profit-maximizing institutions, it is inconceivable that governments would have put them in charge of supervising their competitors. Although supervision was never formally a responsibility of either of the early American central banks, intentionally or not, they nonetheless accomplished some of the tasks that are today explicitly entrusted to banking supervisors.

Finally, and most importantly, modern central bankers undertake a variety of functions related to the conduct of monetary policy. They alter the level of reserves—and through them, the money supply and interest rates—with the twin goals of maintaining price stability and fostering economic growth. They may manage foreign currency reserves and intervene in foreign exchange markets to influence the value of the domestic currency on international markets. They also frequently take a leading role in ensuring financial stability, acting as a lender of last resort. Describing this role requires a slightly more detailed explanation of how the banking system works.

Consider a simplified bank balance sheet, which is nothing more than a record of the bank's assets, or what it owns, and its liabilities, or what it owes. Assets consist of cash, securities it has purchased, and loans it has made. Cash earns no interest but is safe: its price will not change and it can be used to pay depositors who want to withdraw their funds. Securities, typically bonds, and loans earn interest, but their underlying value may fluctuate: if the bond market falters, the value of bonds held will fall; if a company to which the bank has loaned money fails, the loan may become worthless. Further, these earning assets must be converted into cash before they can be used to satisfy depositors' demands. Since there are often no markets in which bank loans can be sold, and because bond markets may become unstable, converting these assets into cash— particularly if the cash is needed quickly—may be costly or, in times of financial instability, impossible. Liabilities consist mainly of demand liabilities, that is, obligations that have to be redeemed in cash on demand. These liabilities are generally spendable and can be thought of as money. In earlier times, the main component of demand liabilities would have been the banknotes that each bank issued; today, it consists primarily of checking account deposits.

The balance sheet highlights an important dilemma that banks face, which can be conveniently summarized as "fear and greed." Since bankers earn returns from their portfolios of securities and loans, and none from their holdings of cash, they have an incentive—let's call it greed—to minimize their holdings of cash and maximize their holdings of loans and securities. On the other hand, if holders of a large quantity of demand liabilities show up at the bank one day demanding funds and the bank has insufficient cash, it will be unable to pay and forced to close. Hence, even if there were no government-mandated requirements to hold a minimal amount of cash, banks would hold more than token levels out of fear.

Today, cash—more properly, reserves—consists of cash *and* deposits held on account at the central bank. Central banks conduct monetary policy by buying and selling securities on the open market. When central banks buy securities, they pay for them by writing a check. The seller of the securities deposits the check in his or her bank, and that bank presents the check to the central bank for payment. The central bank responds by creating a *new* deposit in the account of the security seller's bank, increasing that bank's reserves and the total quantity of reserves of the banking system. This is typically the most difficult part of the monetary policy story to explain. Students usually ask, "Where do the central bank deposits come from?" Or, "Where does the central bank get the reserves to pay for the security?" The answer is that the central bank *creates* new reserves. Unlike banks, governments, firms, or individuals, the central bank can create reserves out of nothing, merely by making a book entry on its own balance sheet.

An increase in reserves permits banks to expand their holdings of loans and securities, if they are so inclined, which leads to an increase in demand deposits—the money supply—and a decline in interest rates. Because the central bank can create reserves out of thin air, either by printing currency or creating reserve deposits, it can lend reserves to banks that have insufficient resources to satisfy their depositors and thus are on the point of failure. This is something that commercial banks, governments, and firms usually cannot do and why central banks are well situated to act as "lenders of last resort."

Central banks face a dilemma in making monetary policy. On the one hand, they have an incentive to increase the level of reserves, since doing so will keep interest rates down, encourage businesses to invest in new plant and equipment (since much of this investment is done with borrowed money), and promote economic growth. If the government can pressure the central bank into lending to it freely, or if the government itself issues currency, it can secure an almost unlimited line of credit and increase spending well beyond tax revenues. If reserves are injected too aggressively, the money supply will increase rapidly, and inflation, or perhaps even hyperinflation, will result. On the other hand, if reserves do not grow rapidly enough, high interest rates will choke off economic activity.

During the nineteenth century, bank reserves consisted largely of monetary metals, typically gold and silver; demand liabilities consisted of banknotes issued by individual banks. Here again, fear and greed come into play. The more banknotes a bank could put into circulation, the more earning assets (loans and securities) it could hold, resulting in greater profits. The farther from the bank its banknotes circulated the better, since notes could only be redeemed at the bank itself, and such far-flung circulations meant that fewer banknotes would be presented for redemption in gold or silver. Of course, if a note holder did present notes for redemption and the bank did not have sufficient reserves of gold or silver to satisfy the demand, the bank would fail.

Central banks were typically founded for one or more of three reasons: to lend money to the government, to establish a coherent monetary order, or to promote credit creation. The Bank of England, as noted earlier, was established primarily as a mechanism for raising money for the government. Similarly, Napoleon, who was deeply suspicious of banks, established the Bank of France to generate income for the state. Even central banks that were not established primarily for fiscal reasons could bring governments some financial benefit. The Swedish Riksbank, for example, was required to split its profit with the crown and the City of Stockholm.

Several central banks were established to clear up chaotic monetary situations, frequently by giving the new institution a monopoly on the right to issue banknotes. The Bank of Finland was established in 1812, just three years after Finland had been ceded by Sweden to Russia, in order to withdraw the circulating Swedish money and replace it with Russian currency. The Austrian National Bank was established with a monopoly on banknote issue following several decades during which the government had consistently overissued currency, resulting in severe inflation. The establishment of central banks in Norway and Denmark followed a similar period of monetary excess during which a predecessor institution had overissued currency. Both of these banks were given a monopoly on note issuing at the time of their founding. Later in the nineteenth century, following national unification, the German Reichsbank and the Banca d'Italia were established, in part, to consolidate the note issues of several preexisting institutions. Although the Swedish Riksbank was not established for monetary purposes, the country's unwieldy copper currency—the 10-daler coin weighed 19.7 kilograms (43 pounds)—virtually guaranteed its success as a note-issuing bank and greatly simplified Sweden's unwieldy monetary arrangements.

Still other central banks were established primarily to create credit, which is vital for the development of commerce. Consider a transaction in which a wholesaler sells goods to a retailer in a distant location. The wholesaler will naturally want payment as soon as possible, since once the goods are shipped it may be difficult to collect the unpaid bill. The retailer may not have sufficient funds to pay for the shipment until it arrives and the goods have been resold. One solution to this problem is the creation of an institution that will provide credit—that is, loan money—to the retailer, using the goods in transit as collateral. Once the goods have been resold, the retailer can pay off the loan. The Riksbank, the world's first central bank and the only credit-creating bank in Sweden at the time of its founding, was established primarily to promote commerce. The Netherlands Bank was also established to promote credit creation. The Netherlands had been home to a number of city-owned, credit-creating institutions dating back to Amsterdam's Wisselbank, which had been established in 1609. The decline of these institutions in the 1790s, combined with a prolonged slump in trade, led the authorities to establish the Netherlands Bank in 1814 in hopes that it would contribute to a revival of trade. The National Bank of Belgium was similarly founded to support domestic commerce following the revolutions and monetary disturbances of 1848, as well as to issue notes and handle public moneys.

The United States might have been proudly independent of its former colonial master following the Declaration of Independence in 1776 and the Treaty of Paris in 1783, but financially it was a mess. At the beginning of 1784, the United States owed more than $39 million; by 1790, its debt was estimated at more than $79 million. Customs revenue, the main source of income for most countries at that time, amounted to about $162,000 during the last three months of 1790, not nearly enough to cover interest payments on either the domestic or foreign debt. And the continental dollar, the currency issued by the Continental Congress during the 1770s, had depreciated so much that by the early 1780s, it was worthless. "Not worth a Continental" became a common derogatory expression of the time.

The 1790s saw something of a financial revolution in the United States. By 1793, the US government had collected about $4.7 million in tax revenue, enough to both fund government operations and meet interest payments on the national debt. The US Mint had been opened in Philadelphia and was producing gold and silver coins denominated in the newly created US dollar. Securities markets had emerged in New York, Philadelphia, and Boston that were making markets for the $63 million of outstanding domestic debt. And in 1791, Congress chartered a central bank.

The Bank of the United States (BUS), which historians today refer to as the First Bank of the United States for reasons that will soon become clear, was established by legislation enacted in 1791. Banks were not a complete novelty in the United States at the time. By the end of 1791, the legislatures of five states had each granted bank charters; by 1811, there were more than a hundred state-chartered banks in the United States. Nonetheless, BUS was unique in that it was the only bank to have a charter issued by the federal government, and therefore it was the only bank allowed to open branches anywhere in the country. The charter also gave the bank a special relationship with the federal government.

BUS was the brainchild of the secretary of the Treasury, Alexander Hamilton. As early as 1779, Hamilton had suggested the formation of a government bank to financier Robert Morris, who would soon assume the newly created post of Superintendent of Finance. Hamilton's arguments in favor of BUS were similar to those made to advance the Bank of England, Riksbank, and subsequent central banks: raising money for the government, monetary stability, and credit creation. Hamilton's plan envisioned a bank that promoted the circulation of a paper currency that was redeemable in gold and silver, in contrast to the unredeemable, and by the time Hamilton began to formulate his plan, largely worthless continental dollar. He also argued that a government bank would provide credit and stimulate commerce, noting that banks "have proved to be the happiest engines that ever were invented for advancing trade." He also argued that it would afford "[g]reater facility to the government, in obtaining pecuniary aids, especially in sudden emergencies"—in other words, it would help the government borrow money.

Hamilton submitted a report to Congress outlining his plans in December 1790. A bill to establish BUS was introduced in the Senate on December 23, 1790, where it passed with a majority and was sent to the House of Representatives on January 20, 1791. Neither the Senate votes nor debates were recorded, so we do not know the extent of the division of opinion in that chamber. Much of the debate in the House focused on whether the federal government had the constitutional authority to charter a bank. Hamilton and other Federalists who favored a strong central government supported the bill; anti-Federalists, including Jefferson, Madison, and others who believed that the powers not explicitly granted to the federal government should be the reserved to the states, opposed it.

The House of Representatives passed the bill on February 8 by a vote of 39 to 19. Washington requested written opinions on the bill from Hamilton, as well as from secretary of state Thomas Jefferson and attorney general Edmund Randolph. Hamilton, of course, supported the bill; both Jefferson and Randolph argued that the bill was unconstitutional and recommended that Washington veto it. Nonetheless, Washington signed the measure into law on February 25, 1791. The vote in the House was not strictly along party lines. Eleven of those who voted to establish BUS were anti-Federalist Republicans, while six Federalists voted against it. The geographic pattern of voting was more striking: only three votes in favor came from southern states (two from North Carolina and one from South Carolina), and only one vote against came from a northern state (Massachusetts). The six votes from Delaware and Maryland were split evenly. The bank's supporters came from the commercial and moneyed classes and from those who believed in a strong central government, a more common view in the north. Opponents were mainly farmers who mistrusted business interests and expansive federal authority, particularly since a powerful federal authority might one day decide to outlaw slavery; these concerns were more common in the south.

The Bank of the United States was headquartered in Philadelphia. Branches were established almost immediately in New York, Boston, Baltimore, and Charleston. By 1804, additional branches had been opened in Norfolk, Savannah, New Orleans, and Washington, DC. Although BUS branches had no official relationship with local, state-chartered banks, they nonetheless exerted an indirect kind of supervisory oversight. Recall that the longer a bank's notes remained in circulation and the farther away from the issuing bank they circulated, the greater that bank's ability—and incentive—to overissue notes. However, when BUS branches received the notes of nearby banks, they promptly returned them to the issuing bank in exchange for silver. Further, because BUS was the only bank in the country with branches in several states, the notes of any bank that might have migrated out of state and into the hands of BUS were more easily returned to the issuing bank for redemption. Since the banks knew that their notes would not remain unredeemed for long, they had an incentive not to overissue notes.

A crucial difference between BUS and both the Bank of England and the Riksbank is that the initial BUS charter was limited to 20 years: without an explicit renewal, BUS's charter would expire in March 1811. In Sweden, the Riksbank's charter was not subjected to any such time limit and could, in theory, continue indefinitely. Bank of England charters were guaranteed to continue for a minimum period of time, ranging from 11 to 33 years depending on the particular rechartering legislation, after which the government could, with one year's notice, repay the loan and revoke the charter. Still, neither the Swedish nor English chartering legislation required rechartering within a certain period of time: in the absence of any legislation to the contrary, both the Riksbank and the Bank of England would have continued indefinitely.

Three years before the BUS charter was due to expire, shareholders sent a request to Congress asking for an extension. The political landscape had changed substantially during the intervening years, however. The Federalist-inclined administrations of Washington and Adams gave way to anti-Federalist administrations of Jefferson and Madison; with the exception of New England, the House and Senate were now solidly in the anti-Federalist camp. Despite their original opposition to the bank, Jefferson and Madison, as well as the Federalists in Congress, recognized the benefits of BUS and were in favor of its recharter. The anti-Federalists, however, were split. Business interests that owned state-chartered banks were wary of

BUS's restraining influence on their ability to issue notes. The legislatures of Massachusetts, Pennsylvania, and Maryland "instructed" their senators to vote against the renewal of the bank's charter. Samuel Taggart, a representative from rural Massachusetts, argued that virtually all the representatives from the great commercial towns had opposed the bank. The vote to recharter BUS lost in both the House and the Senate—by one vote in each chamber.

The period during which BUS operated had been one of near-constant expansion of banking. The first state-chartered banks, the Bank of North America (1782) and the Bank of Massachusetts (1784), received their charters prior to BUS; several more, including the Bank of New York (founded by Alexander Hamilton), Bank of Maryland, and Providence Bank, received charters in the same year as BUS. From these five state-chartered banks in existence at the end of 1791, their numbers increased to more than 110 by 1811. Bank capital increased nearly 15 times during the same period. Banks were present in only five states at the end of 1792; by the end of 1811, they had spread to 21 states and territories and the District of Columbia. The dramatic growth of banking reflected the country's expanding area, population, and interregional and international trade: from 1790 to 1810, the US population increased by 75 percent, and total land area doubled. By aiding monetary stability and fostering sustainable credit growth, BUS had contributed significantly to economic growth.

The demise of the First Bank of the United States marked the beginning of a period of even more rapid, but less solidly grounded expansion of the banking system. During 1811–16, the number of state-chartered banks more than doubled. Now free of the restraining influence of BUS, the value of banknotes in circulation increased by nearly 250 percent. Combined with the fiscal strains brought about by the War of 1812 with Britain, the excessive monetary expansion rendered the financial system and public credit vulnerable to crisis. When the British raided Washington and threatened Baltimore in August 1814, there was a widespread banking panic. Albert

Gallatin, secretary of the Treasury from 1801 to 1814, placed the blame for this excessive expansion, and the subsequent crisis, squarely on the failure to renew the BUS charter.

Even before the panic, proposals to establish a new national bank had been made. At least three bills failed to secure congressional approval; two more were vetoed by President James Madison. The act authorizing the Second Bank of the United States (2BUS) was signed into law by Madison in April 1816. The legislation incorporated many of the same features as the 1791 act. According to one observer, the new charter "differed from the old mainly in terms of verbosity, being about treble the length." Like BUS, 2BUS was to have 20 percent government ownership and a 20-year charter. One-fifth of the bank's capital was to be in the form of gold or silver, and 2BUS had a larger paid-in capital ($35 million) than BUS ($10 million). BUS had been the Treasury's de facto depository; 2BUS filled this role by law.

The political battle over the bank was like that in 1791, except that the supporters and opponents were now reversed. In 1791, with the Federalists in power, northerners had established BUS and southerners had opposed it. In 1816, with the anti-Federalist Republicans in power, southerners and westerners supported the bank's re-establishment and northerners opposed it. Republican support reflected, in part, the pragmatic interest of those in power in having a useful instrument in the form of a national bank. Northern opposition may have reflected the greater political influence of bankers in those states. Bank density in New England and the middle Atlantic states in 1810 was about four times that in southern and western states. If bankers feared that a re-established national bank would restrict their ability to issue notes, they might have brought pressure to bear on their representatives to oppose the new bank.

The Second Bank of the United States did not start auspiciously. Its first president, William Jones, had been President Madison's secretary of the navy and acting secretary of the Treasury. He had also recently gone through bankruptcy proceedings, which was probably not the best advertisement for his qualifications for the job of president of the national bank. The bank was poorly run under Jones's leadership, which was characterized by several dramatic, ultimately destabilizing shifts in policy as well as accusations of fraud and mismanagement. Congress considered revoking 2BUS's charter following the collapse of the Baltimore branch with a loss of $3 million, but the resignation of Jones in 1819 appeased Congress and staved off the bank's untimely demise.

Jones's successor was Langdon Cheves, a Republican congressman from South Carolina who had been Speaker of the House of Representatives. Cheves ran a relatively scandal-free administration during his tenure at 2BUS (1819–22); however, his leadership was less than successful. Cheves was naturally conservative; his critics accused him of being "too conservative. Even for a banker." His conservatism was such that, upon taking the helm of the bank he began to contract its business, closing offices and reducing its loans. This policy was maintained even in the wake of the panic of 1819, when other banks were being forced to restrict their business, exacerbating the monetary and economic contraction that was already under way. One critic characterized Cheves's performance during the crisis as making sure that "the bank was saved and the people were ruined." Cheves was re-elected as president, but the downturn following the 1819 crisis had made the bank so unpopular that he resigned shortly thereafter.

Cheves was succeeded by the remarkable Nicholas Biddle, who would remain president for the remainder of 2BUS's life as a federally chartered institution. Scion of a prominent Pennsylvania family, Biddle had finished the requirements for a degree at University of Pennsylvania at age 13 but was denied the degree because of his youth. He subsequently attended Princeton, where he graduated two years later at the top of his class. He served as assistant to the American ambassador in Paris and was involved in negotiating the Louisiana Purchase and, later, was secretary to the American ambassador to London, the future president James Monroe.

Biddle proved a far more competent and innovative president than either of his predecessors. Under his leadership, 2BUS undertook at least three types of central banking functions that had not yet been employed elsewhere. First, the bank actively managed the money supply in light of underlying economic conditions. This was done by altering the speed with which the bank returned banknotes to state banks. If the economy was expanding too rapidly, which could lead to increased inflation, the bank responded by promptly returning notes to state banks. This forced them to rein in their note issuing, which reduced both the money supply and the threat of increased inflation. When the economy was in a downturn, the bank would return bank notes at a more leisurely pace, which permitted state banks to expand their note issues and provide the weak economy with needed monetary stimulus. Second, as the only financial institution with a nationwide presence, 2BUS was instrumental in keeping the value of the dollar constant across the country. Previously, the value of the currencies issued by state-chartered banks varied from place to place, making commerce more difficult. Finally, 2BUS acted as a lender of last resort, extending loans to banks during times of economic stringency. These loans allowed state-chartered banks to maintain their own loans to businesses instead of having to recall them and force firms to contract their business, worsening the downturn. The bank's lender-of-last-resort operations were particularly important during the British financial crisis of 1825, which put many American banks under stress.

Despite Biddle's obvious competence and the country's financial stability during his tenure, the election of Andrew Jackson in 1828 and his re-election in 1832 cast a cloud over the bank's future. The hero of the Battle of New Orleans during the War of 1812, Jackson was nicknamed "Old Hickory" because of his toughness. Jackson was a frontiersman with limited formal education and a reputation as a dueler and a brawler. Jackson had a deep mistrust of entrenched elites—in short, he was the polar opposite of Biddle. Jackson was an avowed foe of the bank for several reasons, not the least of which was that he believed it had supported John Quincy Adams, his opponent in the presidential election of 1828.

The 1816 charter of 2BUS was due to expire before the end of Jackson's second term, and he made no secret of his opposition to its renewal. Addressing the opening session of the Twenty-First Congress, Jackson said: "Both the constitutionality and expediency of the law creating this bank, are well questioned, by a large portion of our fellow-citizens; and it must be admitted by all, that it has failed in the great end of establishing a uniform and sound currency." This was the opening salvo in what historians have dubbed "the Bank War." In fact, Biddle and Jackson were aligned with opposing political groupings and were both difficult personalities, which no doubt worsened their policy differences. Congress passed a recharter bill in 1832 with comfortable majorities in both houses; however, Jackson vetoed it. The attempt to override the veto and subsequent attempts to pass a new charter failed.

The federal charter of 2BUS expired in 1836. Jackson ordered that federal government deposits be placed in other banks, called "pet banks" by his political opponents, further weakening the bank. Following the expiration of its federal charter, 2BUS was reconstituted with a Pennsylvania charter as the US Bank of Pennsylvania. Biddle retired in 1839, briefly pursuing the Whig Party's nomination for president. He and other former officers of the US Bank of Pennsylvania were subsequently indicted for fraud in connection with cotton speculation, but the charges were dropped. The bank itself failed in 1841, taking much of Biddle's fortune—and reputation—with it. Biddle died in 1844. The American experiment with central banking was over. For the next three-quarters of a century the United States would operate with a variety of monetary arrangements. None of them would involve a central bank.

The demise of 2BUS can be ascribed to a number of factors. Banks, businesses, and farmers resented the restraint that the bank had on the growth of banknote issues and credit creation. Some opposed it as an unwanted federal intrusion to what they considered to be a state matter, since every other bank in the country operated under a state charter. Others mistrusted banks in general and banking corporations in particular. Still others ascribe 2BUS's downfall to the inability of Jackson's administration to extract political "spoils" from the bank, the personality clash between Jackson and Biddle, and New York's determination to overtake Philadelphia as the nation's financial center.

The aftermath of the Second Bank's demise shared some characteristics with that of the First Bank. The expiration of the federal charter was followed by a period of inflation, culminating in financial panics in 1837 and 1839. These boom-bust panics have been blamed on Jackson's veto of the charter renewal and the removal of the bank's restraining hand upon state-bank credit creation, although this view is not universal.

The failure to renew the charters of the first two incarnations of the Bank of the United States had both immediate and longer-term consequences. Although scholars continue to debate whether the dismantling of the central banks was responsible for the financial panics that erupted following their demise, the absence of the banks did remove a potential check to the note-issuing activities of state-chartered commercial banks. History—not to mention the more recent events, such as the subprime crisis—are replete with examples of financial institutions that cannot be restrained by rules that are not backed up by active supervision and regulation. The power to issue banknotes—that is, to print money—presents an almost irresistible temptation to do so to excess.

One indication that dismantling the banks was bad public policy is that proposals to reconstitute them sprang up almost immediately. Despite the fact that the First and Second Banks were each destined to last only 20 years, they enjoyed considerable support across the political spectrum. Thomas Jefferson, like the majority of anti-Federalist Republicans, opposed the initial charter when he was secretary of state. As president, however, he favored renewal, no doubt recognizing its usefulness as an instrument of public policy. Remorse over the First Bank's demise set in rapidly. The re-establishment of a national bank was soon proposed. Within five years a new institution with the same name was established. Similarly, a majority in Congress favored the renewal of the Second Bank's charter—just not by the two-thirds majority necessary to override Jackson's veto. Finally, in 1841, just five years after the expiration of the federal charter of 2BUS, Congress passed a bill establishing a third bank. That bill was vetoed by President John Tyler.

Shortly after the demise of 2BUS, states began enacting so-called free banking laws. Under free banking, individuals could obtain a charter and the right to issue notes by completing some paperwork and depositing a prescribed quantity of state government bonds with the authorities. Easy access to the note-issuing franchise and absence of the restraining hand of a central bank led to excessive note issues and high failure rates among free banks, as well as substantial losses to customers who held their notes. Failures were often blamed on "wildcat banks," so called because they were deliberately set up in remote locations that were not accessible to individuals anxious to redeem notes—locations "where the wildcats roamed." The proliferation of banknotes in circulation—including forgeries and the notes of banks that were no longer in business—led to the publication of a variety of "banknote reporters," magazines that included pictures, descriptions, and the current market value of various banknotes. Such unrestrained overissues had been more difficult in the presence of a central bank with a nation-wide system of branches that ensured that notes were returned to the bank that issued them.

The next major pieces of federal banking legislation were the National Banking Acts of 1862 and 1863. Under these laws, the federal government granted banking charters—and the right to issue notes to banks in return for a deposit of federal government bonds. The goal of this legislation was to sell federal bonds to help finance the Union effort during the Civil War and to institute a more uniform currency. Under the National Banking Acts, the existing hodgepodge of state banknotes was taxed out of circulation and national banks were permitted to issue notes of uniform design that were printed by the federal government, although they were liabilities of the banks issuing them. The national banking era was beset by financial turbulence, however: severe banking crises erupted in 1873, 1884, 1890, 1893, and 1907.

One of the causes of these crises most often cited by contemporaries and subsequent investigators is that the money supply did not sufficiently expand and contract to smooth out the seasonal and cyclical ups and downs of the economy. For example, during the national banking era, interest rates showed a distinct seasonal pattern, rising dangerously high during the autumn months. During the fall, harvested crops were moved from the agricultural regions—primarily in the interior of the country—to large eastern cities, both for consumption and for export. The money to pay for these crops naturally moved in the opposite direction, leading to a shortage of funds in financial centers, accompanied by higher interest rates and a greater risk of financial crisis. This agricultural-based movement of funds explains why the vast majority of financial crises took place during the autumn months. Once the Federal Reserve was established in 1914, seasonal fluctuations—and the threat of autumn panics—were greatly reduced. Given the techniques developed by Biddle as early as the 1820s, it is entirely possible that if there had been a central bank in the United States during the remainder of the nineteenth century, it could have moderated seasonal fluctuations and prevented several of these costly financial crises.

A central bank could have mitigated crises that nonetheless occurred. A crucial aspect of the evolution of European central banks was their development of lender-of-last-resort techniques and acceptance of the responsibility to assume that role. The Bank of England developed into a lender of last resort over the course of the nineteenth century. That evolution was essentially complete by 1873, when Walter Bagehot presented the first comprehensive statement of the role and responsibilities of the lender of last resort in his classic volume, *Lombard Street*. The central banks of France, Sweden, Norway, and Denmark also evolved into lenders of last resort by about the turn of the twentieth century—15 years before the Federal Reserve was established as a response to the financial crisis of 1907. Had it survived, the Bank of the United States could well have been a pioneer in this field, making nineteenth century American banking far less crisis prone.

Given its potential to promote financial stability, the decision not to renew the charter of the Bank of the United States—not once, but twice—was a major public policy error. The failure had two main causes. First, it was due in part to the deep-seated partisan and sectional divisions in the country. The bank was supported by those who thought that it would benefit their economic interests and opposed by those felt it would be detrimental to theirs. Second, ideology was a crucial element of the failure to renew the bank. Jefferson and Madison, who had been ideologically opposed to the bank, were won over by its practical benefits. Jackson's ideological opposition could not be overcome and, because it could not, American banking was condemned to suffer crisis after crisis for the next three-quarters of a century.

Chapter 4

The Great Hunger

Famine in Ireland, 1845–1852

And there shall arise after them seven years of famine; and all the plenty shall be forgotten in the land of Egypt; and the famine shall consume the land; and the plenty shall not be known in the land by reason of that famine which followeth; for it shall be very grievous.

GENESIS 41:30–31

Ireland died of political economy.

JOHN MITCHEL

The Irish famine was one of the worst disasters of the nineteenth century. It left roughly one million people—or about 12 percent of Ireland's population—dead in its wake and led an even larger number to emigrate. The Great Hunger, or *An Gorta Mór* in the Irish language, lives on in Irish oral tradition, as well as in scholarly and popular books with such evocative titles as *Paddy's Lament*, *This Great Calamity*, and *Why Ireland Starved*. The memory of the famine has entered the political realm as well. During the 1990s, Ireland's president, Mary Robinson, invoked the Irish experience in urging greater attention toward modern famine victims, arguing that: "the past gave Ireland a moral viewpoint and an historically informed compassion on some of the events happening now." She further wrote that "we can honor the profound dignity of human survival best...by taking our folk-memory of this catastrophe into the present world with us, and allowing it to strengthen and deepen our identity with those who are still suffering."

The Irish famine was a humanitarian tragedy of massive proportions. Some have framed the calamity in genocidal terms, arguing that the crisis was a result of deliberate British policy. Leading scholars of the famine categorically reject this accusation. However, the charge that British demonstrated a greater commitment to an economic ideology than to the relief of human suffering cannot be dismissed.

Famines have been common occurrences since the beginning of recorded history. The Egyptian famine described at the beginning of this chapter is reckoned by biblical scholars to have occurred around 1650 BCE; famines are mentioned on Egyptian *stelae* (inscribed stone pillars) from as far back as the third millennium BCE. Famines were common in ancient China. According to one researcher, between 108 BCE and 1911 CE there were 1828 famines across China. In other words, for more than 2000 years, there was a famine in one part of China or another in nine out of ten years. Another researcher, writing in the 1920s, emphasized the prevalence of famine in China by noting that "[i]n China, the polite salutation on meeting a friend is 'Have you eaten?' instead of the customary inquiry as to one's health or well-being usually employed in other tongues." Famines were known in ancient Greece and Rome, and elsewhere in the ancient and medieval worlds and were typically the result of human agency (e.g., wars), natural phenomenon (e.g., droughts), or both.

In terms of sheer numbers, the Irish famine was as at least as deadly as the Asian and African famines of the past 40 years. The Ethiopian famine of 1985–86 and North Korean famine of 1995–2000, both of which killed between 600,000 and one million people, come closest in severity. The Chinese famines of 1877–79 (9.5–13 million) and 1927 (3–6 million) and the Soviet famines of 1921–22 (9 million) and 1932–33 (5–6 million) each took much higher tolls than the Irish famine. The 1959–61 famine associated with China's Great

Leap Forward, with excess mortality estimates ranging from 15 million to more than twice that number, is characterized by one famine scholar as being in a "macabre league of its own." All these famines, however, killed a far smaller *percentage* of their country's population, ranging from 1 percent to 7 percent, compared with the Irish famine, which killed about 12 percent. Thus, by historical standards, the Irish famine was severe both in its absolute size and in terms of its impact relative to the size of the population.

The famine had a long-lasting effect on Ireland. On the eve of the famine, Ireland's population was just shy of 8.5 million; by its end, through death and emigration, it had been reduced to less than 6.5 million. Ireland's population decline continued for an entire century. On the eve of World War I, Ireland's population was about 4.25 million, roughly equivalent to its population today. By the early 1960s, it had reached a low point of about 2.8 million. Even today, Ireland's population is only about three-quarters of its pre-famine level.

Numbers, of course, cannot adequately express the misery the famine exacted. On December 15, 1846, Cork magistrate Nicholas Cummins traveled to Skibbereen in the southwestern part of the county and was haunted by what he saw. One week later he wrote a letter describing the scene the to the Irish-born Duke of Wellington, a copy of which he sent to the *Times* of London:

> Being aware that I should have to witness scenes of frightful hunger, I provided myself with as much bread as five men could carry, and on reaching the spot I was surprised to find the wretched hamlet apparently deserted. I entered some of the hovels to ascertain the cause, and the scenes which presented themselves were such as no tongue or pen can convey the slightest idea of. In the first, six famished and ghastly skeletons, to all appearances dead, were huddled in a corner on some filthy straw, their sole covering what seemed a ragged horsecloth, their wretched legs hanging about, naked

above the knees. I approached with horror, and found by a low moaning they were alive—they were in fever, four children, a woman and what had once been a man. It is impossible to go through the detail. Suffice it to say, that in a few minutes I was surrounded by at least 200 such phantoms, such frightful spectres as no words can describe, either from famine or from fever. Their demoniac yells are still ringing in my ears, and their horrible images are fixed upon my brain.

Equally horrific stories of the famine abound.

Cormac Ó Gráda, a leading scholar of the famine, writes: "Whoever says 'Irish famine' says 'potato.' Without the massive and repeated failures of the potato crop in Ireland from 1845 on, there would have been no famine." This assertion contains two important statements. First, the Irish—and particularly, the Irish poor—were inordinately dependent on the potato; second, the potato crop failed on a massive scale in several consecutive years.

The potato originated in the Americas, reaching Ireland via Spain about 1590. Although cultivated in Britain, Alsace, Belgium, Switzerland, and elsewhere in Europe, nowhere was it more important as food—for both humans and animals—than in Ireland. During the early 1840s, the average adult male in Ireland consumed about 5 pounds of potatoes per day. For the poorest third of the population, the rate was even higher: about 10–12 pounds per person per day. By comparison, contemporary daily consumption was far less in France (6 ounces per person in 1852), Norway (20 ounces in the 1870s), and Holland (28.5 ounces). The only areas to come close to Ireland in potato consumption were Belgian Flanders (2.2 pounds in 1800, 4.4 pounds in 1845), Alsace (6.5 to 8 pounds), and Prussia (about half a pound in 1800, about 2.5 pounds by the 1840s).

As a crop, the potato flourished in Ireland because of the country's favorable climate and soil. It is not clear exactly why it became

such a crucial crop and whether its rise to prominence was a cause
or consequence of Ireland's rapid pre-famine population growth.
What is clear is that Irish meals of potato and buttermilk provided
sufficient calories and minerals, as well as almost all the vitamins
required for a healthy population. Pre-famine Ireland had low inci-
dences of scurvy, pellagra, and other vitamin-deficiency-related ill-
nesses common in developed countries during the nineteenth and
early twentieth centuries. Assessing pre-famine Irish diets, modern scholars have concluded that they were "excellent, not merely
when measured by 'recommended daily intake' of the nutritionist,
but also when set against the historical reality of the nineteenth
century."

The prominence of the potato in Ireland was not only acknowledged but also celebrated. Thomas Keating, an Irish émigré in
France at the time of the Revolution, advised the French to follow
the Irish example:

> To be convinced that potatoes are as nutritious and good
> as corn bread one needs only to consider the actual state of
> Ireland. The island contains a little more than three million
> people, and it is incontestable that two thirds of them eat no
> more than twelve pounds of bread a year. The Irish live on
> potatoes, to which they occasionally add a little salt and but-
> ter. And yet the whole world knows that the Irish peasants
> are very strong and very brave.

An important downside to the high reliance on the potato was that
when the crop failed, as it did on several occasions before the famine
considered here, the consequences were dire. The crop failure of the
mid-nineteenth century resulted from the infestation of a fungus,
Phythophthora infestans. This fungus struck the United States during
the summer of 1843 and made its way across the Atlantic by 1845,
although the precise route it took is a matter of debate. The infestation was spotted in England in August 1845. The blight, as it is now

known, had no name when it was first discovered, but was referred to as "the disease," "the blight," "distemper," "the rot," "the murrain" or, perhaps most fittingly, "the blackness" because the afflicted potatoes decomposed into an inedible black mass. The spores of the fungus spread easily and needed only mild temperatures and moisture—both commonplace in Ireland—to multiply.

The blight reached Ireland in September 1845. It was first spotted in Wexford and Waterford counties in the southeast of the country. The potato crop was badly damaged in 1845, with perhaps one-quarter to one-third of the harvest lost to the blight. However, because yields were uncommonly high in that year, the net effect of the disease was not devastating. About 14.8 million tons of potatoes were harvested in 1844; in 1845 the amount fell to about 10 million tons. The destruction of the 1846 crop was far more complete: less than 3 million tons of potatoes were harvested. Because of the fear of the blight, the total acreage planted with potatoes was dramatically reduced—from more than 2 million acres in 1846, to less than 300,000 in 1847. The crop was healthier in 1847, but because far fewer acres had been planted, the total amount of potatoes harvested was again quite small, barely 2 million tons. The respite from the blight led to increased planting, and the area under cultivation in potatoes rose to 800,000 acres in 1848. The blight returned in 1849, however, and wet conditions again resulted in a small potato crop.

Potatoes grow from a plant. Although the plant's leaves are visible, the potatoes themselves develop underground and therefore cannot be seen until they are harvested. Although the blight was first spotted in September 1845, because the potato harvest did not begin in earnest until October, it was difficult to appreciate the severity of the damage to the crop at first. Nonetheless, the Conservative government of Prime Minister Sir Robert Peel acted swiftly. Within a week of the first sightings of the blight, the government ordered the local constabulary in every county to provide weekly reports on the potato crop. By October, Peel had dispatched a scientific commission to Ireland to investigate and offered to provide free of charge any chemical that would halt the disease. The commission's recommendations were widely distributed—the government had 70,000 copies printed and distributed 30 to each parish priest in the country; the Royal Agricultural Society distributed 10,000 copies to local agricultural bodies. Unfortunately, the scientific investigators had misdiagnosed the problem, and the remedies they suggested were completely ineffective.

In November, the government established a temporary relief commission to organize food depots and to coordinate the efforts of local relief committees. Without securing the approval of the Treasury, Peel and the chancellor of the exchequer George Goulburn ordered the import of £100,000's worth of corn from the United States, which arrived during the late winter of 1845 and spring of 1846. Additional corn and oatmeal were imported from Britain. The total amount of food imported, approximately 44 million pounds, was thought sufficient to feed nearly a half-million people for three months.

The government planned to sell the grain at cost to local relief committees. These committees were expected to raise funds, primarily from local landowners. The objective of the imports was neither to replace the domestic market for food nor to provide relief directly to the poor, but to sell grain—and put downward pressure on its price—when local prices rose excessively. To get cash into the hands of the poor so that they could buy food, the government enacted a series of public works projects aimed at making improvements in harbors, piers, and roads. These projects provided employment for up to 140,000 people at a cost of £600,000.

Beyond these measures, the main source of relief was the Poor Relief (Ireland) Act of 1838. Under this legislation, poor law unions supported by local property-tax payers were responsible for the administration of relief. "Relief" in most cases meant confinement in a workhouse. Between the enactment of this law and 1845, some

130 workhouses were established across Ireland. Workhouses were designed to provide relief but not to be sufficiently desirable to provide an attractive alternative to work. Conditions in them were, to put it mildly, unpleasant and included "segregation [from family members] and confinement, physical labor, unpleasant and sometimes inadequate food, and [inmates were forced to wear] a pauper's uniform." Because the workhouse was such an unattractive alternative, it was truly the last resort of the poor. By the end of March 1846, Irish workhouses housed fewer than 50,000 inmates. As conditions in the country deteriorated, the workhouse population grew, reaching its full capacity of 100,000 early in 1847. As the workhouses grew more crowded, conditions within them deteriorated and disease became rampant. According to a report in the *Economist* on January 2, 1847, "the dormitories resembled pig-styes more than habitations of human beings, and the effluvia from them was overpowering to the highest degree."

A variety of responses to the crisis were recommended by the press and by various officials. Some of the proposed remedies had been employed during previous food shortages; others had been adopted elsewhere in response to the potato blight. These suggested measures included a prohibition on distilling grain into alcohol and a ban on grain exports. The fact that Irish grain was being exported in the midst of famine seems perverse. Nevertheless, in the absence of government policy prohibiting its export or higher prices at home, grain producers had no incentive to refrain from exporting. As a practical matter, prohibiting grain exports from Ireland during 1846–47 would have made only a small dent in the food shortage— perhaps one-seventh of the calories provided by the shortfall in the potato harvest. Peel was skeptical of the benefits of such policies. He wrote: "I have no confidence in such remedies as the prohibition of exports or the stoppage of distilleries. The removal of impediments to import is the only effectual remedy."

By "impediments to import," Peel meant the Corn Laws. The Corn Laws, which had existed in one form or another since the seventeenth century, maintained a high domestic price for grain by imposing tariffs (a tax on imports) when the world price was low. In other words, when overseas harvests were abundant and the price of imported grain was therefore low, tariffs raised those prices so that domestic grain producers could charge higher prices without losing out to foreign competition. The law was popular with British and Irish landholders, the mainstays of the Conservative Party, because it kept the price of their crops competitive with imported grain, which at the time came mostly from Russia and Prussia. Thus, Peel's strongest political backers were staunch supporters of the Corn Laws. The famine convinced Peel that the Corn Laws should be repealed. His decision to pursue repeal split the Conservative Party. The repeal was passed with the help of the opposition Whig Party, which favored it as a matter of policy; however, the split led to fall of Peel's government. A Whig government, led by Lord John Russell, came into office in June 1846.

Peel's government had responded to the famine swiftly and effectively. Importing grain increased the availability of foodstuffs; the wages paid by public works projects made it easier for those affected by the famine to buy food. These measures were, to a large extent, based on successful policies undertaken during the earlier food shortages of 1817, 1822, 1831, 1839, and 1842. Peel himself had no doubt been influenced by his experience as chief secretary for Ireland during the 1817 famine.

It is certainly possible to criticize Peel for what he did not do, such as ban food exports and close distilleries. And he can be damned with faint praise because the challenge he faced during 1845–46 was not as severe as that which faced his successor. Nonetheless, the verdict on his administration by historians and contemporary observers alike has been positive. As his ministry drew to a close— well before it was known how severe the famine would become—the *Freeman's Journal*, which was no great fan of Peel, wrote:

> The limited distress which Sir Robert Peel was called upon to meet, he provided for fully and fairly. No man died of famine

during his administration, and it is a boast of which he might well be proud. Widen the circle of destitution in 1845 and it could be effectually encountered by the proper extension of the same policy.

It is not entirely fair to compare Peel's approach to the crisis with that of his successor, Lord John Russell. The situations they encountered were of completely different magnitudes. Peel faced only the partial destruction of the potato crop. The 1845 harvest amounted to perhaps two-thirds of the crop of the previous year. Russell became prime minister just months before the far more complete devastation of the subsequent crop. The harvest in 1846 was less than one-third of the already reduced crop of 1845, and famine would continue to oppress Ireland for another six years. Nonetheless, the differences in the approaches of Peel and Russell are noteworthy.

Ideologically, Russell and the Whigs were committed to laissez-faire economic policies. That is, they opposed government interference with market mechanisms. This ideology was responsible for their support of the repeal of the Corn Laws. Almost immediately upon entering office, Russell made it clear that his government's approach to the crisis would differ from that of Peel's. Speaking of the previous government's decision to import grain, Russell told Parliament on August 17, 1846:

In the first place, I think that the supply of Indian corn in the emergency which happened, was a measure of great prudence; but if it were to become established practice for the Government of this country, out of the resources of the Treasury, to purchase food for the people, and that this food should be sold by retail at a low price, it is evident that trade would be disturbed; that the supplies which are brought to us by the natural operations of commerce would be suspended; that the intermediate traders who deal in provisions in local districts would have their business entirely deranged; and that Government would find themselves charged with that which it is impossible they can perform adequately—I mean, the duty of feeding the people.

Or, as he put it more bluntly in correspondence with the Lord Lieutenant of Ireland in October 1846: "It must be thoroughly understood that we cannot feed the people. It was a cruel delusion to pretend to do so."

Russell discontinued Peel's policy of using government-imported grain to counter spikes in domestic prices. Instead, he closed the food depots in the eastern part of Ireland, where the government mistakenly assumed that the distribution system worked well, and maintained them only in the west. Further, when grain was sold from these depots, it was not sold at or below cost in an effort to lower market prices, as had been done during Peel's government, but rather at the prevailing local price—even if that price was high because the local market was controlled by a monopolist. Like Peel, Russell refused to impose restrictions on the export of grain from Ireland. Having just succeeded in repealing the Corn Laws, Russell was not about to reverse his stance on intervening in the market. "The fetish of free trade," wrote a later historian, "had tied their hands." In time, and against Russell's originally stated intention, the government did eventually authorize grain purchases, although these were small relative to the shortfall.

During the same speech, and with similar economic logic, Russell criticized the public works project adopted by the previous administration as having interfered with the free market for labor:

With respect to many of the public works, for which advances were granted, although they were themselves use-ful, yet the effect was that ordinary work was abandoned, and that the public works sought in preference to other works, so that here again the ordinary operations of work were disturbed.

He further noted that because of the availability of public-works employment, Irish workers had opted not to undertake seasonal agricultural employment in Scotland and the north of England, and as a result "the harvest has been delayed from want of labourers, and I believe that a great deal of the food of the country has in this way been lost." Blaming the Irish for a poor harvest in Britain no doubt did nothing to enhance Russell's popularity in Ireland.

Despite these objections, Russell did not propose to abandon the system of public works, but he changed their character. Under the new system, public works projects were to be planned and controlled by a central body (the Board of Works), but the financial responsibility for those projects was to fall more heavily on local taxpayers than on the government in London. In the words of English politicians and civil servants, "Irish property must support Irish poverty." The new public works scheme failed miserably. It was inconceivable that Ireland could afford these projects.

Despite Russell's skepticism, public works grew dramatically from the fall of 1846. The total number of people employed by the Board of Works rose from 26,000 at the beginning of October 1846 to 286,000 at the end of November to 441,000 in December, and peaked at over 714,000 in March 1847. Workers were paid less than a subsistence wage, doing jobs that had little economic justification. By the time the public-works projects were terminated in the spring of 1847, the cost of the relief schemes had totaled £4.85 million.

In place of public works, the government instituted soup kitchens which provided free food directly to the poor. These were modeled on the soup kitchens established by the Quakers in Cork and elsewhere, which had been widely praised. The soup kitchens were intended only as a temporary measure to bridge the gap between the end of the public-works schemes in March 1847 and the implementation of a new poor law. The new law shifted an even larger portion of the expense of relief to local taxpayers, who could not afford it, and led to an increase in number of tenants evicted from their homes. During early July when the soup kitchens were busiest, they served as many as three million people. In terms of cost and numbers fed, the soup kitchens have been judged to have been among the more effective solutions for relieving the famine. They were also among the shortest lived.

The verdict on Russell's handling of the Irish famine by historians and contemporary observers alike has been deservedly harsh. In one of the many coroners inquests that followed a famine death, a jury held that "death was caused by negligence of the government in not sending food to the country in due time." Yet another appended a rider to its finding of "death by starvation," recommending that a charge of willful murder be brought against Lord John Russell.

It is difficult to state with precision when the famine ended. Various authorities place the date in 1847, 1849, 1850, and 1852. In the summer of 1849, the workhouses were overflowing, with a quarter-million inmates; more than three-quarters of a million people were receiving relief outside the workhouse under the Poor Law. The famine ended in different regions at different times. Although death rates in Ulster had fallen back to 1846 levels by 1850, elsewhere the high workhouse mortality persisted into 1851. Famine-induced emigration, some supported by landlords eager to get their tenants to leave, was common. Emigration had totaled about 50,000 in 1844 and grew to more than 100,000 in 1846 and 1848; it exceeded 200,000 in every other year between 1847 and 1852.

In recent years, some have portrayed the Irish famine in genocidal terms. Some US states have mandated that the famine be taught in their high schools as an example of genocide, sometimes in courses originally intended for the study of the Holocaust. This is misguided. The vast majority of scholars of the famine do not view it as part of a genocidal plot on the part of the British. What is true is that British policy makers showed insufficient regard for Irish suffering. British policies to assist the Irish—particularly during Russell's ministry—were "tardy and half-hearted." As the crisis deepened, so did British insistence that solutions to the Irish problem be paid for by Irish taxpayers. Given the magnitude of the crisis, this was an impossible demand.

There is little doubt that a more effective approach to the Irish famine on the part of the British would have saved lives. Similarly, there is little doubt that if famine had struck Britain, the response would have been more energetic—as it was, the government was more worried about the lack of seasonal workers to assist in the harvest in Britain than in the suffering of the Irish. This indifference was not lost on the Irish. William Smith O'Brien, an Irish MP bitterly complained: "If there were a rebellion in Ireland tomorrow, they would cheerfully vote 10 or 20 millions to put it down, but what they would do to destroy life they would not do to save it."

The Great Irish Famine was, sadly, not the world's last famine. In the years since its end, severe famines have wracked China, the Soviet Union, Africa (most recently Somalia), the Indian subcontinent, and other countries. These and other countries that have endured famine in the subsequent years were already poor. They were often at war. And they generally did not have modern governmental or societal institutions. By contrast, Ireland in the mid-nineteenth century, if not rich, was by no means poor. It was at peace, possessed of a high standard of governmental and societal institutions, and was in a political union with the world's leading economic and military power. How did policy makers allow the tragedy to happen?

The commitment to free and unfettered markets made it impossible to act effectively in the face of Ireland's grave emergency. The primary culprit was the Whig administration of Lord John Russell, which balked at importing grain for fear of interfering with the workings of the market mechanism. Russell's blind devotion to ideology in the face of widespread suffering had tragic consequences.

Chapter 5

The Krauts Will Pay

German Reparations after World War I

Le Boche paiera tout (The Krauts will pay for everything).
LOUIS LUCIEN KLOTZ
French Finance Minister, 1917–1920

If we aim deliberately at the impoverishment of Central Europe, vengeance, I dare predict, will not limp. Nothing can then delay for very long that final civil war between the forces of Reaction and the despairing convulsions of Revolution, before which the horrors of the late German war will fade into nothing, and which will destroy, whoever is victor, the civilization and the progress of our generation.
JOHN MAYNARD KEYNES
The Economic Consequences of the Peace

The American Civil War general William Tecumseh Sherman is credited with coining the phrase "War is hell." Sherman, it should be remembered, was on the winning side. Although death and destruction afflict both sides in war, the vanquished typically suffer more than the victors. From time immemorial, defeat in war has led to the loss of political independence, territory, treasure, and more. Following the First Punic War (264–241 BCE), Rome stripped Carthage of Sicily and required it to pay an indemnity of 3200 talents of silver. Following the Second Punic War (218–201 BCE), Carthage lost Iberia, agreed to limits on its ability to raise an army or navy, and paid Rome 10,000 talents of silver. At the end of the Third Punic War (149–146 BCE), Carthage was razed and its population killed or sold into slavery. Hell, indeed.

The English economist John Maynard Keynes famously called the peace imposed on Germany in the aftermath of World War I "Carthaginian" and resigned in protest from the British delegation to the Paris peace conference. Although Germany's population and property fared far better at the hands of the Allies than those of Carthage at the hands of the Roman Republic, the conditions of the Versailles peace treaty were nonetheless harsh. Germany forfeited territory to surrounding countries and lost its colonial empire. The German army and navy were subjected to a variety of restrictions. The import and export of munitions was prohibited, and their manufacture in Germany was strictly limited. Finally, Germany was required to pay, by the standards of the time, extremely high levels of reparations. The crushing burden of these reparations contributed to Germany's economic and political instability during the interwar period. That instability helped pave the way for the rise of the Nazis and, ultimately, the German aggression that led to World War II.

The human toll of World War I was enormous. About 8.5 million military personnel lost their lives during the conflict, and another 15 million or so were wounded. To get a sense of the magnitude of the carnage, consider that the combined number of military deaths in *every single war during the preceding hundred years*—both wars between countries and civil wars—amounted to about 5.6 million. The number of civilian fatalities due to World War I is harder to calculate. If deaths stemming from the Russian Revolution are included, the total was probably somewhere between 5 and 10 million. The material cost of the war was similarly staggering. Writing shortly after the war's end, the economist Ernest Bogart estimated the "direct cost" of the war, that is, money spent by the combatants, to be $186 billion and its "indirect cost," the value of life and property lost, to be $152 billion. To put this total of $338 billion in context, it represented an amount greater than one and one-half times the total output of goods and services produced by the United States during the war's four years.

The Treaty of Versailles, signed six months after the armistice, placed blame for the war squarely on Germany and her allies, and made it clear that Germany would be made to pay substantial reparations. Articles 231–232 of the treaty stated:

> The Allied and Associated Governments affirm and Germany accepts the responsibility of Germany and her allies for causing all the loss and damage to which the Allied and Associated Governments and their nationals have been subjected as a consequence of the war imposed upon them by the aggression of Germany and her allies.
>
> The Allied and Associated Governments recognize that the resources of Germany are not adequate . . . to make complete reparation for all such loss and damage.
>
> The Allied and Associated Governments, however, require, and Germany undertakes, that she will make compensation for all damage done to the civilian population of the Allied and Associated Powers and to their property during the period of the belligerency of each as an Allied or Associated Power against Germany by such aggression by land, by sea and from the air . . .

Although the treaty enumerated several types of damages for which Germany was bound to provide compensation, it specified neither the total amount nor the time period within which the sum would have to be paid. According to the treaty, Germany was required to discharge its obligations within 30 years, although the Allies could postpone some payments if Germany's economic situation warranted it. There was to be no cancellation of any of the debts without the explicit agreement of the Allied governments. Instead of setting a the total amount of reparations, the treaty provided for the establishment of an inter-Allied commission, the Reparation Commission, that would determine both the amount and schedule of payments on or before May 1, 1921. The uncertainty surrounding both the amount and timing of payments—which persisted throughout the 1920s—made it impossible for the Germans to know exactly what would be demanded of them and when it would be demanded. This prolonged uncertainty exacerbated the burden of reparations.

Despite not fixing the total reparations bill, the treaty did specify an initial interim payment of 20 billion gold marks (about $4.76 billion) to provision the occupying armies and to pay for a variety of deliveries in kind that Germany was required to make to the Allies. These included a proportion of German's existing merchant ships and river fleet, as well as 200,000 gross tons annually of new merchant vessels. The Germans were required to deliver a variety of machinery, tools, reconstruction materials, and farm animals, including 700 stallions, 40,000 fillies and mares, 4000 bulls, 140,000 dairy cows, 1200 rams, 120,000 sheep, 10,000 goats, 40,000 heifers, and 15,000 sows. Further deliveries in kind included up to 43.5 million tons of coal to France and Belgium, 50 percent of the stock of dyestuffs and chemicals on hand at the time of the treaty's signature, plus 25 percent of normal production through January 1, 1925.

The leaders of the Allied powers held a series of meetings during 1920–21 to discuss postwar arrangements, including reparations. These meetings took place in Italy (San Remo), England (Hythe and London), France (Boulogne and Paris), and Belgium (Spa and Brussels). France was the most determined of the Allies to impose severe penalties on Germany. France's resolve can be traced to three factors. First, much of the fighting during World War I—and the greatest amount of physical destruction—had taken place on French soil. Second, the London conference on reparations took place practically on the 50th anniversary of France's defeat—and loss of the recently regained territory of Alsace-Lorraine—at the hands of

the Germans in the Franco-Prussian War. Finally, France was concerned about Germany's economic ascendancy. At the time of the
Franco-Prussian War—even after the loss of Alsace-Lorraine—
France and Germany had similarly sized populations and were at
roughly equivalent levels of economic development. By 1914, however, the population of Germany was nearly 70 percent larger than
that of France, and Germany, in terms of trade, industry, and technology, had far outpaced France.

By the time the Allies convened in London in May 1921 to establish the schedule of reparations payments, it had become clear that
the United States Senate would not ratify the Treaty of Versailles.
Hence the United States, the Allied power that was the least inclined
to extract harsh reparations form Germany, was reduced from
one of the "Big Four" (along with France, Great Britain, and Italy)
to observer status. This limited the Americans' ability to support
Britain's opposition to the more extreme demands of the French
and Italians.

The London negotiations resulted in a total reparations bill of
132 billion gold marks, or about $31 billion. This was reduced from
an earlier demand, expressed in the Paris resolutions of January
1921, of 226 billion gold marks ($53 billion) but was still about three
times the $10 billion that Keynes had estimated Germany could
afford to pay. Under the London Schedule of Payments, Germany
was to begin service on 50 billion gold marks (about $11.7 billion)
immediately, with the remaining 82 billion marks deferred pend-
ing an increase in Germany's capacity to pay. Debt service (principal
and interest) plus occupation costs resulted in initial payments of
four billion gold marks, or slightly less than $1 billion, per year.

The London Schedule of Payments can be put into historical
perspective by comparing it with reparations imposed on France in
the aftermath of the Napoleonic (1815–19) and Franco-Prussian
(1871) wars, and those imposed on Germany, Italy, and Japan
following World War II. By almost every standard, reparations
assessed at the London conference far exceeded those imposed in

the aftermath of these other conflicts. Germany's post–World War I reparation obligations were equivalent to approximately 83 percent of one year's total economic output, 350 percent of one year's tax revenues, and 500 percent of one year's exports. By contrast, the reparations imposed on France in the aftermath of the Napoleonic and Franco-Prussian wars were 25 percent or less of total output, about 200 percent of one year's taxes, and 200 percent to 400 percent of one year's exports. The reparations payments imposed on Germany, Japan, and Italy in the aftermath of World War II—perhaps in light of the post–World War I experience—were far lower by all these measures.

Although the reparations burden imposed on Germany in 1921 was enormous, its magnitude cannot be laid solely at the feet of the European allies. By the war's end a substantial amount of inter-Allied debt had accumulated. The United States entered the war in April 1917 and began lending to its allies on a large scale soon afterward. By the war's end, the United States was owed about $11 billion and was by far the largest net creditor. The British were owed approximately the same amount, including a substantial sum from Russia (the repayment of which was in doubt following the Russian Revolution); however the British, in turn, owed the United States $4.7 billion, giving them a net credit balance of $6.4 billion. Similarly, the French were owed about $3.5 billion—approximately 40 percent of which was due from Russia—but had borrowed $4 billion from the United States and $3 billion from Britain, leaving them with a net debt of $3.5 billion. Proposals to negotiate a reduction or cancellation of British and French debt to the Americans—including one to make French payments to the Americans conditional on German payments to France—which would have made it more palatable for the British and French to ease their financial demands on Germany, were rebuffed by the United States.

The accumulation of debts was, in part, a result of the haphazard ways in which the economic and military costs of the war were shared among the Allies. Writing in the early 1920s, one observer noted that the British had provided six-inch howitzers to the Italian army to be fired by Italian gunners in support of Italian infantry. The cost of these guns was added to Italy's debt to the United Kingdom. However, when British howitzers, horses to transport them, and gunners to fire them were sent to Italy as part of the British army, the cost was borne by the British Treasury. Furthermore, the cost of the maintenance for British personnel and livestock in Italy, such as food and rail transportation, was billed to the British government.

A notable characteristic of virtually all the agreements pertaining to reparations, starting with the Treaty of Versailles, is that they were vague. Given clauses in many of the agreements that tied the level of reparations to Germany's ability to pay, several scholars have argued that there was little prospect—or expectation—that the assessed amount would ever be paid in full. Clearly, German officials had every incentive to understate their capacity to pay—and did. When the reparations assessed were nonetheless severe, the German government proved itself, as we will see below, willing to wreck its own economy rather than submit to allied demands.

The massive scale of reparations—and German resistance to them—took their toll on the economy. They also took a toll on the political stability of the new Weimar Republic that had been established to succeed the imperial government that had led Germany into war. The government's budget was in deficit throughout 1920–22, due in large measure to reparations payments. German deliveries in kind to the Allies fell short of prescribed amounts almost immediately and, in December 1922, the Reparation Commission declared Germany to be in default for failing to meet its assigned timber deliveries. In January 1923, French and Belgian troops occupied the Ruhr valley—a center of German industry and coal production—in an effort to extract reparations directly. German workers went out on strike and were supported by the government with direct payments, further contributing to the growth of the government's deficit.

Although the German government raised taxes in an effort to cope with the burden of reparations payments, the taxes raised were not sufficient to balance the budget. Government spending—including payments in support of striking workers—was financed by borrowing from the Reichsbank (Germany's central bank), which met the government's loan demands by printing more money. The resulting increase in the currency supply—by about 7500 times between January 1921 and December 1923—set the stage for one of the world's most famous episodes of hyperinflation. German prices rose to 10 times their pre–World War I level (July 1914) by January 1920—or over the course of about five and one-half years. This represents a substantial inflation by the standards of a modern industrial economy. For example, the US price level increased 10 times between 1946 and 2005, a period of 59 years; British prices increased 10 times between 1972 and 2007, a period of 36 years.

The next tenfold increase of German prices occurred by July 1922—taking only about a year and a half; the next such increase took place in less than six months; and the next in less than four months. By the end of the hyperinflationary period, tenfold increases in the price level were taking place within a matter of days, with the price level rising nearly 300 times in October 1923 alone. Concurrently, the international value of the mark fell dramatically: from between about 1.5 and 2.5 US cents throughout 1920 and the first half of 1921 to less than 0.00000000003 US cents by the end of 1923.

The sharp increase in prices was reflected in the similarly dramatic increases in the denominations of bills issued, since so many more marks were required to make ordinary purchases. Before the war, the highest denomination issued was the 1000 mark note, which was at the time equivalent to about $240. In January 1922, a 10,000 mark note was introduced, followed by a 50,000 mark note in November of that year. In 1923, denominations skyrocketed: a 100,000 mark note was introduced in early February, followed less than three weeks later by a 1 million mark note. By June, a 5 million mark note was introduced; in July, 10, 20, and 50 million mark denominations debuted; in August, the first 100 million mark note was produced, followed by 500 million and 1, 5, and 10 billion mark notes in September. Notes in the trillions (including 100 trillion) were issued in October and November. When a new currency, the Rentenmark, was introduced in November 1923, the rate of exchange between the new currency and the old was set at one trillion to one.

Evidence illustrating the severity of the hyperinflation abounds, including photos showing Germans burning banknotes to generate heat and using banknotes as wallpaper. According to one story, a suitcase filled with money was left by its owner on the sidewalk while he went into a store. When the owner returned to retrieve the suitcase, he discovered that a thief had emptied out the money and stolen the now much lighter suitcase. Another story, which resonates with college students, is of the growing practice of ordering two beers at once, since by the time the first beer was consumed, it would have been more expensive to purchase a second. Real or apocryphal, these stories are indicative of the disruption of normal economic life caused by the hyperinflation.

Stabilization took place in November 1923. Key elements included a currency reform, consisting of the establishment of a new currency, and a commitment to fiscal austerity. A law passed in August 1924 increased the Reichsbank's independence by limiting the government's power to appoint senior officers, a job that was taken over by the General Council, a new body that would consist of seven Germans elected by the bank's shareholders and seven foreigners. The law strictly limited the government's access to new credit from the Reichsbank, reducing the possibility that future deficits would be financed by printing money. The government's payroll was slashed dramatically, by cutting both the numbers and pay of government employees. Passive resistance in the Ruhr ended. Industrialists came to an agreement with the Allied authorities and increased their deliveries of coal and other products, and government subsidies to workers ended. Despite these measures, which led to a stabilization of the price level and exchange rate, Germany still faced a large reparations bill.

A measure of relief came with the implementation of the Dawes Plan. This plan emerged from a committee of experts appointed by the Allies in November 1923 to assess Germany's capacity to pay reparations. The committee was chaired by Charles G. Dawes, who had been the director of the US Bureau of the Budget (forerunner of today's Office of Management and Budget) and would subsequently serve as Calvin Coolidge's vice president. The committee made its recommendations in April 1924, and the proposals were accepted at the end of August. The Dawes Plan envisioned reduced reparations payments for the subsequent two years, followed by a gradual increase. Other aspects of the plan included the reorganization of the Reichsbank described earlier and a statement that German economic activity should be unhampered by foreign organizations, implying an end to the occupation of the Ruhr.

The Dawes Plan did not reduce the total amount of reparations or inter-allied debt, but by postponing the bulk of payments, provided some breathing room for the German government. The plan paved the way for an international loan of the equivalent of 800 million gold marks in foreign currencies: half of the loan was raised in the United States, a quarter in Britain, and the remainder in France, Italy, Belgium, the Netherlands, Sweden, and Switzerland. Although the loan was not large relative to German reparations payments under the Dawes Plan—the first year's payments under the plan were to be 1 billion gold marks—it played a crucial role in supporting German stabilization and encouraged a flood of private US lending to Germany. The plan was considered a success, and Dawes was awarded one-half of the 1925 Nobel Peace Prize for his contribution.

Despite the early success of the Dawes Plan, as the 1920s wore on doubts began to grow about the sustainability of Germany's financial position. Payments under the Dawes Plan were scheduled to grow from 1 billion gold marks in its first year to 2.5 billion by its fifth year. By 1928, S. Parker Gilbert, the American official supervising reparations payments on behalf of the Allies, was worried that the German government was again lapsing into fiscal irresponsibility. This led to the creation of yet another committee of experts, this time under the chairmanship of Owen D. Young, the president and chairman of General Electric, who had been a member of the Dawes Committee. The Young Committee, which met in Paris from February to June 1929, was charged with making a final adjustment to reparations payments, setting a definite total sum to be paid.

The Young Plan further reduced the reparations burden. It divided annual payments into two components: "unconditional" payments of about 660 million gold marks per year that could not be rescheduled in any way, and "conditional" payments of varying magnitudes (starting at about 1 billion gold marks), which were, under certain conditions, subject to postponement but not cancellation. The total of these two components was to be substantially less than the 2.5 billion gold marks due in 1929 under the Dawes Plan. The Young Plan included a provision stating that German reparations payments would be decreased if any of the inter-Allied debt was forgiven. It also included provision for a new 1.3 billion gold mark loan to Germany.

The Great Depression soon intervened. The collapse of the Austrian Credit Anstalt in May 1931, to which we turn in the next chapter, and the subsequent worldwide financial crisis led US president Herbert Hoover to propose a one-year moratorium on both reparations and inter-Allied debt payments. At the Lausanne conference the following year, Britain and France declared an end to German reparations. Although the cancellation was technically subject to agreement with the United States on a release of debtors from their obligations, the United States never agreed. When the one-year moratorium expired, both France and Britain defaulted on the American portion of their inter-Allied debt. Fourteen years after the last shot was fired, reparations had been finally laid to rest.

John Maynard Keynes was a British Treasury representative to the Paris Peace Conference. Keynes had argued long, hard, and ultimately unsuccessfully against making harsh reparations demands on Germany. Slightly more than three weeks before the treaty was signed, Keynes left Paris in disgust, writing to Prime Minister David Lloyd George:

> I ought to let you know that on Saturday I am slipping away from the scene of the nightmare. I can do no more good here. I've gone on hoping even through these last dreadful weeks that you'd find some way to make of the Treaty a just and expedient document. But now it is apparently too late. The battle is lost.

Less than six months later, Keynes published an extended indictment of the treaty entitled *The Economic Consequences of the Peace*. Brilliantly written and blatantly polemical, the book quickly became a worldwide best seller. It was especially popular in Germany. The book set the tone for much of the modern debate over the consequences of the Versailles treaty. An editor's introduction to a later edition of the volume summarizes this view:

> Germany was "broke"...with the best will in the world it could not have paid...[It is] possible, even plausible, that if the wartime victors had instead framed a generous settlement, cancelled reparations and inter-Allied debts, promoted free trade and international cooperation, and spared Weimar the humiliating admission of war guilt, German democracy might have thrived. The hyperinflation that destroyed the mark and the middle classes in 1923 and the severe Depression of 1929 might never have taken place. Hitler might never have risen to power. World War II might not have occurred. The Nazi death camps might never have existed.

The reality was, in fact, more nuanced. A number of scholars have argued that that the London Schedule of Payments and subsequent modifications "demanded less than met the eye," since there was little expectation that the entire amount of Germany's debt would ever be paid.

Despite these arguments, it is hard to view reparations as being anything other than oppressive. Even the 50 billion mark sum that Germany was required to service under the London Schedule of Payments—reduced from an original demand of 226 billion and a nominal liability of 132 billion assessed at London—was high relative to that assigned in the wake of previous conflicts. And the harshness of the reparations payments was not meant to achieve some reasonable economic policy but to advance the more ideologically grounded goal of enfeebling Germany. And Germany was, in fact, weakened. The reparations burden undermined the fiscal position of the German government and led to conditions under which the occupation of the Ruhr and hyperinflation were likely, if not inevitable.

The reparations were oppressive not only because they were high, but because of the uncertainty surrounding them. Every time reparations were set, they were set conditionally. The Treaty of Versailles itself did not specify a definitive amount of reparations, only an interim payment until the Allies could "finalize" the amount. The London Schedule of Payments set a very high—132 billion marks—level of reparations, but required immediate service on only 50 billion, leaving 82 billion marks that Germany might—or might not—have to service in the future. The Dawes plan reduced and rescheduled payments, but again left a great deal of uncertainty surrounding Germany's eventual liability. The Young Plan, which was intended as a final settlement was, even at the time, clearly not. Hoover's moratorium was similarly short-lived. This uncertainty made it harder for the government, domestic business and financial interests, consumers, and foreign creditors to anticipate and plan for upcoming economic disturbances.

The harshness and ambiguity of reparations, economic uncertainty, and the fragility of the Weimar Republic provided fertile ground for extremism. Hitler attracted his first crowds in early 1921 with speeches denouncing the London Schedule of Payments. In an eerie parallel, extremist parties in Europe today—including the avowedly neo-Nazi Golden Dawn party in Greece—have used the strict austerity measures brought about by the euro crisis as a soapbox for their unsavory views. It would be too strong to assert that there was a direct link from reparations to the rise of Hitler and Nazism. It is, however, impossible to ignore the contribution of reparations to Germany's descent into hyperinflation, depression, and political instability during the 1920s.

Have policy makers learned from the disaster of German reparations after World War I? Yes. Following the end of World War II, the victorious powers were again faced with the question of how to rehabilitate a defeated Germany. There were those, among them US Treasury secretary Henry Morganthau Jr., who argued forcefully that Germany should be completely deindustrialized—that is, turned from a manufacturing powerhouse to an agricultural economy. Morganthau claimed that if Germany were deprived of its industrial base, it would not have the capability to rearm and so would never become a threat to its neighbors. Despite support for this view within the corridors of power, the Allies took a very different approach. Although Germany remained occupied for several years—and East Germany for much longer—Germany was allowed to rebuild its industrial base. Further, Marshall Plan aide helped Germany to recover from wartime destruction and become one of the leading industrial powers in the world today. Although German reparations policy after World War I was an unmitigated disaster, policy after World War II suggests that policy makers can—and sometimes do—learn from their mistakes.

Chapter 6

Shackled with Golden Fetters

Britain's Return to the Gold Standard, 1925–1931

...England, that was wont to conquer others,
Hath made a shameful conquest of itself.

RICHARD II (II, i)

There are few Englishmen who do not rejoice at the breaking of our
gold fetters.

JOHN MAYNARD KEYNES

Essays in Persuasion

Long before he had his own economic disaster to worry about, Federal Reserve chairman Ben Bernanke wrote:

> To understand the Great Depression is the Holy Grail of macroeconomics. Not only did the Depression give birth to macroeconomics as a distinct field of study, but also—to an extent that is not fully appreciated—the experience of the 1930s continues to influence macroeconomists' beliefs, policy recommendations, and research agenda.

Bernanke's awe is well-founded. The Great Depression was the longest and most severe economic contraction the industrialized world has ever known. Almost all developed economies experienced a decline in their aggregate output of goods and services during 1929–34; in some cases, the cumulative loss was greater than one-fifth of a year's total output. International trade and industrial production fell dramatically. Unemployment rates exceeding 20 percent were common. And financial and currency crises were widespread.

"We do not yet have our hands on the Grail by any means," Bernanke wrote in 1995, "but during the past fifteen years or so substantial progress toward the goal of understanding the Depression has been made." A key development in that progress has been the recognition of the crucial role played by the gold standard in intensifying and propagating the Great Depression. The near-universal adoption of the gold standard during the interwar period, in turn, can be explained in large part by the decision of Britain—the preeminent economic power prior to World War I—to return to gold in 1925. That policy decision had catastrophic consequences.

Gold, silver, and other precious metals have been used as money since antiquity. They are well suited to this role for at least four reasons. First, because precious metals are prized as decoration, they are valuable whether or not they are officially designated as money. Second, because mining and refining precious metals is a slow, expensive process, the supply of these metals is limited and not liable to fluctuate wildly in the short run—another desirable feature in something used as money (consider Germany's hyper-inflationary overissue of marks after World War I described in the preceding chapter). Third, precious metals can be weighed and measured, so the amount of gold or silver they contain—and therefore their value—can be determined. Finally, because precious metals have a high value-to-weight ratio, they are more convenient to use in large-scale transactions than less valuable metals.

Coins minted from precious metals are also of ancient vintage. By stamping coins with identifying marks—a likeness of the king was common—and a denomination, the minting process helped to indicate exactly how much precious metal was contained in a coin and, therefore, how much the coin was actually worth, its "face value." Such official certification was frequently undermined by "clipping" (cutting small pieces of metal from the edge of the coin), "sweating," (shaking coins vigorously in a bag so that they shed some gold dust), and other ingenious methods of removing small amounts of precious metal from coins. Such practices left the perpetrator with both their original coins which, if the counterfeit was not discovered, would retain its full value, plus some surplus gold which could be melted down and coined. The great incentive to engage in clipping, sweating, counterfeiting, and other such fraudulent practices led governments to impose harsh penalties—including death—on those caught doing so and encouraged the development of improved minting techniques that made it easier to detect counterfeited or otherwise altered coins. Counterfeiters and coin clippers were not the only ones with an incentive to undermine the currency. By minting coins containing less precious metal than promised on their face, the king could produce more money with less gold, enriching himself in the process.

Until the middle of the nineteenth century, silver was the most common monetary metal. Because gold was so expensive—about 15 times as valuable as silver by weight—gold coins would have been too small to be useful for normal day-to-day transactions. Copper, on the other hand, was not nearly valuable enough to be a convenient form of money. Sweden, a large copper producer, adopted copper as a monetary metal early in the seventeenth century in an effort to increase the demand for copper and therefore to increase its price. Because silver was nearly one hundred times as valuable as copper by weight, copper coins were massive: the 10 daler piece weighed 19.7 kilograms, or about 43 pounds; the standard copper coin measured 24 centimeters (9.5 inches) across. This system rendered large-scale transactions all but impossible without the use of a cart and horse, and explains why Swedes were the first in Europe to use paper money on a large scale.

The rise of the gold standard in Britain is usually attributed to the great mathematician and scientist, Sir Isaac Newton. In 1717 Newton, who was master of the mint, was called upon to determine the price of the guinea, a coin minted from West African gold, in terms of silver. By setting a too low price for the coin, Newton made it cheaper to use gold than silver, effectively eliminating silver from circulation. This is an example of Gresham's Law, under which "bad" (cheap) money circulates, driving "good" (expensive) money, which is hoarded, out of circulation. A modern example will be illustrative. Many countries now issue gold coins. The market price of gold has exceeded $1000 per ounce since 2009, yet the face—and legal tender—value of the one ounce gold coin issued by the US Mint is just $50. It is therefore not surprising that these gold coins are not used to buy groceries and that vending machines are not set up to accept them, since they are far more valuable for the gold that they contain than as currency. If the price of gold were to drop below $50 an ounce, these coins *would* circulate, since they would be more valuable as currency than for the metal they contain. Although such a situation seems fanciful, it is not: the US Mint implemented regulations in 2006 prohibiting the melting down of pennies and nickels, because the value of their component metals (nickel, copper, and zinc) exceeded the face values of these coins. Although the disparity between the face value and market price of the gold coins issued under Newton's stewardship was nowhere near as large as those of the gold coins issued by the mints of the United States and many other countries today, the economic forces worked just as efficiently. Newton's action led to an exodus of silver coins from circulation; from that point onward, England's currency circulation consisted primarily of gold coins and gold-backed banknotes.

During the first three-quarters of the nineteenth century, several countries, including France and the United States, operated under bimetallic systems. Under bimetallism, the money supply consists of both gold and silver coins and banknotes backed by gold and or silver. Maintaining a truly bimetallic system—one in which gold and silver coins circulate side by side and neither is driven out of circulation by Gresham's Law—is complicated because if the ratio of the face value of the coins deviates substantially from the ratio of the value of their metallic content, one or the other of the coins will be driven out of circulation. In the United States from 1792 until 1834, the face value of gold coins was 15 times that of silver coins of equal weight. Since the market price of gold was slightly more than 15 times the market price of silver—approximately 15.5 to 1—silver, the cheaper money, circulated and gold was hoarded. When the US changed the mint ratio to 16 to 1 in 1834 (the market price remained less than 16 to 1), silver was overvalued and gold became the circulating medium—another example of Gresham's Law in action.

One reason for the persistence of bimetallism into the nineteenth century was the state of minting technology. Because the smallest gold coin was worth several days' wages and was thus too valuable to be used for day-to-day transactions, the currency supply had to be supplemented with lower-denomination coins. These could be made out of either silver or some much less valuable metal, such as copper. Because coins produced by early nineteenth-century minting techniques were relatively easy to copy, requiring that lower-denomination coins be made out of silver reduced the incentive to counterfeit. That is, the profit—assuming you don't get arrested—from counterfeiting a one shilling coin out of nearly a shilling's worth of silver is far less than from counterfeiting a one shilling coin one out of a quantity of copper worth a small fraction of a shilling.

Two additional factors contributed to the persistence of bimetallism. First, mining interests exerted political pressure in favor of the continued minting of silver coins, since it increased demand for silver and gave an economic boost to the silver mining regions of the country. Second, highly indebted sectors of the economy, such as agriculture, advocated for the coining of both gold and silver, since more monetary metal in circulation meant a greater money supply, higher inflation, and less costly borrowing—particularly important to those in debt—than limiting the currency supply to gold alone.

Aside from Britain, only Australia and Canada, which had substantial gold deposits, and Portugal, which had access to large supplies of gold from South America, were on the gold standard by the mid-1850s. Most other countries remained on silver or bime-tallic standards until the early 1870s. Because Britain was such an important player in international trade and the source of a great deal of international lending during the nineteenth century, other countries had an incentive to adopt the gold standard because of what economists refer to as "network externality effects." That is, switching to the gold standard made it easier for these countries to engage in trade and financial transactions with the world's economic superpower. A threshold seems to have been crossed when the newly formed German Empire used the war indemnity paid by France after the Franco-Prussian War (1870–71) to buy enough gold to establish the gold standard in 1872. The addition of this rising industrial power to the ranks of gold standard countries led to something approaching a stampede: Denmark, Norway, and Sweden adopted the gold standard in 1873; the Netherlands in 1875; Finland in 1877; Belgium, France, and Switzerland in 1878; the United States in 1879; Italy in 1884; and Japan in 1897.

What did being "on the gold standard" mean during the half century prior to World War I? It did not necessarily mean that many, or even most, cash transactions were concluded with gold coins. Certainly, in Britain, France, Germany, and the United States, gold coins were widely used and circulated side by side with banknotes; however, in other gold standard countries, the circulation consisted almost entirely of gold-backed banknotes. Maintaining the gold standard meant that the monetary authorities were committed to exchanging gold for banknotes—and vice versa—at a fixed price.

Adhering to the gold standard also committed the authorities to allow the free import and export of gold. To demonstrate the indispensability of this second requirement, consider the following example. Assume that Germany and France are both on the gold standard and that the German central bank stands ready to exchange its currency, the mark, for two ounces of gold while French central bank stands ready to redeem its currency, the franc, for one ounce of gold. Naturally, the exchange rate between the two currencies will be two francs per mark, since the gold content of the mark is twice that of the franc. Suppose, however, that the French suddenly forsake wine in droves and start drinking German beer. In order to quench their newfound thirst, the French will need to sell francs and buy marks. If they do this in sufficient quantity, the price of the mark will rise and that of the franc will fall—let's say to three francs per mark. At this new exchange rate, a savvy individual can profit by selling one mark in exchange for three francs, redeeming those three francs at the French central bank for three ounces of gold, taking those three ounces of gold to the German central bank, and exchanging them for 1.5 marks. The result of this series of transactions yields a tidy 0.5 mark profit on a one mark investment—a 50 percent return. The high profit insures that the transaction will be made again and again until the sales of marks (and purchases of francs) and flow of gold from France to Germany returns the exchange rate to the original two-to-one ratio. In the absence of a relatively free market for gold, this adjustment would not be possible and market exchange rates between currencies could permanently deviate from the ratio of their gold content.

With so many countries on the gold standard between 1880 and World War I, it was as if the industrialized world shared a common currency: gold. Countries might call their money marks, pounds, francs, or dollars, but the value of these monies was determined by their gold content. In fact, the exchange rates among the gold standard currencies remained fixed for so long, it is said that schoolchildren learned them by rote because they were as stable as the multiplication tables. This rock-solid stability removed a significant source of uncertainty for individuals and firms selling products, lending money, and investing abroad since payments would always be made in a gold-backed currency at a predictable exchange rate. Thus, the gold standard during the 40 or so years before World War I is credited with having facilitated the dramatic growth in the international movement of goods and services, money, and people during what scholars have dubbed "the first era of globalization."

The eruption of World War I rendered the gold standard untenable. Governments discouraged the export of gold, which might find its way into the hands of the enemy, preferring to conserve domestic gold holdings to use for the purchase of war supplies. Those who wished to export gold were required to secure licenses from the authorities to do so; such licenses were almost never granted. Even if there had been no legal restrictions against exporting gold, the high cost of insuring that it was not sunk or seized in transit would have made such shipments prohibitively expensive. Thus, the outbreak of hostilities effectively—if not officially—ended the gold standard.

Had the exigencies of war not brought about the end of the gold standard, those of war finance would have. Paying for the war led governments to borrow heavily and to print money to finance the war effort. Consider the situation in the United Kingdom. Britain's budget had been in surplus during nine of the ten years preceding World War I; but during the war years government expenditures were between three and four *times* government revenues. By 1920, British public debt was ten times its 1914 level. By 1923, interest and principal on the public debt accounted for more than 40 percent of the government's annual budget, nearly three times its share of the budget in 1914. The price level also rose dramatically during the course of the war: by 1920, currency in circulation, wholesale prices, and the cost of living had all risen to between two and one-half and three times their prewar levels. Such explosions in debt, deficit, money supplies, and prices were common among belligerents; more extreme inflationary episodes occurred in Austria, Germany, Hungary, and Poland.

As the war's end drew near, the expectation in Britain—as in other countries—was that a swift return to the gold standard was both desirable and inevitable. The government committee appointed to consider postwar currency and foreign exchange arrangements, appointed in early 1918, praised the prewar gold standard's promotion of Britain's financial stability and well-being, concluding: "[I]n our opinion, it is imperative that after the war the conditions necessary to the maintenance of an effective gold standard should be restored without delay." The desire to return to the relative financial, economic, and political stability of the prewar period was strong, leading the British economic historian A. J. Youngson to conclude:

> To a world which was seeking to recreate that stability and prosperity which was attributed, rightly or wrongly, to what men called "the nineteenth century," the gold standard was at the heart of the matter, the ark of the covenant. Its restoration did not complete the task of reconstruction, but what remained to do would follow easily, perhaps inevitably. Or so, at least, it was hoped.

The historical appeal of the gold standard was amplified by British pride. Germany and Austria—both defeated in war and subsequently wracked by devastating hyperinflations—had stabilized their currencies in terms of gold by 1924, albeit at a lower exchange rate than before the war. Perhaps an even greater blow to British pride was the fact that the United States had returned to the gold standard at the prewar exchange rate as early as 1919. The United States was left relatively unscathed by World War I and, unlike Britain, was economically ascendant. Contemporary authors wrote of Britain's desire for the pound to "look the dollar in the face." A French observer noted that the return to gold was for the British, "a question of prestige, a question of dogma...almost a question of religion."

Nor did policy makers seriously consider returning to the gold standard at a rate other than the prewar $4.86 parity, even though it was clear that achieving and maintaining that rate would pose serious challenges. A. C. Pigou, an eminent professor of economics at Cambridge University and a member of a government committee considering the return to gold in 1924, wrote that returning to gold at a rate below $4.86 "... need only to be mentioned to be dismissed, [it] could not seriously be considered as a policy for the United Kingdom."

The central character in Britain's efforts to re-establish the gold standard was Bank of England governor Montagu Norman. Norman was an extraordinarily complicated figure. Something of a recluse, he frequently traveled under assumed names and went to great lengths to avoid the press. He was also a towering personality in British finance, presiding over the Bank of England for 24 years. To put that tenure in context, during the Bank's previous two and one-quarter centuries of existence, the typical governor's term had been two years, with a few maintaining the post for three years, and one—during World War I—serving for five.

In seeking to engineer a return to the gold standard, Norman was cheered on by the domestic and international financial communities. He received practical help and moral support from fellow central bankers, particularly Benjamin Strong. Strong had been president of Banker's Trust in New York and in 1914 was appointed as the first governor of the Federal Reserve Bank of New York, part of America's newly established central bank. Strong and Norman first met in 1916 when Strong, one of the more internationally minded of America's financial leaders, visited London. One year later Norman was appointed deputy governor of the Bank of England; three years later he became governor. Norman and Strong became close friends, meeting regularly and maintaining an extensive correspondence about personal and professional matters. The friendship lasted until Strong's untimely death at the age of 55 in 1928.

Norman's commitment to the gold standard was unshakable. In a letter to Strong dated October 8, 1923, he wrote: "We can have nothing and perhaps deserve nothing but troubles until we are again anchored to gold. How and when can we do it?" To re-establish the gold standard, Norman needed to raise the exchange rate to $4.86, an extraordinary task given that it had been as low as $3.20 in February 1920. He accomplished this by maintaining high interest rates throughout the early 1920s, leading British economist T. E. Gregory to characterize his relentless pursuit of the prewar parity as "the Norman Conquest of $4.86."

The path toward the gold standard was cheered by the financial community. When the Bank of England raised interest rates in March 1925, seemingly in preparation for a return to gold, the *Economist* magazine urged that "the moment is not one for relaxation. It is rather the occasion for one more great national effort to bring the good ship *Great Britain* safely into port." After the decision to return to gold was announced by the chancellor of the exchequer Winston Churchill during his budget speech of April 28, the *Economist* positively blustered:

> Great Britain has made its gesture to the world in the grand manner: "Gentlemen, the war, with its temporary interruption of our mutual affairs, is over. We have the honour to pay in our accustomed manner if it so be that your account is in credit in our ledgers."

The achievement was applauded by Norman's central banking colleagues, notably by Strong, who cabled after the resumption, "We are all delighted and send hearty congratulations." Strong sent more than congratulations: the Federal Reserve Bank of New York and J. P. Morgan provided the Bank of England with $300 million in credits—to supplement the nearly $750 million in gold reserves that the Bank had accumulated during the run-up to resumption—to enable the Bank of England to buy up pounds in order to defend the new exchange rate. The return took place without incident and the credits were not used.

Britain's return put it in the company of the United States, Austria, Germany, Poland, Hungary, and several Latin American countries that were already on gold. Britain's return was clearly a turning point: spurred on by the British example, the Netherlands, South Africa, Australia, New Zealand, and Switzerland soon announced that they would also return to the gold standard. Belgium stabilized its currency in terms of gold later in 1925; France did so in 1926, and Italy, in 1927. By the end of the decade, nearly 50 countries were on the gold standard.

Although Churchill's announcement was welcome in financial circles, there were dissenting voices. Throughout the 1920s the prominent Swedish economist Gustav Cassel had warned about the dangers of returning to the gold standard. In Britain, prominent Liberal Party politicians, including former chancellor of the exchequer Reginald McKenna and press baron Lord Beaverbrook, decried the return to gold. John Maynard Keynes eloquently opposed the return in a short pamphlet entitled *The Economic Consequences of Mr. Churchill* (the US edition carried the slightly less provocative title: *The Economic Consequences of the Sterling Parity*), published just months after the announcement. Keynes argued that Britain's wartime inflation, which was more severe than that in the United States, combined with a return to the gold standard at the prewar parity would make British exports uncompetitive in world markets.

Keynes's argument can be illustrated with the following example. Consider identically sized shipments of British and American coal of equal quality. In 1913, the British shipment cost £100, while the American shipment cost $486. Assuming that shipping costs were comparable, at the prewar exchange rate of $4.86 per pound, importers of coal around the world would have been indifferent between spending £100 on British coal or $486 on American coal, since £100 at an exchange rate of $4.86 per pound is equal to $486. Between 1913 and 1925, prices of American goods—including coal—rose by about 48 percent, so the $486's worth of US coal in 1913 would have cost $721 in 1925; British prices increased by about 64 percent during the same period, so the shipment of coal that had cost £100 before World War I would have sold for £164 in 1925. At the $4.86 per pound exchange rate restored by Britain in

1925, the dollar price of British coal would have been $797 (equal to £164 times $4.86/£), or well above the $721 price for US coal. Under these circumstances, importers choosing between British or American coal would have chosen to buy American. For British coal to again be competitive with American coal, its price in dollars would have to fall to $721. This could be achieved through either (1) a decline in the price of British coal from £164 to about £148, since £148 times the old exchange rate of $4.86/£ equals $721, or (2) a reduction of the exchange value of the British pound to about $4.40, since £164 times $4.40/£ equals $721.

Given the situation described above, there were only two ways of making British exports competitive: (1) reduce the value of the exchange rate to about $4.40 per pound (i.e., devalue); or (2) engineer a decline in domestic prices (i.e., deflation). Since the government and Bank of England had just restored the gold standard at the prewar exchange rate, devaluation was out of the question. Hence, the only option was to bring about a decline in the level of domestic prices. Keynes argued that the only way this could be accomplished was by restricting credit—that is, by raising interest rates and driving the economy into recession so that workers would accept lower wages, allowing sellers to lower the prices of their goods and make them again competitive on world markets. Keynes stated the case starkly:

> By what *modus operandi* does credit restriction obtain this result [of lower prices]?
> *In no other way than by the deliberate intensification of unemployment.* The object of credit restriction, in such a case, is to withdraw from employers the financial means to employ labour at the existing level of prices and wages. The policy can only attain its end by intensifying unemployment without limit, until workers are ready to accept the necessary reduction of money-wages under pressure of hard facts.

This observation was prophetic. When owners of coal mines tried to impose wage reductions in 1926, the miners went out on strike in a bitter labor dispute that lasted nine months—and ended with the wage reductions remaining in place. The miners were joined in a general strike by more than a million and a half workers. The general strike lasted nine days and disrupted virtually all facets of the economy, including food production and distribution. The situation was so dire that the government enlisted a naval destroyer to import a shipment of yeast.

Because of the tight credit conditions imposed by the Bank of England, British prices fell throughout the 1925–31 gold standard period. In addition to the constant deflationary pressure, the Bank of England had to guard against any substantial short-term deviation of the exchange rate from parity to protect its gold reserve. Consider what would happen if the market value of the pound fell to $4.40. Individuals could sell one pound to the Bank of England in return for $4.86's worth of gold (the official price). They could use $4.40 of the $4.86 to buy another pound on the international market and pocket a net profit of $0.46 on their original investment. This arbitrage process could, in theory, continue until the Bank of England's gold reserve was exhausted. In order to counteract any downward pressure on the exchange rate, the Bank of England would have to buy pounds with its holdings of gold and foreign currencies and to increase domestic interest rates in order to encourage holders of gold and foreign currencies to buy pound-denominated assets with high interest rates and to prevent holders of pounds from exchanging them for gold and foreign currencies.

The need to balance the requirement to maintain the gold standard with concern about the deteriorating employment situation put the Bank of England under substantial pressure. Statistical analysis indicates that the Bank of England raised its main interest rate, the bank rate, when it began to lose gold. However, the bank was also concerned about the domestic economic effects of high interest rate policy, and was reluctant to raise bank rate further when

it was already high. An examination of public statements and private correspondence of the policy makers at the time confirms that
although the Bank of England was committed to the gold standard,
deteriorating domestic conditions put it under substantial pressure
to moderate any increases in the interest rate. Each time the bank
raised interest rates it sought to justify it as a necessary reaction to
some external event. As early as June 16, 1924—before the gold
standard had been re-established but during the period when the
Bank of England was gradually engineering a return to the prewar
exchange rate—Norman wrote to Strong following a lowering of
interest rates by the Federal Reserve Bank of New York:

> The reduction in your rate to 3-1/2 percent may, at first sight,
> lead one to believe that our rate ought to remain at four per-
> cent. I do not think so. I want to get our rate up, but it is
> necessary to find an excuse for raising it and at this moment
> no excuse is very apparent.

Strong, advising Norman of an impending rise in the Federal Reserve
Bank of New York's discount rate later that year, cabled to ask if Norman
would prefer to raise his bank rate first. Norman replied on December
8 that if Strong raised its rate by one-half of one percent, the Bank of
England would use the opportunity to raise bank rate by a full percent,
"and so appear to have our hand forced by you." Clearly, Norman was
concerned about the consequences of the restrictive monetary policy
required to re-establish and maintain the gold standard.

The interwar gold standard functioned poorly from the start.
Countries with overvalued exchange rates, like Britain, ran persistent balance-of-payments deficits throughout the period, which led
to substantial gold outflows and forced the authorities to maintain
high interest rates, which further dampened domestic economic
activity. This put policy makers in the politically uncomfortable

position of "sacrificing domestic industry on the altar of the gold standard." Countries with undervalued currencies, like France, enjoyed consistent trade surpluses and gold inflows; policy makers in these countries were under no pressure to undertake measures to reverse these flows. As money supplies contracted and deflation progressed, the gold standard began to crumble. Australia, New Zealand, Canada, and a number of countries in Latin America experienced substantial gold outflows and adopted policies making it practically impossible to export gold, ending the gold standard in all but name.

The final unraveling of the gold standard began with the collapse of Austria's Credit-Anstalt in 1931. Founded by the Rothschilds in 1855, the Credit-Anstalt was the largest bank in Austria. By absorbing the troubled Boden Credit Anstalt in 1929, the Credit-Anstalt had become larger than all other Austrian commercial banks combined, with a balance sheet that exceeded the Austrian government's total budget. The economic downturn had weakened the bloated Credit-Anstalt; when news of the bank's situation became public in May, the bank collapsed. The panic soon spread to Hungary, where the Credit-Anstalt owned a controlling interest in that country's largest bank. Concerns about the Credit-Anstalt's solvency led to massive withdrawals from Budapest banks, forcing many to close. The crisis then spread to Germany, where the collapse of the Credit Anstalt combined with the bankruptcy of a large textile company to lead to the failure of Danat-Bank, one of the country's largest banks, in July. That bank failure led panicked creditors not only to remove their money from German banks, but also from Germany. To stem the outflow of gold, the German government imposed exchange controls in July, barring the export of gold and effectively suspending the gold standard. Austria imposed exchange controls three months later.

Pressure soon fell on London. Because Britain had not suspended the gold standard, those with claims on London were able withdraw gold; by contrast, some £70 million of British assets were frozen in Europe. This led to a net outflow of gold, which severely reduced the Bank of England's gold reserve. In response, the bank raised bank rate twice during the last days of July to stem gold outflows and on August 1 secured a $250 million loan from the Federal Reserve Bank of New York and Bank of France to satisfy increased gold withdrawals. By this time, however, the momentum was overwhelming. Britain's gold standard was officially suspended on September 21; very shortly thereafter, a number of countries, including the Scandinavian countries and Japan, also departed from gold. By December, the pound had fallen by about 30 percent to $3.37. Norman suffered a nervous breakdown and took an extended leave of absence from the bank.

The end of the gold standard was liberating for policy makers. Freed from their "golden fetters," the Bank of England and central banks of other countries that had left the gold standard were free to conduct expansionary monetary policy. This led to currency depreciation, which helped increase exports, and to lower domestic interest rates, which stimulated investment. The economies of countries that clung to gold, including the United States (which did not leave the gold standard until 1933), Belgium (1935), France (1936), and the Netherlands (1936), continued to deteriorate until they left the gold standard. Countries that departed from gold early and experienced substantial currency depreciation enjoyed more robust industrial recoveries, greater growth in export volume, increased investment in plant and equipment, and were less likely to suffer further banking instability.

To a world that was still recovering from ravages of war, the idea of the gold standard was appealing. To the British, the lure of the gold standard was irresistible, conjuring up an era of political, military, and economic preeminence. Yet the idea of the gold standard was more appealing than the reality that emerged during the interwar period: exchange rates were misaligned, gold holdings were inadequate and poorly distributed, and the equally unappealing alternatives of leaving the gold standard or maintaining it at the cost of domestic economic prosperity put central bank governors on the horns of a dilemma.

Few scholars argue that the gold standard "caused" the Great Depression. They argue that the gold standard played a crucial role in transmitting the shock internationally, amplifying its effects, and making it harder for policy makers to find ways out of the Great Depression. Countries that left the gold standard early were more competitive in export markets. They were better able to conduct expansionary monetary policy, which was crucial for the recovery of domestic investment and industrial production. And they recovered from the Depression more rapidly than those that did not leave gold.

Britain was not the first country to return to the gold standard after World War I. However, because it had played such an important role in the prewar gold standard, its return provided the signal for many other countries to also re-establish the gold standard. The widespread return to gold played an important role in propagating and intensifying the Great Depression, as well as in preventing policy makers from undertaking steps to counteract the downturn.

Britain's decision to return to the gold standard was made for largely ideological reasons. Britain had operated under a gold standard longer than any other country, so returning to gold was not viewed as some sort of experiment but as a return to normal. Additionally, the gold standard had been synonymous with Britain's nineteenth-century financial, economic, and military dominance; the re-establishment of the gold standard held out the promise of a return to those heady days. Further, a return to gold had the backing of London's powerful financial community. Despite the loud and eloquent opposition of Keynes and others to the gold standard, the ideological argument won the day.

Even if policy makers had been convinced that returning to the gold standard was a bad idea, it is possible that the ideological appeal of the gold standard would have made it politically unstoppable no matter what policy makers thought. This reality was not lost on Norman who, after the gold standard collapsed, wrote in a letter to another central banker:

> Yes I have made mistakes also. I am now accused for having gone back to the gold standard. It was probably a mistake. And still in those circumstances I should do the same thing again. It is easy to see it afterwards. But a great deal of what happened in the meantime was not necessary but depended on policy. It might have been different.

It might have been different. However, because of Britain's emotional and ideological commitment to the gold standard, it was not.

Chapter 7

Trading Down

The Smoot-Hawley Tariff, 1930

The history of the American tariff is the story of a dubious economic policy turned into a great political success.

E. E. SCHATTSCHNEIDER

If there were an Economist's Creed, it would surely contain the affirmations "I understand the Principle of Comparative Advantage" and "I advocate Free Trade."

PAUL KRUGMAN

Few tenets of economics have been as firmly established for as long as the desirability of free trade. And none has been ignored for longer.

Countries that abide by free trade allow goods and services to flow across their international borders with as few obstacles as possible. Tariffs, taxes on imports designed to raise their price and to discourage domestic residents from buying them are the most well-known impediment to free trade, but by no means the only one. Quotas, quantitative limits on the amount of an item that may be imported, and subsidies, payments to exporters to encourage them to sell their wares overseas, also run against the principle of free trade. These policies and others like them that attempt to discourage the free flow of goods and services are termed "protectionist."

Despite economists' long-standing preference for free trade, much of the past three centuries has been characterized by tariffs, quotas, subsidies, and other barriers to trade. Notable exceptions to this protectionist trend include the half century prior to World War I and the years since World War II. Both of these periods of trade liberalization were characterized by a consistent lowering of trade barriers. Sandwiched between these two eras of relatively free trade, the period between World Wars I and II stands out for the opposite reason. So severe and widespread were the protectionist measures adopted during the interwar period, that it almost appears as if the industrialized countries were in competition with each other to see who could impose the most stringent barriers to trade. This "trade war" contributed to the collapse in international trade that accompanied the Great Depression. One of the first shots in this war—and one with serious repercussions—was America's Smoot-Hawley tariff of 1930.

Countries have long imposed protectionist barriers. Arguments in favor of protectionism usually revolve around defending domestic industry against "unfair" foreign competition. The modern version of this argument made most often in industrialized countries is that protection is needed to shield workers from "cheap foreign labor." This line of reasoning asserts that if foreign workers are paid less than domestic workers, the items they produce will be less expensive than similar items produced domestically. In the absence of trade barriers that raise the price of imported goods, consumers will purchase cheaper imports in preference to higher-priced domestic products. This forces domestic firms to close and workers to lose their jobs. Tariffs and other trade barriers raise the price of imports, allowing domestic firms to compete with lower-cost foreign producers and increase their sales at the expense of imports. Although barriers to trade are a boon to the protected domestic producers and their employees, they are more often than not offset by the losses faced by domestic consumers, who pay higher prices for both imports and the domestic products that compete with them.

Among the earliest advocates of free trade was Adam Smith, who argues in the *Wealth of Nations* (1776) that tariffs give a monopoly to domestic producers, which hurts domestic consumers:

> To give the monopoly of the home market to the produce of domestic industry, in any particular art or manufacture, is in some measure to direct private people in what manner they ought to employ their capitals, and must, in almost all cases, be either a useless or a hurtful regulation. If the produce of domestic can be brought there as cheap as that of foreign industry, the regulation is evidently useless. If it cannot, it must generally be hurtful.

In other words, if our industries can sell their goods more cheaply than imports, tariffs are not necessary; if tariffs are necessary to protect our domestic industries, then they hurt consumers. Smith further argues that the division of labor between workers with different skills is analogous to that between producers in different countries:

> The tailor does not attempt to make his own shoes, but buys them of the shoemaker. The shoemaker does not attempt to make his own clothes, but employs a tailor. The farmer attempts to make neither the one nor the other, but employs these different artificers. All of them find it for their interest to employ their whole industry in a way in which they have some advantage over their neighbors, and to purchase with a part of its produce, or what is the same thing, with the price of a part of it, whatever else they have occasion for . . . If a foreign country can supply us with a commodity cheaper than we ourselves can make it, better buy it of them with some part of the produce of our own industry employed in a way in which we have some advantage.

Smith's notion is that if an industry is efficient, it will flour-
ish without tariffs; if it is not efficient, it should not be the business of government to prop it up. Subsequent authors concluded
that trade benefits all who participate voluntarily, whether or not
their economies are particularly advanced. This argument in favor
of what economists call "comparative advantage" was first asserted
by Robert Torrens in *An Essay on the External Corn Trade* (1815)
and was formalized by David Ricardo in *On the Principles of Political
Economy and Taxation* (1817). According to the theory of comparative advantage, two countries can always benefit from trade, even if
one country is more efficient in all areas of production.

An example from introductory economics textbooks will illustrate the principle. Consider two brothers, Milton and Paul. Milton
is a freshman in college and has a term-paper assignment in his economics class; Paul is his 14-year-old brother. Milton is no doubt better at conducting economic research and more proficient at using
a word processor than Paul. In economics terminology, Milton has
an "absolute advantage" in both activities. Nonetheless, Milton can
still benefit from trade with Paul by spending his time conducting
research and hiring Paul to type up the paper. Paul has a "comparative advantage" in typing, since the cost of having him do the typing,
in terms of economic research given up, is lower if Paul types than
if Milton does. An important implication of comparative advantage
is that reducing tariffs permits more trade to occur and makes *all*
parties better off, even if one party has an absolute advantage in all
products.

The superiority of completely free trade has been challenged on
various grounds since Adam Smith's time. Among the oldest objec-
tion to free trade is the "infant industry" argument, which posits
that protection may be warranted—on a temporary basis—to allow
new, small enterprises to compete during their start-up phase with
larger, more established foreign firms. For example, if the early
American cotton-cloth industry operated with smaller, less efficient—and therefore higher-cost—factories than the competition

in Britain, tariffs could provide temporary protection, allowing American firms to grow in size, sophistication, and efficiency until they are able to compete on an equal footing with British firms. This argument was advanced by the first US secretary of the Treasury, Alexander Hamilton, in his *Report on Manufactures* (1791). Another argument against completely free trade is that tariffs can help defend sectors that are deemed "economically (or militarily) strategic" from foreign competition. Such arguments have been advanced to support a variety of protectionist policies in the auto, steel, and aeronautics industries. A more modern argument is that free trade is only beneficial when international markets are perfectly competitive; if they are not because, for example, there is a dominant firm, tariffs may actually increase economic welfare.

Each of the foregoing exceptions to the free trade argument comes with its own caution. How long does it take for infant industries to become mature and therefore able to survive without protection? Once an industry enjoys the benefits of trade protection, it has powerful incentives to lobby the government to maintain that protection, even after it has matured. Which industries are strategic and therefore worthy of protection? And who makes these determinations? Since tariffs are generated by the political process, industries and regions that are effectively represented are more likely to receive protection than those that are not, regardless of their actual strategic import or the maturity of their industrial base. Despite the various intellectual challenges to free trade, the economics profession—if not the public and politicians—remains solidly in favor of free trade: according to a survey of 210 economists published in 2006, an overwhelming 87.5 percent supported the elimination of remaining US tariffs and other barriers to free trade.

Nearly all European states emerged from the medieval period with high tariffs. Tariff barriers were not limited to national frontiers: even countries that were politically united often retained internal tolls. England and Scotland were united under one monarch from 1603 but did not achieve a customs union (in other words, "free trade") for another century. France, although governed by one monarch, was divided by 1600 internal tolls and tariffs prior to the French Revolution. The many states that would later become Germany were divided by some 1800 customs frontiers prior to the establishment of the Zollverein (customs union) in 1834—Prussia alone (which was about the size of Arizona or New Mexico) had 60 internal tariff frontiers covering nearly 2800 classes of goods. A ship carrying cargo from Mainz to Bamberg on the Main and Rhine rivers—a distance of about 170 miles—would have had to pay more than 30 separate tolls along the way, on average one every five to six miles.

The loss of the North American colonies—French Canada to Britain and the thirteen colonies to American independence—during the last part of the eighteenth century led to a major disruption of the colonial powers' trade patterns. British exports fell by about one-fifth following the American Revolution, and as a result the proportion of Britain's trade with northwestern Europe nearly doubled. This led Britain to seek bilateral trade treaties with other European countries. Aside from a short-lived accord reached with France in 1783, "Britain's unprecedented attempt at trade negotiations was most notable for its utter failure. From 1785–93, interminable negotiations with Portugal, Spain, Poland, Prussia, and several other important trading partners in Europe (and even Ireland) failed to produce any agreements." The French Revolution and subsequent Napoleonic Wars prevented any substantive progress being made on trade liberalization into the early nineteenth century. Further attempts by the British to negotiate bilateral tariff reductions during the 1830s and 1840s also failed.

One of the first major breakthroughs toward trade liberalization was the repeal of Britain's Corn Laws. The Corn Laws—"corn" being British English for "grain" of all types—had regulated the import and export of grain in England since the seventeenth century for the purpose of preventing "grain from being at any time, either so dear that the poor cannot subsist, or so cheap that the farmer cannot live by the growing of it." The price of grain, which had been high during the Napoleonic Wars, fell dramatically in their aftermath. In response, Parliament enacted the Corn Law of 1815, which allowed the tariff-free importation of grain when the price exceeded a certain level and prohibited entry when it was lower. A subsequent act (1828) introduced a sliding scale of duties on grain; this scale was further refined in 1842. By preventing the entry of less expensive grain imports, the Corn Laws benefited land-owning aristocrats, who reaped profits from their own agricultural activities as well as rent from their tenants, who were also engaged in agriculture.

The Corn Laws were phased out under the Conservative government of Prime Minster Sir Robert Peel in 1846. Because the Conservatives' strongest support came from the landed classes, many of them opposed repeal. Nonetheless, there were several crucial factors that contributed to the sentiment in favor of repeal. A nearly 50 percent rise in the population between 1811 and 1841 had increased the demands on domestic agriculture and resulted in high food prices. Industrialization and the growing importance of Britain's export industries, especially cotton textiles, increased pressure in favor of free trade as manufacturers increasingly complained about the protection afforded to agriculturalists and the resulting higher food prices their workers paid. An economic downturn in the mid-1830s, combined with already high food prices and high unemployment led to the rise of the first nationwide political-pressure group in Britain, the Anti-Corn Law League. The Irish famine, which emerged in 1846, further impressed on Peel the benefits of cheap foreign grain.

A striking aspect of the repeal of the Corn Laws is that it was completely unilateral and was not made conditional on equivalent tariff-lowering by any other country—attempts to reach reciprocal arrangements had been completely unsuccessful. As Prime Minister Peel explained in Parliament on January 27, 1846:

> Wearied by our long and unavailing efforts to enter into satisfactory commercial treaties with other nations, we have resolved at length to consult our own interests, and not to punish those other countries for the wrong they do us in continuing their high duties upon the importation of our products and manufactures, by continuing high duties ourselves.

Although some countries did ease their tariffs following the repeal of the Corn Laws, the movement was not widespread.

A second major push toward free trade came in the form of the Anglo-French Commercial Treaty of 1860, also known as the Cobden-Chevalier Treaty, which reduced tariffs on both sides. The treaty was pursued by Emperor Napoleon III, in large part due to France's isolation within Europe following its intervention in a war between Italy and Austria. Because Napoleon did not require legislative approval to ratify treaties, adopting the treaty allowed him to circumvent protectionist sentiment in Parliament. An important element of Cobden-Chevalier was a "most favored nation" (MFN) clause, which stated that if either country extended tariff reduction to a third country, the other party to the treaty would be entitled to the same treatment. Although Britain had already extended its new lower tariffs unilaterally, France's lower MFN tariffs only applied to Britain, leading many other European countries to seek treaties with France so their exports would be treated as favorably as those of Britain. The French subsequently concluded treaties with Belgium in 1861, the German Zollverein in 1862; Italy in 1863; Switzerland in 1864; Sweden, Norway, the Hanseatic cities, Spain, and the Netherlands in 1865; Austria in 1866; and Portugal in 1867.

Before proceeding further, we need to explain why it is difficult to characterize precisely how high tariffs have been set. Economists frequently calculate an economy's *average tariff rate* by adding up all the tariff revenue collected and dividing it by the total value of imports. Thus, if the US government collects $5 of total tariff

revenue on $100's worth of imports, the average tariff rate is esti-
mated to be 5 percent. Although the average tariff rate provides a
useful guide to the level of protection, and is one we will make use
of here, it may obscure some important features of a tariff regime.
Because it is a simple average, the average tariff rate cannot cap-
ture the fact that tariff regimes typically consist of many classes of
imports—each of which may be subject to widely differing tariff
rates. In the example above, for example, $5 of tariff revenue could
have been generated by a system that levied a 5 percent tariff on
all imports or by a system which imposed no tariffs on 95 percent
of imports but a 100 percent tariff on the remaining 5 percent of
imports. Further, the average tariff rate does not take into account
nontariff barriers. If the United States charges a low—or no—tariff
on the few items it allows to be imported, but prohibits the importation of the vast majority of items or charges such a high tariff on
them that no one ever imports them, the average tariff rate would
appear to be low, since imports would consist overwhelmingly of
low-tariff items, even though the trade regime was characterized by
a high level of protection.

Interpreting tariff rates is further complicated by the fact that
tariffs are assessed in two different ways: some are assessed on an
ad valorem basis, that is, as a percentage of the value of the item
imported; others are assessed as *specific duties*, that is, as a certain
amount of money per quantity of item imported (e.g., 20 cents per
ton). This means that the average tariff rate depends crucially on
the prices of items that carry specific duties. Changes in the prices
of items that face a specific duty can dramatically affect the tariff
rate. For example, a $0.20 per ton tariff on an item that costs $1.00
per ton constitutes a tariff rate of 20 percent; if the price of the item
falls to $0.50 and the specific duty does not change, the effective
tariff rate would rise to 40 percent.

Tariffs were imposed not only to protect domestic producers but
also to raise revenue. In fact, tariffs during the nineteenth century
were usually a government's largest source of revenue, so no country

ever reduced tariffs continuously or seriously considered eliminating them completely. Because all trade (aside from smuggling) came in through ports and under the watchful eye of customs inspectors, tariffs were a relatively efficient means of raising revenue—far more easily collected than a sales tax or an income tax. Even Britain, the most free-trade country in Europe, collected tariffs at a rate of about 5 percent from 1880 onward. France and Germany had similarly low tariffs as early as 1865; these were increased during the 1870s and 1880s for budgetary reasons before being reduced to near-British levels at the beginning of the twentieth century. Despite the presence of revenue-raising tariffs and the many complexities in characterizing tariff regimes precisely, it is safe to say that European tariffs declined consistently during the second half of the nineteenth century and that they were, on average, lower in 1913 than they had been prior to 1850.

In contrast to the main European powers, the United States maintained high average tariff rates—ranging between 20 and 40 percent—during the half century prior to World War I. US tariffs had not been uniformly protectionist during the early years of the republic. Hamilton's *Report on Manufactures* recommended only moderate tariffs, and, to a certain extent, this approach was adopted. Even without substantial tariffs, however, the high cost of transport from Europe to the United States imposed tariff-like costs on European importers and offered some protection to American producers. With the increase in imports following the conclusion of the Napoleonic Wars and the War of 1812, political sentiment in favor of protection grew and tariff increases followed, beginning with legislation enacted in 1816 and culminating with the Tariff Act of 1824, which had as its chief objective the protection of domestic manufacturers.

Nineteenth-century American tariff policy was often a partisan, and almost always a sectional issue. Because the American South was a heavy exporter of raw materials, particularly cotton, and less industrialized than the North, southerners were wary of tariffs. If foreigners raised their own tariffs in response to increased US tariffs, southern exports bore the brunt of the retaliation. Also, since the South had to either import many of its manufactured goods or buy them from the North, higher tariffs raised the cost of goods from both of these sources. The Tariff Act of 1828, which was even more protectionist than that of 1824, enraged southerners who labeled it the "Act of Abomination." The Tariff Act of 1828 contributed to the 1833 Nullification Crisis, in which South Carolina declared the 1828 law and the subsequent Compromise Tariff of 1832, which had lowered tariffs in an attempt to appease southerners, unconstitutional and unenforceable in the state. This set up a potentially violent confrontation between South Carolina and the federal government, although the conflict never came to blows. The bad feelings engendered during the Nullification Crisis may go some way to explaining why South Carolina was the first state to secede from the Union before the Civil War.

Tariffs followed a zigzag pattern between 1832 and the outbreak of the Civil War, rising under (primarily northern) Whig rule and falling when the (primarily southern) Democrats held sway. The fiscal demands of the Civil War led the Union to raise both taxes and tariffs substantially, as well as to devise new ways of borrowing money. Congress raised import duties during the summer session of 1861 and again during the winter session later that year. From that time through the war's end in 1865 " no session, indeed, hardy a month of any session, passed in which some increase of duties in imports was not made." By 1865, tariffs were higher than they had been at any time during the previous 30 years, although they fell from wartime highs through the early 1870s. During the subsequent half century tariffs rose and fell in a distinctly partisan/sectional pattern, declining under the southern-dominated Democrats with the Wilson-Gorman (1894) and Underwood-Simmons (1913) Acts, and rising under northern Republicans with the 1883 Tariff, the McKinley Tariff (1890), the Dingley Tariff (1897), and the Payne-Aldrich Tariff (1909).

Following World War I there were broad increases in tariffs on both sides of the Atlantic. Justification for tariff increases included the desire to protect new industries that had grown up during the war, to protect the new countries created by the breakup of the Austro-Hungarian Empire, and to protect against the growth in exports by countries with substantially depreciated currencies. Further, the extensive reparations imposed on Germany and the substantial inter-Allied debts encouraged countries to seek means— including protection—of generating export surpluses with which to pay off the debts. Britain raised tariffs in 1915 with the McKenna duties, which imposed a 33-1/3 percent tariff on a number of items as a wartime measure. After the war, Britain's Key Industries Act 1919 and Safeguarding of Industries Act 1921 imposed high tariffs on a long list of goods. By 1918, French minimum tariff rates were raised from 5 percent to 20 percent, and maximum rates from 10 percent to 40 percent. Germany had been required by the Treaty of Versailles to grant the Allied Powers most favored nation status for five years; as soon as the period ended, Germany raised tariffs.

No major US tariff legislation was passed during World War I, although the average tariff rate fell from the beginning of the war through 1920. This was due to the combination of wartime inflation and the fact that many tariffs were specific duties: with the wartime prices of imports rising and the tariff per item fixed, the average tariff rate fell. The return of the Republicans to power after the election of 1920 and the decline in agricultural prices following the end of the World War I boom, which increased agitation among agriculturalists for tariff protection, led to the enactment of the temporary Emergency Tariff Act of 1921, followed by the Fordney-McCumber Tariff in 1922. The enactment of new, higher, tariff rates, combined with a sharp deflation in 1920–21 resulted in the average tariff rate more than doubling, from about 6.5 percent to about 15 percent.

The tariff increases, particularly the Fordney-McCumber Tariff, were not well-received abroad, and led to protests and retaliation, as well as attempts to negotiate a tariff truce. Between 1925 and 1929, there were 33 general revisions and substantial tariff changes in 26 European countries and 17 revisions and changes in Latin America. In August 1926 both Bulgaria and Czechoslovakia protested against Fordney-McCumber and threatened retaliation if rates were not lowered. France had been hard hit by both Fordney-McCumber, as well as by Prohibition's Volstead Act (1919), which barred wine imports. France raised import duties in April 1927, specifically targeting American automobiles, but at the same time suggested that compromise with the United States was possible. The following month, Spain announced a 40 percent increase in duties on American imports. International conferences at Brussels (1920), Portorose (1921), and Genoa (1922) strongly endorsed a tariff truce, as did the League of Nations' 1927 World Economic Conference in Geneva, with little effect.

During the election campaign of 1928, Republican presidential candidate Herbert Hoover pledged to increase tariffs on agricultural goods in an attempt to support farmers. After a dramatic decline during 1920–21, farm prices rose through 1925 before falling slightly during 1926 and 1927. Despite their recovery during the first half of the decade, farm prices lagged behind the overall level of consumer prices throughout the 1920s. Therefore, a farmer producing the same quantity of output in 1929 as in 1919 would have been able to afford fewer manufactured items with the cash realized by selling the harvested crop. Although the Hoover campaign emphasized agricultural tariffs, the Republican platform was committed to raising tariffs more broadly. Six weeks after his inauguration, Hoover called Congress into special session to consider tariff legislation. The session lasted 14 months, the record of public hearings ran to 20,000 pages, and the final bill included tariff schedules for more than 20,000 items.

The Tariff Act of 1930, known as Smoot-Hawley after its sponsors, passed the Senate by a 44–42 vote on June 13 and the House by a 245–177 vote the following day, with overwhelming Republican support. Hoover signed the bill into law on June 17, 1930. Strictly speaking, the law should be known as Hawley-Smoot, since under the US Constitution revenue bills must originate in the House of Representatives and its lead House sponsor was Oregon Rep. Willis C. Hawley. It was popularly known as Smoot-Hawley because of the prominence of Hawley's Senate cosponsor, Utah's Reed Smoot. The Smoot-Hawley Act raised the tariff on dutiable items by between 6 percent and 15 percent. The average tariff rate rose from about 13.5 percent in 1929 to nearly 20 percent by 1932, although some of this increase occurred because of the combination of falling prices and specific duties. Although the increase was substantial, it was not unprecedented: the increases imposed by the 1922 Fordney-McCumber Tariff and the decreases under the 1913 Underwood-Simmons Tariff were substantially larger.

Why was Smoot-Hawley passed? In an early and comprehensive study of the tariff, E. E. Schattschneider argues that the pattern of protection in the legislation was the result of intensive lobbying by various agricultural and industrial special interests. He ascribes the political forces in favor of tariffs as being aided by the fact that the benefits of any given tariff are typically concentrated in one industry, while its costs are usually spread more broadly across the economy. Put more succinctly: "Benefits are concentrated while costs are distributed." Others paint Smoot-Hawley as resulting from party politics, and hence the inevitable result of the Republican Party's election victory in 1928. Still others suggest that the tariff resulted from the cooperation between northern farmers and those involved light industry, both of whom benefited from the tariff. An analysis of a series of Senate roll-call votes on the tariff finds that economic interests motivated individual senators to support the law. Further evidence suggests that the measure passed, in part, because of "log-rolling," or "vote-trading," that is, Senator A supporting tariff protection favorable to Senator B's constituents in return for Senator B's vote in favor of tariff protection for Senator A's constituents.

Economists, not surprisingly, opposed the tariff. On May 17, a petition signed by 1028 professors of economics from 179 colleges and universities was sent to Washington, urging Congress to vote down the legislation and, if it should pass, for Hoover to veto it. The academics had little impact on either Congress or the president. Senator Samuel Shortbridge (R-CA) declared that he was "not over-awed or at all disturbed by the proclamation of the college profes-sors who never earned a dollar by the sweat of their brow by honest labor." Shortbridge, it should be noted, did not make his living by the sweat of his brow either—he was admitted to the bar in his early twenties and made his living by practicing law before being elected to the Senate.

Almost as soon as it was enacted, Smoot-Hawley was viewed as having been a dubious policy choice. Because it was enacted just as the world economy was heading into the most catastrophic eco-nomic decline the industrial world has ever known—which was accompanied by a collapse in world trade—Smoot-Hawley has been permanently linked to the Great Depression. The League of Nations saw it as the first shot in a tariff war. According to one contempo-rary observer: "As a score of writers have pointed out, the world depression and the Hawley-Smoot Tariff are inextricably bound up one with the other, the latter being not only the first manifesta-tion of but a principal cause of the deepening and aggravating of the former." Even those who argue that Smoot-Hawley was not a major factor in the advent or propagation of the Great Depression acknowledge the harsh judgment of history, noting that it "ranks among the most infamous pieces of Congressional legislation in this century." Other modern observers go even further: "Apart from the Fugitive Slave Act, the 1930 Smoot-Hawley tariff bill is probably the most infamous piece of legislation in U.S. history."

Did Smoot-Hawley cause the Great Depression? No. The tar-iff increase embodied in Smoot-Hawley was substantially less than that generated by the Fordney-McCumber tariff. And Fordney-McCumber itself was followed by a seven-year-long economic boom during America's Roaring Twenties. Although some modern authorities maintain that Smoot-Hawley had a major impact on trade and aggregate economic output of the United States, the consensus view is that although it worsened the Great Depression, its direct effect on the American economy was modest. This is not to say that Smoot-Hawley was in any way wise or enlightened policy, or that it did not have detrimental effects on the longer-term economic health of the United States or on international trade more generally. The tariff has been characterized—quite accurately—as "unnecessary" and "futile." It was singularly unsuccessful in achieving President Hoover's objective of raising agricultural prices: at the time of the law's passage, the United States was already large net exporter of agricultural products, and so a tariff on farm imports did relatively little for farmers. Further, Smoot-Hawley was the epitome of what we would consider today "smoke-filled room politics." Congressmen noted at the time that the tariff schedules for the 20,000 items covered by the tariff were constructed for the benefit of various private interests and with very little regard for the public interest.

Smoot-Hawley also contributed to the breakdown of international trade during the Great Depression, aggravating an already severe economic crisis. According to the League of Nations, aggregate imports of the 75 countries for which it collected data declined by about two-thirds between 1929 and 1933. Much of this decline can be accounted for by falling incomes and the accompanying decreased demand for imports. However, a substantial portion of this reduction can be laid at the feet of trade and exchange rate policies adopted by many countries to direct domestic spending away from imports and onto domestic products. And many of these policies can clearly be identified as retaliation against the United States for imposing Smoot-Hawley. According to the League of Nations, Smoot-Hawley "was the signal for an outburst of tariff-making activities in other countries, partly at least by way of reprisals. Extensive increases in duties were made almost immediately by Canada, Cuba, Mexico, France, Italy, and Spain."

Several countries made serious lobbying efforts to head off Smoot-Hawley, and its passage led to popular outrage against the United States and in several cases retaliation. Spain withdrew the MFN treatment of US imports. Italy's fascist government discouraged citizens from buying American goods. Switzerland boycotted American products. And Britain returned to protectionism, granting trade preferences to countries in the Empire and raising tariffs on goods coming from other countries, including the United States.

Canada, the United States' largest trading partner, retaliated quickly. Prime Minister William Lyon Mackenzie King, who expected that any American tariff increases would carve out an exception for Canadian goods, had been contemplating a downward revision in Canada's tariffs as late as February 1929. However, in September of that year, he noted in his diary "If the Americans put up their tariff against us, I am inclined to take that method of retaliation against them." It probably did not help that Congressional negotiations over Smoot-Hawley coincided with a general election in Canada. Richard Bedford Bennett, the leader of the Conservative Party—and therefore already more likely to be a protectionist than the Liberal Party's Mackenzie King—stated his intention to retaliate while campaigning in Quebec just a week before Hoover signed Smoot-Hawley:

How many tens of thousands of American workmen are living on Canadian money today? They've got jobs and we've got the soup kitchens...I will not beg of any country to buy our goods. I will make [tariffs] fight for you. I will use them to blast a way into markets that have been closed.

For many years, Smoot-Hawley stood accused as having been an important cause of the Great Depression. Modern economic thinking suggests that, although Smoot-Hawley did contribute to a reduction in world trade at a moment when expanding trade would have been welcome, its net effect on the US economy was negligible. Some scholars suggest that Smoot-Hawley may even have had a slightly positive effect on the US economy. Although Smoot-Hawley certainly did not cause the Great Depression, it did have serious repercussions. Not only did world trade decline during the Depression, but when it began to revive, it did so in a Balkanized manner, with revived trade developing primarily within trading blocs and regions, rather than across the board. It would take nearly 20 years to reverse the damage to international trade done by Smoot-Hawley.

Have policy makers learned from the mistake of Smoot-Hawley and similar restrictive interwar trade legislation? Yes. The lessons were learned quickly and—importantly—they have not been forgotten.

With the election of Franklin Delano Roosevelt and a Democratic Congress in 1932, Smoot-Hawley's days were numbered. The 1934 Reciprocal Trade Agreements Act (RTAA) gave the president unilateral authority to negotiate trade treaties and offer reciprocal concessions of up to 50 percent off the price of tariffs via bilateral treaties. The RTAA was renewed in 1937 and 1940. By 1939, the United States had signed 20 MFN treaties with countries accounting for 60 percent of its trade. The desire for a more open trading system was not just an American phenomenon. Since the end of World War II, tariff reduction has been vigorously pursued on a multilateral basis. The General Agreement on Tariffs and Trade (GATT) was established with 23 members in 1947. By the time GATT was succeeded by the World Trade Organization (WTO) in 1994, it had 123 member countries. The WTO now has 159 members, and the world's average tariff rate is lower than it has been at any time during the past 150 years.

Although great progress has been made on trade liberalization, a number of thorny issues remain. If a country holds its manufacturers to a high standard of pollution control, raising the cost of domestic output, should it be allowed to impose tariffs on the imports from neighboring countries where manufacturers use cheaper, but more polluting means of production? Can countries where workers are guaranteed certain minimum workplace standards impose tariffs against countries with lower workplace standards that produce lower-cost goods?

Because of improvements in communications technology, services as well as goods can move internationally. Thus, although we typically think of protectionist sentiment as coming from manufacturing industries, it may come from the service sector as well. A phone call to your credit card company may well be answered in a call center halfway around the world. In many circumstances, computer programmers need not be physically present to do their jobs effectively. Even medical services can be imported: radiologists in India can read X-rays and MRI scans taken in America without leaving their home country—at a fraction of the cost of American doctors. In fact, the only hate mail I have ever received in my professional life was from a radiologist in response to a letter to the editor in which I suggested that outsourcing the reading of MRIs and X-rays might not be a bad way to cut domestic health-care costs. But despite these and other real challenges to free trade, even in the midst of the recent subprime and euro crises there has been no rush to return to the high levels of protectionism of the interwar period.

The Smoot-Hawley tariff was a major policy mistake, made largely for ideological reasons. High tariffs were a central part of the Republican Party's political creed—and had been common Republican practice—for decades. Hence, the passage of Smoot-Hawley provides a good example of a political party applying its "tried and true" recipe, in a sense relying on its instincts rather than hard-headed analysis. Of course, there were other causes, including a desire to redistribute economic welfare toward agriculture and some other sectors, as well as a desire to shift some of the cost of the declining economy onto foreign producers. Nonetheless, a commitment to an out-of-date ideology was at the heart of this policy blunder.

Chapter 8

Why Didn't Anyone Pull the Andon Cord?

Japan's Lost Decade

*[Calvin Coolidge's] characteristic way of dealing with [public problems]
is simply to evade them, as a sensible man evades an insurance solicitor
or his wife's relatives.*

H. L. MENCKEN

*Only yesterday, it seems, Americans were obsessed with Japan. The
successes of Japanese industry inspired both admiration and fear;
you couldn't enter an airport bookstore without encountering rows
of dust jackets featuring rising suns and samurai warriors. Some of
these books promised to teach the secrets of Japanese management;
others prophesied (or demanded) economic warfare. As role models
or demons, or both, the Japanese were very much on our minds.
All that is gone now.*

PAUL. KRUGMAN

The Toyota Motor Corporation is the largest automobile producer
in the world. In fact, it is one of the largest manufacturing firms
on the planet. Toyota is not only big, but it is widely admired.
Toyota's Total Production System (TPS), developed after World War
II, has provided instructional material for generations of business
school students and inspiration for other manufacturing firms.
A distinctive characteristic of TPS is its emphasis on learning from
mistakes. When assembly line workers spot a problem—or even a
potential problem—they are encouraged to pull the *andon cord* that
runs along the assembly line. Pulling the andon cord lights up a

signboard; this alerts managers to the problem and initiates a diagnostic problem-solving process. Production continues unimpeded if the problem can be fixed in less than a minute; otherwise, production is halted—despite the substantial cost involved—until the issue is resolved.

Unfortunately, Japanese authorities were not operating under TPS rules during the 1990s, but were instead devoted to maintaining the status quo. When a serious financial crisis emerged early in the decade, rather than pulling the andon cord—that is, allowing poorly performing banks to fail—policy makers hid the problem in hopes that it would go away and that their powerful position atop Japan's financial system would remain secure. In doing so, they made a severe financial crisis far worse than it needed to be and sent Japan into a "lost decade" characterized by slow economic growth, high unemployment, and a long, costly cleanup of its financial system.

The sluggish growth, high unemployment, and battered financial system that characterized Japan during the 1990s and into the 2000s stands in marked contrast to its economic performance during the quarter century following World War II. From 1948 through 1973, real gross domestic product (GDP) per capita in Japan—that is, the total quantity of goods and services produced per person, a rough approximation of the standard of living—grew on average by more than 8 percent per year. This represents extraordinarily high growth by historical standards: the annual growth rate among industrialized countries during the past century and a quarter has averaged slightly over 2 percent per year. Although many industrialized countries have experienced periods of high economic growth, none has ever sustained comparable growth over such a long period.

To put the above in perspective, as a result of rapid economic growth between World War II and 1973, the standard of living in Japan doubled roughly every nine years. By contrast, average annual growth rates in Britain, Canada, and the United States during the same period—about 2.5 percent—were sufficient for the standard of living to double every 30 years or so. At the same time, Japan enjoyed low and stable unemployment. Although cross-country comparisons of unemployment rates are notoriously unreliable, the Japanese unemployment rate was below 1.5 percent for almost all of the 1960s, at or near the low end for all industrialized economies.

Even after the 1973 oil shock ended the "golden era" of rapid economic growth that had characterized the industrialized world during the early post–World War II period, Japan's economy continued to outpace those of other developed countries. The growth of Japan's real GDP per capita during 1974–90 fell to about 3 percent per year—a considerable drop from the 8 percent that reigned during the previous quarter century, but still above the rates of 2 percent or less that characterized Canada, the United States, and the majority of Western European economies. By the end of the 1970s, Japan's unemployment rate had edged up to about 2 percent, still mild by industrial country standards.

The bursting of Japan's so-called bubble economy in the early 1990s led to a prolonged economic slowdown. Japanese economic growth fell to 1.2 percent during the 1990s, less than half of its rate during 1974–90, and, for the first time since the 1950s, below the growth rates of other industrialized countries. Japan's unemployment rate continued to rise, reaching a post–World War II record of 5 percent before the close of the 1990s and exceeding it early in the 2000s.

Like most developed economies, Japan's financial system was tightly controlled during the quarter century following World War II. Domestic stock and bond markets were kept deliberately underdeveloped, and foreign securities markets were off limits for Japanese firms and individuals, so savers with funds to lend and firms that required loans had no viable alternative to the domestic banking system. The government used the banking system as an instrument of industrial policy, channeling domestic savings toward investment in export-oriented industries, which fueled Japan's impressive growth during these years.

The heavy hand of regulation not only contributed to Japan's growth by providing industry with ample funding but also kept banks profitable. Interest rates were controlled by the government and the spreads between borrowing and lending rates were kept high, guaranteeing banks substantial interest income in excess of interest expenditures. Interest rate controls and other administrative rules limited competition between banks and further contributed to bank stability and profitability. The banking system operated under what was known as the "convoy system," in which competition within the financial sector was discouraged. The result was that all banks were allowed to grow at approximately the same speed, and none was allowed to fail. Banks that found themselves in trouble were typically merged—often with the assistance and at the behest of government authorities—with healthier institutions.

Overseeing the Japanese financial system from a lofty perch was the Ministry of Finance (MoF), which has been described as

> much more than an office of government. It is a political, economic, and intellectual force without parallel in the developed world. It enjoys a greater concentration of powers, formal and informal, than any comparable body in any other industrialized democracy. In Japan, there is no institution with more power...
>
> On induction into the Finance Ministry, recruits are told that its earliest known incarnation dates from at least AD 678, when the ancient imperial court comprised three main components: an inner shrine for the gods, an outer shrine for the man-god (the emperor), and the treasure store, or *Okura*. It is from this term that the Ministry of Finance takes its Japanese name, the Okura*sho*—literally, great storehouse ministry. And so it is that in Japan, after the deities of heaven and earth comes that of the Ministry of Finance.

The Ministry of Finance's influence was extensive in part because it exerted authority over areas of policy that in most industrialized countries were split among different departments. The ministry held both major levers of macroeconomic policy, with authority for the government's fiscal policy and enormous influence over the Bank of Japan and, hence, over monetary policy. It was the lead regulator and supervisor for banks and the securities and insurance industries, as well as holding the reins in many other important areas, such as managing national property (e.g., the Imperial Palace Grounds) and controlling the national tobacco monopoly.

The relationship between the MoF and the banking sector has been characterized as: "personal...informal...opaque." Although Japanese law established detailed banking regulations, officials within the MoF had great latitude to direct banks though "administrative guidance." That is, ministry officials could "suggest" that a bank pursue a particular course of action, including making business decisions that might not have been in its best interest. For example, when Japanese stock prices fell dramatically in the early 1990s, MoF officials called up several investment banks and pointed out just how detrimental the depressed stock market was for the overall economy. The banks are believed to have bought large quantities of shares of Japan's flagship companies shortly thereafter.

Other examples include MoF suggestions to stock brokers that they not accept buy or sell orders from a particular foreign investor and recommendations that certain poorly performing banks might be excellent targets for acquisition. Although these suggestions did not have the force of law, failure to follow them had subtle and not-so-subtle consequences. For example, the MoF controlled a number of permits and licenses that financial institutions needed in order to conduct their business and was not shy about using their power to retaliate against firms that did not follow administrative guidance. After Daiwa Bank ignored MoF suggestions that it not enter the trust business, the bank suddenly found it harder to obtain permission to open new branch offices.

Banks maintained a good relationship with the ministry through their *mofutan* (variously translated as "MoF liaison" or "MoF handler"), whose job it was to establish a rapport with a relatively junior civil servant at the ministry. A *mofutan* would be in daily contact with his counterpart. After hours, if he was not wining and dining his contact in the ministry, the *mofutan* would be on call in case the official needed any information—both to maintain good relations and to prevent the MoF official from deepening his ties with another bank's *mofutan*. These informal discussions and the information-sharing they fostered served the interests of both the banks and the ministry: banks could seek informal guidance on plans that would subsequently require formal approval, such as opening new branches or starting new product lines. The ministry used the contacts to sound out the industry on regulations under consideration and to provide administrative guidance. For banks in Japan's tightly regulated environment, contacts with the ministry were prized as an important way of keeping up with competitors.

Ties between banks and the ministry were further strengthened by the practice of placing MoF officials in high positions in banks immediately following their retirement from the civil service. Ministry ex-officials, known as *amakudari* (descent from heaven), were often employed at the "suggestion" of the MoF. Officials from the banking sector who were temporarily assigned to the MoF, yet another means of reinforcing the relationship between the two, were known as *ama-agari* (ascent to heaven). Ties between the ministry and the Diet (parliament), particularly the ruling Liberal Democratic Party, were even more intimate—cemented by marriages between MoF recruits and daughters of prominent party officials.

The cozy relationship between the banks and the ministry complicated a system that was already characterized by weak oversight and a lack of transparency. Because the MoF's Banking Bureau was not regarded as the most prestigious area within the ministry—the tax and budget areas were more central to the ministry's political power base—its resources were limited, and it was able to conduct fewer bank examinations than was the norm in other industrialized countries. When examinations did occur, they tended to focus on compliance with administrative rules rather than on the composition of assets and liabilities, which were far more germane to questions of bank solvency and stability. Further, bank examinations rarely came as a surprise to those being examined. Obtaining the inspection dates was a central part of a *mofutan*'s responsibilities; an inability to obtain this information would call the *mofutan*'s competency into question. Information that *was* relevant to bank solvency was often not gathered during bank examinations but was provided to the ministry by the banks themselves. Such figures were later found to be incomplete and inadequate. Further, information that was collected was often not made public, preventing depositors and investors from disciplining poorly performing banks by removing deposits and selling equity.

Two key events in the 1970s set the stage for the subsequent boom—and bust—of what became known as Japan's bubble economy: the breakdown of the Bretton Woods system during 1971–73 and the OPEC oil shock of 1973.

The Bretton Woods system was established prior to the end of World War II under agreements signed in Bretton Woods, New Hampshire, in July 1944. Under these agreements, countries fixed the value of their exchange rates vis-à-vis the US dollar, adjusting them only occasionally and only in the face of persistent trade imbalances. If a country consistently imported more than it exported, indicating that the value of its currency was too high— since an overvalued exchange rate makes a country's exports more expensive to foreigners and imports of foreign goods cheaper for domestic residents—the currency would be devalued. A system of fixed exchange rates will not be credible if exchange rate adjustments are too frequent, because it suggests that policy makers are not committed to the fixed rates. Nor will fixed exchange rates be sustainable if the rate of inflation differs substantially across countries, since higher inflation combined with a fixed exchange rate will render the exports of the inflating country more expensive to its trading partners and will lead to a trade deficit. Persistent differences in inflation across countries, due in large measure to the high inflation rate in the United States in the late 1960s, eventually led to the abandonment of Bretton Woods in favor of a regime of floating—and often volatile—exchange rates. The collapse of the fixed exchange rate system reduced the incentive for policy makers to keep inflation under control.

The OPEC oil embargo in the aftermath of the 1973 Yom Kippur War further increased inflation through at least two channels. First, since energy is an important input into all sectors of economic activity, the substantial increase in oil prices from about $2 per barrel in 1973 to nearly $10 in 1974 had a dramatic impact upon the prices of many goods and services. Second, the expansionary fiscal and monetary policies adopted by many countries to fight the ensuing economic downturn exacerbated inflation.

The consequences of the oil shock and the end of Bretton Woods were particularly severe for Japan. With a rapidly growing industrial sector and minimal domestic energy supplies, the Japanese economy was hard hit by the rise in the price of imported oil. In the aftermath of the shock, real GDP per capita declined by 2.5 percent in 1974—Japan's first decline during the post–World War II period. The recession had a dramatic impact on the government's budget: the economic slowdown reduced tax collections from firms and individuals, while expansionary fiscal policy kept government expenditures high. The budget deficit, which had been equal to 2 percent or less of Japan's GDP during the early 1970s, rose to 3.5 percent in 1975 and to 6 percent by 1979. The oil price increase, combined with expansionary monetary policy used to combat the economic slowdown, helped to ratchet up inflation from 5 percent to 6 percent per year during the early 1970s to more than 23 percent in 1974.

One response of Japanese policy makers to these changes was a gradual liberalization of the financial system. The sudden increase in the government's need to fund an ever-growing debt led to an easing of restrictions on the bond market, making it easier for the government—and also for private firms—to raise money by issuing debt. Subsequent measures during the late 1970s and into the 1980s liberalized other securities markets, such as those for short-term debt (i.e., money markets), equity, and foreign exchange, each of which had been under formal or informal government control, and eventually gave households greater access to the expanded offering of financial products.

The liberalization of the bond market opened up alternative funding sources for corporations, allowing them to bypass banks and borrow directly (and more cheaply) by issuing bonds. Deregulation aimed at expanding the options of individual depositors was slower to develop. Thus banks were left with substantial deposit bases but fewer willing borrowers. This encouraged banks to expand their lending—typically collateralized by real estate—to small- and medium-sized businesses, especially property development firms, which could not borrow money in the bond market as easily or cheaply as large firms. The resulting boom in real estate prices, which was particularly intense during the closing years of the 1980s, was further supported by expansionary monetary policy undertaken by the Bank of Japan during the second half of the 1980s. The boom in real estate and equities collapsed at the beginning of the 1990s, with stock prices falling by 60 percent during the early 1990s and land prices falling by roughly 50 percent over the course of the entire decade.

The best way to understand the consequences of the asset price declines is to consider a simplified bank balance sheet. A balance sheet consists of everything that the bank owns or is owed (i.e., assets), like outstanding loans, securities owned, and cash; and everything that it owes (i.e., liabilities), primarily deposits of various types. The excess of assets over liabilities is the bank's capital, also known as shareholder equity, which serves as a buffer to protect depositors against losses in the value of the bank's assets. Because capital serves an important role, governments typically mandate that banks maintain the equivalent of something like 10 percent of their assets in capital.

The decline in the value of real estate left those who had borrowed using land as collateral unable to repay their loans. Since the price of land had fallen dramatically, banks could not make up their losses by seizing collateral and selling it. Because loans accounted for about one-half of all Japanese bank assets, a 20 percent decline in the value of outstanding loans could essentially wipe out the capital of Japan's entire banking system. Moreover, because of the dismal condition of the securities markets (not to mention the banks themselves), it was not possible for banks to raise additional capital by selling shares on the stock market. In short, the banks were bankrupt. Because of obfuscation by the banks and the government, it was not entirely clear just how bankrupt they were.

The government's reaction to the emerging financial crisis was painfully slow. Fully eight years passed from the beginning of the crisis until substantial measures were put into place. This delay resulted in a longer, deeper, and more costly crisis than would otherwise have occurred. By way of comparison, governments responded with lightning speed to the banking crises of the Great Depression of the 1930s. In the United States, the Reconstruction Finance Corporation made substantial loans to banks in 1932 and 1933; major banking reforms, including the introduction of deposit insurance, were introduced in 1933 and 1935. The German government took substantial equity stakes in the nation's banks, accumulating about 70 percent of the ownership capital of the large banks by 1934. And in Italy and Sweden, holding companies were created shortly after the onset of the crisis to take substantial amounts of banks' troubled assets off bank balance sheets. Responses to the banking problems in the 1990s in Scandinavia and elsewhere were even faster, with successful government resolutions taking place in some instances within 10 months of the onset of the crisis.

Rather than confronting the financial distress swiftly and decisively, the Japanese government's response during the first half of the 1990s was one of denial and forbearance. Although the MoF was well aware of the seriousness of the banks' problems, it used all the tools in its arsenal—from changing accounting rules and permitting (and even encouraging) shady accounting practices, to intervening in the stock market—to prevent the emergence of any news about banking problems in hopes that real estate and stock markets would rebound and come to the rescue. The *Economist* magazine summarized the ministry's strategy:

> The mandarins of Japan's Ministry of Finance used to pride themselves on artful cover-ups. They concealed weakness in the stockmarket by propping up security prices. They threw a veil over the weakness of the banking system by discouraging the disclosure of bad loans. By these ploys the ministry hoped to conceal the true awfulness of the troubles plaguing Japan's financial system after the popping of the financial bubble in 1990. Time and economic recovery would, it thought, heal all. But half a decade after the bubble burst the economy has yet to recover, the banks' woes are getting worse, and the cover-up increasingly hard to sustain.

Although some small banks were allowed to fail in the early 1990s, for the most part the convoy system persisted. The standard method for dealing with troubled banks was for the government to arrange the merger of ailing institutions with stronger ones, sometimes with the Bank of Japan providing loans or equity participation. This path was followed despite the October 1994 statement of Yasushi Mieno, then governor of the Bank of Japan, that "[i]t is not the business of the central bank to save all financial institutions from failure. On the contrary, failure of an institution that has reasons to fail is even necessary from the viewpoint of nurturing a sound financial system." Occasionally, banks were liquidated and reconstituted as new institutions. In most cases, however, banks were not allowed to fail.

Banks had little incentive to acknowledge problem loans, since in doing so they would be forced to recognize the need for additional capital. Nor were banks pressured by the Ministry of Finance to confront their capital shortage. Instead of pressing troubled borrowers for repayment or cutting off the flow of loans, banks often continued to lend to these firms, in effect throwing good money after bad, to forestall the day of reckoning. These "living dead" or "zombie" firms had little or no hope of recovery but nonetheless avoided failure—at least temporarily—thanks to continued bank support, further worsening the eventual fallout from the crisis.

Nor was the public made aware of the extent of the bad loans problem. Information about banks that could unnerve depositors and shareholders was withheld: estimates of nonperforming loans for the 21 largest banks were not reported by the MoF until 1992; those for smaller banks were not made until 1994. When official estimates finally were made, they relied on bank self-reporting—and depended on flexible definitions—which seriously understated the problem. Accurate information using a consistent standard across banks was not available until March 1998.

The opacity of the system kept the public in the dark as long as possible. As late as 1995, the MoF publicly denied that any large banks were endangered, although it did issue a blanket guarantee of all deposits that remained in force until 2001. The MoF's willingness to bury unpleasant news is exemplified by the Daiwa Bank scandal that broke in 1995. On August 8, the president of Daiwa, Akira Fujita, took the director of the Banking Bureau, Yoshimasa Nishimura, to dinner and informed him that Daiwa's New York branch had, over the course of the previous 11 years, lost $1.1 billion in unauthorized bond trading. There is some dispute about exactly what transpired during the meeting. According to one account, Nishimura suggested that Daiwa conduct its own investigation—effectively letting the matter drop. Another account, on the basis of correspondence with

Nishimura, reports that Daiwa requested additional time to fully investigate the affair, which Nishimura accepted as necessary. In either case, US regulators were not informed for another 41 days—during which the unauthorized bond trading continued. For its role in the cover-up, Daiwa was fined $340 million and banned from operating in the United States.

The government undertook a number of cosmetic fixes during the first half of the decade, none of which made fundamental changes to the financial system or imposed any penalties on bankers, bank shareholders, or uninsured depositors. For example, with the erosion in bank capital, the MoF "encouraged" insurance companies—which, conveniently, the ministry also regulated—to invest in banks, bolstering bank capital ratios at the expense of the insurance industry. One mechanism devised for getting bad loans off bank balance sheets involved the Cooperative Credit Purchasing Corporation (CCPC), which was established with the encouragement of the MoF in 1992 with funds pooled from 162 banks. A proposal to secure public funding for the CCPC was derailed by complaints that this would unfairly favor banks over nonfinancial firms. The CCPC was not especially effective. Banks were fearful of drawing attention to their bad loans; since CCPC could only purchase loans that were offered by banks, it acquired a limited number of loans. Further, the loans that the CCPC did take on were generally not sold, meaning that they were "warehoused" rather than "resolved," and very little cash was realized from their sale.

Part of the direction—or lack of direction—of public policy can be traced to an unwillingness to commit public funds to a rescue, particularly during the first half of the 1990s. Instead of purchasing bad loans or bank capital directly, the government provided tax breaks to banks, allowing the government to contribute a relatively small amount of money in order to attract less attention from the public. For example, taking advantage of CCPC facilities granted banks a tax break related to the decline in the value of their real estate. The eventual consequences of these efforts were substantial: by 2002, approximately one-third of

Japanese banks' "core" capital, or half of the total required capital, was in the form of tax breaks of one sort or another.

Another approach, adopted because it required little government expenditure, was a series of major financial system reforms, called Big Bang. Announced in 1996, Big Bang was to be phased in over several years. These measures were aimed at liberalizing financial markets, clarifying opaque rules, and upgrading the accounting, supervisory, and legal framework. The roadmap provided by the Big Bang announcement (specific legislation was neither proposed nor enacted until later) did suggest a path toward enacting needed long-term reforms, although they were of little use in addressing the problem at hand. It may be that these reforms were proposed at this time to take the voters' minds off of the poor record of the government in addressing the short-term financial situation.

By the second half of the decade, it had become obvious that the strategy of propping up unsound banks was not viable. On November 18, 1996, in a statement eerily reminiscent of that made by Governor Mieno's two years earlier, Federal Reserve chairman Alan Greenspan told the Japanese Federation of Bankers, "Our goal as supervisors should not be to prevent all bank failures, but to maintain sufficient prudential standards so that banking problems which do occur do not become widespread." Three days later Hanwa Bank was allowed to fail. Nevertheless, the MoF continued to engineer convoy operations, such as the 1997–98 restructuring, and eventual nationalization, of the Nippon Credit Bank and the Long Term Credit Bank.

The Asian financial crisis, which had erupted in the summer of 1997 in Thailand, Malaysia, and Indonesia, reached Japan in November, when Sanyo Securities, Hokkaido Takushoku Bank, Yamaichi Securities, and Tokyo City Bank failed. The Asian crisis threw a spotlight upon the precarious position of Japanese banks, which was reflected in the emergence of a "Japan premium," a higher interest rate charged to Japanese banks vis-à-vis their European and American counterparts due to the perceived higher risk of failure.

By March 1998, the Diet enacted the Financial Function Stabilization Act, which authorized the Bank of Japan and Deposit Insurance Corporation to provide as much as ¥30 trillion (approximately 6.25 percent of GDP) to protect depositors (¥17 trillion) and to inject capital into "undercapitalized, but presumably healthy" banks (¥13 trillion). Although a much larger expenditure had been authorized, only ¥1.8 trillion of capital was, in fact, provided. The plan injected the same amount of capital into each bank, an amount based on what the strongest bank requested. This small amount of capital proved to be inadequate and, one year later, the Rapid Recapitalization Act provided for an injection of ¥8.6 trillion in capital. Although this was inadequate to solve the long-term capital shortage among Japanese banks—estimates place the cumulative losses to Japanese banks from bad loans during 1992–2006 at about ¥96 trillion, or approximately 19 percent of GDP—it was seen as a more serious attempt to calm the market and led to the elimination of the Japan premium.

The fallout from the crisis has been long-lasting. The 1990s was dubbed Japan's "lost decade," and banking problems and sluggish economic performance continued into the 2000s. The MoF was viewed a major culprit in the crisis and was punished by having many of its powers stripped away. Where it had once been the all-powerful *Okurasho*, the "great storehouse ministry," in 2001 it was renamed *Zaimusho*. Although the new name also translates as Ministry of Finance, it carries with it the more prosaic connotation of "manager of fiscal policy"—taxing and spending—to which it has since been relegated. The MoF suffered more than a downgrading of its name. The Bank of Japan, which had been heavily influenced by the MoF, was reformed in the late 1990s, making it more independent of the ministry, although it has been criticized for not taking stronger measures to combat deflation both before and after the reform. A series of organizational changes beginning in 1998 gradually stripped from the MoF its role as banking supervisor as well as supervisor of the securities and insurance industries. Authority for supervision was first moved to the prime minister's office and, by 2001 to a new cabinet officer, the Minister for Financial Services, under which the new Financial Services Agency operates.

Japan's financial crisis can be blamed on many factors. Among the most important of these was poorly timed deregulation that contributed to a massive asset bubble. When the bubble burst, both the financial and non financial sectors of the economy suffered. Japan's financial crisis was not unique, however. Sweden, Norway, and Finland all endured severe financial crises during 1987–94, each of which resulted in large measure from the ill-timed deregulation of a tightly controlled financial system. Because of swift and decisive government action that both publicly acknowledged the failures and instituted a resolution plan, the Nordic countries were able to resolve their crises more rapidly and with far less economic pain than Japan. The crucial difference between Japan and the Nordic countries was Japan's commitment to maintaining the status quo— both in the banking system and in the regulators' place in it—rather than the health of the economy. It is inconceivable that Japan could have escaped from the 1990s without enduring a severe financial crisis. Had the authorities pulled the andon cord, however, the consequences of that crisis would have been far less dire.

Chapter 9

The Worst Financial Crisis since the Great Depression

The Subprime Meltdown

O gods! Who is't can say, "I am at the worst"?
I am worse than e'er I was....
And worse I may be yet: the worst is not
So long as we can say, "This is the worst."

KING LEAR (IV, i)

I've had it up to my keister with the banking industry.

RONALD REAGAN

If financial crises came with their own nicknames, the subprime meltdown surely would have earned the sobriquet "worst financial crisis since the Great Depression." That mantra has been chanted over and over again, not only by leading academics and media pundits, but at the highest levels of policy making. When President Barack Obama selected Christina Romer, an economic historian from the University of California, Berkeley, as chairman of his Council of Economic Advisors, some carped that the president should have selected an economist with a deeper background in policy rather than in economic history. When Romer herself later asked President Obama's chief of staff Rahm Emmanuel why she got the job, Emmanuel answered: "You're an expert on the Great Depression, and we really thought we might need one." Given how close the subprime crisis came to economic Armageddon, it is important to understand the series of policy mistakes behind it.

For the most part, previous chapters in this book have focused on particular policies that have had disastrous results, rather than on economic disasters and the policies that led to them. The three policy failures of the interwar period discussed earlier in this book—German reparations after World War I, the interwar gold standard, and the increasing trade protectionism of the 1930s—each merited its own chapter instead of being discussed in a single chapter on the Great Depression. The approach adopted here is different. Rather than starting with a failed economic policy, this chapter starts with a disaster—the subprime crisis—and examines the policies that contributed to it. There are good reasons for proceeding in this way. The interwar policies discussed earlier had their origins in different countries and occurred under widely differing circumstances. World War I reparations resulted from fears that an isolationist United States would not be able to counter future German aggression, the heavy burdens of inter-Allied debts, and a French desire to punish Germany. The worldwide return to the gold standard was galvanized by the British precedent, which was based on a desire to return to the monetary "normalcy" of the nineteenth century. And the rise of trade protectionism, spurred by the United States's Smoot-Hawley tariff, was a response to the beginnings of a global economic down-turn and domestic political factors. By contrast, the subprime crisis originated almost entirely in the United States, although it subse-quently spread far and wide. The main culprits behind the crisis were ill-conceived and ideologically motivated fiscal and monetary policies, which were aided and abetted by inadequate regulation and a variety of other policy mistakes.

Despite the severity of both the Great Depression and the subprime crisis, neither was completely unprecedented. Banking crises were common during the nineteenth and early twentieth centuries: there were more than 60 such crises in the industrialized world during 1805–1927. Many of these crises shared a common "boom-bust" pattern. Boom-bust crises occur when business cycles—the regular, normally moderate upward and downward movements in economic activity—become exaggerated, leading to a spectacular economic expansion followed by a dramatic collapse. Boom-bust crises play a central role in formal models of financial crises dating back at least as far as Yale economist Irving Fisher, who wrote about them in the 1930s. In Fisher's telling, economic expansion leads to a growth in the number and size of bank loans—and even the number of banks themselves—and a corresponding increase in borrowing by non-bank firms. As the expansion persists, bankers continue to seek profitable investments, even though as the boom progresses and more investment projects are funded, fewer worthwhile projects remain. The relative scarcity of sound projects does not dissuade eager lenders, however, who continue to dole out funds. Fisher laments this excessive buildup of debt during cyclical upswings: "If only the (upward) movement would stop at equilibrium!" But, of course, it doesn't.

When the economic expansion ends, the weakest firms—typically those that received loans later in the expansion—have difficulty repaying and default. Loan defaults lead to distress among the banks that made the now-impaired loans, panic among the depositors who entrusted their savings to these banks, and a decline in the wealth of bank shareholders. Even if no depositor panic ensues, banks under pressure will become more defensive by reducing their loan portfolio, both by making fewer new loans and by refraining from renewing outstanding loans that have reached maturity. Banks and individuals will sell securities in an attempt to raise cash, leading to declines in stock and bond markets. The contraction in the availability of loans will hurt firms and further exacerbate the business cycle downturn. The deepening contraction will lead to more loan defaults and bank failures, which will further depress security prices and worsen the business cycle downturn that is already underway.

Two other distinctive features characterize boom-bust crises. First, the economic expansion is typically fueled by cheap and abundant credit. That is, bankers have a lot of money to lend, which they are willing to lend at low interest rates. This often occurs when the central bank follows a low interest rate policy. In earlier times, when gold constituted a substantial portion of the money stock, credit expansion could be the result of gold discoveries or gold imports, which made loanable funds plentiful and cheap. It could also be a consequence of an increased willingness on the part of banks to lend the funds that they already have on hand, or from the emergence of new ways of lending money, including the creation of new types of securities. Second, boom-bust cycles are often accompanied by increased speculation in a particular asset or class of assets, the price of which, fed by cheap and abundant credit, rises dramatically during the course of the boom—and then collapses catastrophically during the bust.

The scenario described above aptly describes many nineteenth and twentieth century crises. For example, England suffered crises in 1825, 1836–39, 1847, 1857, 1866, and 1890. Each of these was preceded by several years of rapid economic growth, frequently fueled by gold imports and accompanied by increased speculation. The object of speculation varied from crisis to crisis and included at different times grain, railroads, stocks, and Latin American investments. Similar stories can be told about US crises of 1837, 1857, 1873, 1893, and 1907, and many others in Australia, Canada, and Japan, and across Western Europe.

As the world economy became more interconnected during the course of the nineteenth century, increasing numbers of these crises took on an international character. During the weeks following the outbreak of a panic in London in August 1847, business failures spread outward from London to the rest of Britain, to British colonies, and to continental and American destinations. Similarly, the 1857 crisis, which started in the United States, soon spread to Austria, Denmark, and Germany. The even more severe crises of the mid-1870s, early 1890s, 1907, and early 1920s, not to mention the Great Depression of the 1930s, also traveled extensively.

It is impossible to identify precisely when the run-up to the sub-prime crisis began. According to the National Bureau of Economic Research, the private academic organization that is the arbiter of when business cycle expansions and contractions begin and end, the longest-ever US business cycle expansion began in March 1991 and lasted until March 2001. Following an eight-month down-turn—among the shortest in US history—the business cycle turned upward again in November 2001. That expansion ended late in 2007, about the same time that the subprime meltdown began. The boom, like countless others before, was fed by expansionary fiscal and monetary policies.

The business cycle expansion that began in 2001 was given a substantial boost by a series of three tax cuts during the first three years of the administration of President George W. Bush. President Bush was ideologically committed to lower taxes and had pledged, if elected, to cut taxes. In his acceptance speech to the Republican National Convention in Philadelphia on August 3, 2000, Bush said:

> Today, our high taxes fund a surplus. Some say that grow-ing federal surplus means Washington has more money to spend. But they've got it backwards. The surplus is not the government's money. The surplus is the people's money. I will use this moment of opportunity to bring common sense and fairness to the tax code. And I will act on prin-ciple. On principle...every family, every farmer and small businessperson, should be free to pass on their life's work to those they love. So we will abolish the death tax. On prin-ciple...no one in America should have to pay more than a third of their income to the federal government. So we will reduce tax rates for everyone, in every bracket.

Supported by a Republican majority in the House of Representatives and a nearly evenly divided Senate, Bush signed into law the Economic Growth and Tax Relief Reconciliation Act of 2001

(EGTRRA), the Job Creation and Worker Assistance Act of 2002, and the Jobs Growth and Tax Relief Reconciliation Act of 2003. These laws lowered tax rates in all brackets, reduced taxes on capital gains and some dividends, and increased a variety of exemptions, credits, and deductions. Some of the tax cuts, which were to be phased in under EGTRRA, were accelerated under the 2003 legislation.

Further fiscal stimulus was provided by the invasion of Afghanistan the month following the terrorist attacks on September 11, 2001 and the war in Iraq, which began in March 2003. The war led to the deployment of 5200 US troops in Afghanistan during the fiscal year 2002; by 2008, the combined in-country forces in Afghanistan and Iraq had reached nearly 188,000. Thanks in large part to the collapse of the Soviet Union, US military spending had been relatively flat in the 1990s, never exceeding $290 billion in any year. By 2008, annual military spending had more than doubled, to $595 billion.

President Bush was faithful to his pledge to eliminate the federal government's budget surplus. The net effect of the tax cuts, combined with the additional expenditure related to the overseas conflicts, turned the federal government's $236 billion surplus in 2000 to a $458 billion deficit by 2008. This fiscal stimulus encouraged more spending by households and firms and contributed to the economic boom that lasted from 2001 to 2007.

The boom was also fueled by expansionary monetary policy, as the Federal Reserve kept interests rates low for a prolonged period. At the end of 2000, the federal funds rate, a key indicator of Federal Reserve monetary policy, stood at 6.5 percent. Following a sharp decline in stock prices in March 2001, primarily the result of the collapse of internet stocks (the "dot-com bubble"), the Federal Reserve lowered interest rates swiftly and dramatically in an effort to cushion the effects of the fall on the wider economy. By the end of March 2001, the federal funds rate had been reduced to 5 percent, and by June it was 4 percent. In August it stood at 3.5 percent, and was further reduced following the terrorist attacks of September 11. By the end of 2001, the federal funds rate was below 2 percent—its lowest level in more than 40 years. The rate remained at or below 1 percent for nearly a year during 2003–04, and below 2 percent until the middle of November 2004. The low interest rate policy, especially during 2003–04, helped to ignite a speculative boom.

The Fed kept interest rates low for two reasons. First, employment had recovered more slowly than expected from the 2001 recession, the so-called jobless recovery, indicating that a more prolonged period of lower interest rates was needed to stimulate the economy. Second, Fed policy makers were concerned that the country might fall into a Japanese-style "lost decade" if they did not make a clear and convincing case through bold actions that low interest rates would persist as long as required to boost the economy. A less charitable view holds that Fed chairman Alan Greenspan's motives were less economic and more ideological and self-serving—supporting easy monetary policy to increase the re-election prospects of fellow Republican George W. Bush, who was locked in a tight re-election race, or to curry favor with the administration so that he would be reappointed Fed chairman when his term expired after the presidential election. And, in fact, President Bush did nominate Greenspan for an unprecedented fifth term in May 2005. Whatever the reason for the prolonged monetary easing, it was crucial to the development of the boom.

As previously noted, boom-bust cycles are often accompanied by increased speculation in a particular asset or class of assets. During the subprime meltdown, the object of speculation was real estate. Housing prices, which had risen by about 25 percent during the entire decade of the 1990s, more than doubled between 2000 and 2006. The amount of debt undertaken to finance housing purchases also increased dramatically. Although expansionary fiscal and monetary policies undoubtedly fueled the explosion in house prices, the boom was enabled by a variety of legal and financial developments that eased constraints on the housing finance market, particularly the subprime mortgage market.

Subprime mortgages are housing loans made to less creditworthy borrowers. They include loans to borrowers who have a history
of late payments or bankruptcy, who are not able to document their
income sufficiently, or who are able to make only a small down payment on the property to be purchased. Because subprime loans are
considered risky, financial institutions will only make them if they
can charge higher interest rates than they charge more creditworthy borrowers. Subprime mortgage lending became more common
in the 1980s when federal legislation deregulated interest rates
and preempted state interest rate ceilings, allowing lenders to issue
higher-interest-rate mortgages. Subsequent legislation eliminated
the tax deductibility of consumer credit interest, but permitted the
continued deductibility of home mortgage interest on both primary
and secondary residences. This encouraged consumers to engage
in cash-out refinancing, that is, refinancing an existing mortgage
with a new, larger loan and taking the difference in cash. The net
effect was to shift what might otherwise have been credit-card
debt to mortgage debt. When interest rates increased during the
mid-1990s, reducing loan demand from high-quality borrowers,
lenders sought out new opportunities among the less creditworthy,
which contributed to a further increase in new subprime mortgage
loans.

The expansion of the subprime market was aided by securitization, a process that involves bundling a group of individual loans
together into a mortgage-backed security (MBS) and selling pieces
of that security to investors. A benefit of securitization is that it
makes it relatively easy for firms and individuals to invest in mortgages and therefore increases the overall amount of money available
for mortgage lending. The average individual investor would have
no interest in buying the mortgage loan on my house. Anyone who
bought my loan would have to assume administrative costs such
as billing, record keeping, and tax reporting. And even if I appear
to be good credit risk and hence unlikely to default, the investor
who bought my loan would risk a substantial loss if through some

unforeseen event I was unable to make my mortgage payments. On the other hand, that average investor would be much more likely to buy a share of a pool of several thousand mortgages like mine, where the administrative costs could be divided up among many investors and the default of a few loans (out of thousands) would not jeopardize the value of the investment. In this way, securitization increased the funding available for housing finance.

Although mortgage securitization had been popularized in the 1980s, the securitized loans at that time were typically "conforming" mortgages, that is, of a standard size with a relatively creditworthy borrower and high quality collateral. Securities backed by pools of conforming mortgages were eligible to be guaranteed by the quasi-government Federal National Mortgage Association ("Fannie Mae") and Federal Home Loan Mortgage Corporation ("Freddie Mac"), and hence carried a low risk of default and, therefore, low interest rates. In an effort to increase home ownership by the less affluent during the 1990s, government policy encouraged Fannie Mae and Freddie Mac to increase the flow of mortgage lending to low and moderate income areas and borrowers, including relaxing lending standards. These policy actions gave a boost to the subprime market: subprime mortgage-backed securities made up 3 percent of outstanding MBSs in 2000 and 8.5 percent of all new issues; by 2006, they constituted 13 percent of outstanding MBSs and nearly 22 percent of new issues. More than 80 percent of all new subprime loans were financed by securitization during 2005 and 2006, up from about 50 percent in 2001.

The proliferation of subprime mortgage-backed securities led them to be used in a variety of even more complex securities, such as collateralized debt obligations (CDOs) and credit default swaps (CDSs). CDOs consist of a portfolio of debt securities (including subprime MBSs), which are financed by issuing even more securities. These securities are classified into higher- and lower-risk portions, called "tranches," with higher-risk tranches providing higher returns. The tranches were assigned risk ratings by the credit ratings agencies Moody's, Standard and Poor's, and Fitch, which were harshly criticized in the wake of the crisis for having been overgenerous in their ratings. One of the main complaints against the ratings agencies is that since they are paid by issuers, who pay a lower interest rate if they receive a higher rating, they have an incentive to be overly generous in assigning ratings. As a managing director of Moody's, one of the big-three ratings agencies, said anonymously in 2007: "These errors make us look either incompetent at credit analysis or like we sold our soul to the devil for revenue, or a little bit of both."

Credit default swaps are contracts in which one party (the protection seller) agrees to pay, in return for a periodic fee, another party (the protection buyer) in the case of an "adverse credit event," such as bankruptcy. The availability of CDSs encouraged financial firms to hold CDOs, since they believed that CDSs insured them against losses on their CDOs. However, even though a CDS sounds very much like conventional insurance, it is not. A life-insurance company issues many policies; since the likelihood of death is small for any given policy holder, claims against the insurer are typically paid off from the proceeds of premia paid by policy holders that do not die. CDSs involve no such pooling of risk, so the extent to which the protection seller is able to pay off in the case of an adverse event depends solely on the value of the assets—which might fall during a crisis—it has to back up the contract.

It is well beyond the scope of this chapter to explain the veritable alphabet soup of derivative securities—including CDO^2s, synthetic CDOs, multisector CDOs, and cash flow CDOs—that emerged during this time. Even without details, it is clear that the development of these instruments, combined with elements of deregulation and misguided policy, made it easier and more profitable for less-creditworthy borrowers to obtain mortgage loans. Because of securitization and the attractive returns paid by these new securities, it was much easier for subprime-related securities to be sold in the United States and abroad. When the US housing boom collapsed, the value of many of these securities fell sharply and led to the collapse of institutions that held or had loaned money against them.

It is clear that there were misaligned incentives every step of the way toward the subprime crisis. Edmund Andrews, at the time a *New York Times* economics correspondent who was caught up in his own subprime nightmare, explained the chain of events.

> My mortgage company hadn't cared because it would sell my loan to Wall Street. Wall Street firms hadn't cared, because they would bundle the loan into a mortgage-backed security and resell it to investors around the world. The investors hadn't cared, because the rating agencies had given the securities a triple-A rating. And the rating agencies hadn't cared, because their models showed that these loans had performed well in the past.

The collapse of the real estate market led to a sharp decline in the value of mortgage-backed securities that had supported it and widespread distress among financial institutions—in short: the type of bust that Irving Fisher had written about more than three-quarters of a century earlier.

An additional factor contributing to the growth of the speculative bubble was the absence of effective regulation and supervision of the new and complex securities and of the institutions that employed them. To explain the importance of government regulation, we must return to fear and greed, first discussed in chapter 3. Virtually any financial decision can be framed in terms of these twin motives. Should I invest my life savings in a risky venture that will either make me a millionaire or put me in the poorhouse? Or should I restrict myself to only the bluest of blue chip stocks and the safest, if low yielding, bonds? Greed will steer me toward the former choice; fear to the latter. If there is a boom in risky ventures and their owners all seem to be making money hand over fist, my greed might get the better of my fear. Typically, the government doesn't get involved in my decision-making process. I am free to choose to take as much risk as I see fit. The government maintains bankruptcy courts that will help my creditors carve up my assets if I do go bankrupt, but the government will not prevent me from making choices that might increase the probability that I become bankrupt.

Bankers are also subject to fear and greed. Because most of the funds that banks use are entrusted to them by depositors, governments establish rules to ensure that bankers' greed does not overwhelm their fear. Among the most important of these rules are capital requirements. Capital requirements prevent banks from relying solely on deposits to fund their operations, forcing them also to use money that they and their shareholders put up. This money is known as capital. Capital requirements protect depositors in several ways. If a bank fails, capital can be used to pay off depositors. Additionally, holding capital encourages banks not to behave in an excessively risky way, so as not to jeopardize their own money. Capital also provides a concrete signal to depositors that the bank will not undertake excessive risk. The capacity of capital to reduce risk taking is sometimes described as putting banks in the position of having "skin in the game." Governments have set bank capital requirements for many years, and in the Basel (1988), Basel II (2004), and Basel III (2010) Accords, an international consensus was reached on minimum capital standards. Under the Basel Accords, banks are required to hold proportionately more capital against inherently riskier assets.

In 1996, the Federal Reserve permitted banks to use CDSs as a substitute for bank capital under certain circumstances. Thus, holding CDSs for which the protection seller was a highly rated company, such as American International Group—which was bailed out by the Federal Reserve in 2008—allowed banks to hold less actual capital, making them more vulnerable to failure if the protection seller was unable to fulfill its part of the bargain. Regulators became aware of the potential problems surrounding some of these CDSs as early as 2004, but did not take any action. Further, in 2004 the Securities and Exchange Commission (SEC) ruled that the five largest investment banks (Morgan Stanley, Merrill Lynch, Lehman Brothers, Bear Stearns, and Goldman Sachs) would be permitted to use their own internally created risk models to determine the levels of capital required rather than some government-mandated amount: in other words, these institutions became—to some extent—the judge of how much capital they needed to hold to insure their safety. Although the SEC announced its determination to hire more staff and have regular meetings with the investment banks to monitor the situation, capital ratios declined at all five investment banks following the ruling.

Another criticism of the regulators is that they did not impose more transparency on the derivatives market. That is, because these securities were so complex and were not traded on securities exchanges, it was easy for clients to misunderstand—or be misled—about the risky nature of these investments. Such allegations were made in connection with the derivatives transactions at the heart of the bankruptcy of Orange County, California, and in lawsuits brought against Bankers Trust by Gibson Greetings and Proctor and Gamble in the mid-1990s. Efforts to increase disclosure initiated by the Commodities Future Trading Commission (CFTC) met with opposition from the Federal Reserve, Treasury, and Congress; the Commodity Futures Modernization Act of 2000 exempted these derivatives from government supervision.

The subprime crisis has indeed been the longest, deepest, and broadest—in short, the worst—financial crisis since the Great Depression. Although the severity of the crisis was extraordinary, its origins were not: the boom-bust pattern of financial crises has been repeated again and again during the last 200 years.

When J. P. Morgan was asked about what the stock market would do, he famously replied, "It will fluctuate." And, indeed, that is what most markets—be they markets for securities, currency, commodities, or real estate—do, rising and falling in an unpredictable manner. When the value of an asset, or a class of assets, continually rises for a prolonged period of time, investors often come to believe that increases will continue indefinitely: fear is banished and greed becomes the watchword. Once the belief that market prices can only go up is established, it makes good sense to borrow money to invest in that market—after all, the loan can be repaid with the proceeds from sale of the appreciated asset. The more firmly entrenched the belief that the asset will continue to rise, the greater the lengths reasonable people will go to take advantage of the seemingly free lunch.

The housing boom, fueled by ideologically driven expansionary fiscal and monetary policies, encouraged the development of new and increasingly risky ways of taking advantage of its apparently limitless profit possibilities. Mortgage lending, which previously had been confined to those most able to afford it, was made available—also for ideological reasons—to individuals of more precarious means: those with less-solid credit histories, with less money to make a down payment, and with lower incomes. There are sound public policy arguments for promoting home ownership among all sectors of society; however, encouraging the less well off to take on debt that may be beyond what they are able to service—particularly in the event of a decline in the economy and house prices—dramatically increases the risk of a severe crisis. Further, because subprime lending was profitable, financial institutions regularly devised new and increasingly risky means of raising even more money to pour into the housing market. This further inflated the bubble and made its collapse that much more painful. Finally, the supervisory and regulatory apparatuses that were specifically mandated to protect the system utterly failed.

It would be an oversimplification to place the blame for the subprime crisis solely on ill-conceived fiscal and monetary policies. Fingers have been pointed—with good reason—at a host of alternative villains, including Fannie Mae, Freddie Mac, the credit ratings agencies, and the SEC. And, of course, borrowers themselves were not blameless. According to Edmund Andrews:

> Nobody duped me, hypnotized me, or lulled me with drugs. Like so many others—borrowers, lenders, and the Wall Street deal makers behind them—I thought I could beat the odds. Everybody had a reason for getting in trouble. The brokers and deal makers were scoring huge commissions. The condo flippers were aiming for quick profits. The ordinary home buyers wanted to own their first houses, or bigger houses, or vacation houses. Some were greedy, some were desperate, and some were deceived.

Nonetheless, the bulk of the blame for the crisis must be assigned to the Bush administration's fiscal policy and the Greenspan Fed's monetary policy. Why? Quite simply: fear and greed. The economic and speculative boom launched by the fiscal and monetary policies of the early 2000s raised the returns to greed—that is, the incentive to take on additional risk—to extraordinary levels. No matter how fear-inspiring the regulation and supervision was—and it was not—it would have been overwhelmed by dangerously high levels of greed.

Chapter 10

I'm OK. Euro Not OK?

A day will come when the only battlefield will be the market opening to commerce and the mind opening to new ideas. A day will come when bullets and bombshells will be replaced by ballots, by the universal suffrage of nations, by the venerable arbitration of a great sovereign senate, which will be to Europe what the Parliament is to England, what the Diet is to Germany, what the Legislative Assembly is to France. A day will come when a cannon will be exhibited in public museums, just as an instrument of torture is now, and people will be amazed that such a thing could ever have been.

VICTOR HUGO

Address to Paris Peace Congress (1849)

It can't happen. It's a bad idea. It won't last.

RUDIGER DORNBUSCH

Describing the American attitude toward the euro

The astute reader will have noticed that title of this chapter is punctuated by a question mark. Why a question mark and not an exclamation point? After all, as the quote by Rudiger Dornbusch demonstrates, economists have been skeptical about the euro since even before it was introduced. Writing early in the second decade of the twenty-first century, it is hard to imagine how the euro can be seen as anything but a disaster. The subprime meltdown, although born in the USA, ravaged the eurozone. The financially weaker eurozone countries—particularly Cyprus, Greece, Ireland, Italy, Portugal, and Spain—by now have spent months or years teetering on the edge of bankruptcy. As the fiscal positions of these countries have deteriorated, yields on their national debt have been driven to record heights to compensate bondholders for the increased possibility of default. Every interest-rate spike seems to result in an emergency summit of European leaders—typically lasting well into the night—trying desperately to find a way to shore up the embattled country's finances and to save the euro itself.

Nor have fiscally sound countries been immune to the crisis. Europe-wide growth is at post–World War II lows; unemployment at postwar highs. In December 2011, the ratings agency Standard and Poor's put all eurozone countries on notice that their sovereign bond ratings were under review and might well be downgraded—and subsequently downgraded nine of them, including France, Europe's second largest economy. During the same month, 50 percent of Dutch people surveyed agreed with the statement "we never should have joined the euro," while 47 percent disagreed.

The economic crisis has also contributed to greater political instability. In Greece, the inability of the political parties to reach agreement on economic policy led to the appointment of the former governor of the central bank as prime minister in November 2011. The subsequent election, in May 2012, resulted in a parliament in which no coalition of parties could command a majority, leading to a second election six weeks later. In Italy, the unwillingness of political parties to undertake economic reforms pressed on it by the EU led to the selection of an academic and international civil servant, Mario Monti, as prime minister and an entire cabinet composed of nonpartisan technocrats. More ominously, the economic crisis has led to the rise of extreme right-wing parties across Europe, including the avowedly neo-Nazi Golden Dawn in Greece, and the racist Jobbik in Hungary.

Why, then, the question mark?

To paraphrase Mark Twain, reports of the euro's death are greatly exaggerated. Because there is no cheap or easy way to break up the euro area, policy makers have no choice but apply bandages that will allow the euro to survive in the short term. If they are farsighted enough, European leaders will also adopt changes to put the euro on a healthier long-term course. Although this will be a costly and difficult exercise—as many aspects of implementing the economic and monetary union already have been—if done correctly, the rewards for Europe, and the world, will be substantial. The success of these reforms will determine whether the euro becomes one of the keys to European prosperity that its founders imagined or just limps along, another great policy failure.

Generals, politicians, and philosophers have planned the unification of Europe for more than two thousand years. The most successful military effort to that end was undertaken by the Roman Empire. During the second century of the Common Era, Rome ruled virtually all of Europe south and west of a line running approximately from Hadrian's Wall in the north of England to Romania's Black Sea coast. More than 700 years later, Charlemagne united much of central and western Europe under his rule, including almost all of modern France and large portions of what are now Germany and Italy. The armies of Napoleon during the early nineteenth century and of Hitler in the twentieth conquered substantial portions of Europe; however, these empires were short-lived.

Schemes for peaceful political and economic cooperation among European countries, including the establishment of joint legislative and judicial bodies, date from the medieval period. Utopian plans were spelled out in the work of Pierre Dubois (1306), Henry IV of France (1603), Eméric Cruce (1623), and William Penn (1693–94). Philosophers Jean Jacques Rousseau (1712–78) and Jeremy Bentham (1748–1832) proposed the establishment of an international tribunal; Immanuel Kant (1724–1804) explicitly called for a federation of states.

Not all early plans for greater international cooperation were purely theoretical. The German Zollverein, or customs union, was established in 1834. The Zollverein reduced internal customs barriers between German states, set a common external tariff, and established a customs parliament, paving the way for national unification later in the century. The International Telegraph Union (1865) and the General Postal Union (1874) set administrative and technical standards to promote international communication. Other practical international agreements that were established include the International Metric Convention (1875), the Geneva Convention for the Amelioration of the Condition of the Wounded and Sick in Armies in the Field (1864), the International Convention for the Protection of Industrial Property (1883), and the Berne Convention and of Works of Literature and Art (1886).

The devastation wrought by World War I led to the creation of several organizations aimed at fostering improved international relations. The League of Nations was established at the end of the war

> [i]n order to promote international co-operation and to achieve international peace and security by the acceptance of obligations not to resort to war by the prescription of open, just and honourable relations between nations by the firm establishment of the understandings of international law as the actual rule of conduct among Governments, and by the maintenance of justice and a scrupulous respect for all treaty obligations.

At its height, the League had nearly 60 member countries, although the United States never joined because the US Senate failed to ratify the Treaty of Versailles under which the League was established. The Pan-European Union was established in 1923 by Austrian Count Richard Coudenhove-Kalergi, who argued that if Europe did not achieve a closer integration it would again be devastated by war. Pan-Europeanism was supported by number of prominent politicians, including future French premiers Edouard Herriot and Aristide Briand as well as German foreign minister Gustav Stresemann and

Cologne mayor and post–World War II West German chancellor Konrad Adenauer.

Despite the desire for a warmer rapport between countries, international relations during the period between the two world wars were anything but harmonious. The Treaty of Versailles imposed severe conditions on Germany. In addition to financial and in-kind reparations, Germany was forced to cede territory to neighboring countries, give up its colonial empire, and submit to a variety of constraints aimed at crippling its war-making capability, including limitations on the size of its armed forces and on the import or manufacture of munitions. The heavily industrialized and coal-rich Saar basin was placed under French and British administration for 15 years; at the end of that period, the inhabitants voted to return to Germany. When Germany was unable to meet its reparations obligations in 1923, French and Belgian troops occupied the Ruhr valley, which, like the Saar, was an important mining and industrial region. The harshness of the postwar terms was intended both to punish Germany and to keep it industrially and militarily weak.

The best evidence of the failure to achieve better international relations after the end of World War I is, of course, World War II. At the conclusion of that war, the Allies were again confronted with the question of how to treat a defeated Germany. The US secretary of the Treasury, Henry Morganthau Jr., took a hard line, arguing that Germany should be transformed into an agricultural country. Eradicating its industry would deprive Germany of the means to rearm. According to Morganthau, these harsh terms would lead the way toward "the establishment of conditions which would prevent Germany from imposing devastation and terror upon a helpless Europe for a third time in a single century." Others argued for a softer approach, believing that the Soviet Union posed a greater threat to the post–World War II world, and hoped to bind Germany firmly to the western Allies—rather than to the Soviets and the Soviet-occupied zone of eastern Germany.

Morganthau counted Eisenhower among his backers, and quoted Ike as saying:

> I want to say that I am not interested in the German economy, and personally would not like to bolster it if that will make it easier for the Germans. The soft peace demands came from people who wanted to make Germany a bulwark against Russia. True, the strength of Russia was fantastic. But Russia now had all she could digest, and her present problems would keep her busy until long after we were dead. The whole German population is a synthetic paranoid, and there is no reason for treating a paranoid gently. The best cure would be to let the Germans stew in their own juice.

Initially, Morganthau's opinion held sway. Issued in May 1945, Joint Chiefs of Staff Directive 1067 (JCS 1067) mandated that the US commander should do nothing to restore Germany's economy beyond the minimum required to prevent disease and unrest that might endanger the occupation forces. This stricture was eased in July 1945, when an order was given to stimulate German coal production for export to Belgium, the Netherlands, and France. By 1947, concerns about the Soviet threat began to outweigh the desire to stifle the German economy, and JCS 1067 was rescinded. At about the same time, the European Recovery Program, also known as the Marshall Plan, was established to provide economic assistance to a number of European countries, including Germany.

Despite the softening of the attitude toward Germany, the Saar region was placed under French supervision and the Ruhr area's coal and steel output was put under the administration of the western Allies. As compensation for this territorial imposition, the Allies allowed the establishment of the Federal Republic of Germany in 1949 in the zones occupied by American, British, and French forces. In what may possibly have been a case of "if you can't beat them, join them," French foreign minister Robert Schuman proposed the establishment of a common Franco-German market for coal and steel under a supranational authority. Other European nations were invited to participate, and in 1951 the European Coal and Steel Community (ECSC), consisting of Belgium, France, Germany, Italy, Luxembourg, and the Netherlands, was established by the Treaty of Paris. According to the treaty, the ECSC would eliminate tariffs, quotas, subsidies, restrictive practices, and price discrimination between members, establish a common external tariff, and set a formula for apportioning customs revenues among the countries. By binding Franco-German production and sale of two products that were vital to war making, it was hoped that the ECSC would reduce the likelihood of a future war.

Although Winston Churchill had called for the creation of a "United States of Europe" as early as 1946, and a (largely consultative) Council of Europe had been established in 1949, the formation of the ECSC was the most concrete step ever taken toward the peaceful economic integration of Europe. The European Economic Community (EEC), established under the 1957 Treaty of Rome, pushed economic cooperation even further, establishing a road map for a common market within Europe: the elimination of tariffs between countries, the establishment of a common external tariff, and the gradual elimination of all national quotas and subsidies. Given the benefits economists ascribe to free trade, the EEC was well placed to deliver both substantial political and economic benefits.

The road to European unity had its costs, however. An important exception to the free market was agriculture. Farmers all over Europe, particularly those in France and Germany, had long operated in markets that were both tightly controlled and protected against foreign competition. Germany was a rising industrial power; the new EEC would grant its industry access to markets throughout Europe. France, however, had a large and politically influential agricultural sector and President Charles de Gaulle was not prepared to go forward with the EEC treaty unless substantial exceptions were made for agriculture. The result was Europe's Common Agricultural

Policy (CAP). The CAP provided for a free internal agricultural market, with a common system of external tariffs. Farm prices were determined centrally by European authorities and prices were set artificially high—that is, above those that would have been determined in a competitive market—in order to placate farmers.

The CAP had a number of negative effects. First, it raised the cost of agricultural products to European consumers, since prices were set at above-market rates. Second, it raised the tax burden on EEC citizens, who paid the bill for agricultural price supports. Third, it led to massive unsold surpluses of agricultural products that were purchased by the EEC: because producers were paid above-market prices, they produced more output than they could sell on the market. These surpluses were given evocative names like the "butter mountain" and the "wine lake." Although the CAP has been substantially reformed, it has not quite disappeared: as recently as February 2009, the EU bought 30,000 tons of butter, two years after its surplus had been exhausted. This is a drop in the bucket next to the 1.23 million tons of butter purchased by the EEC in 1986, but indicative the CAP has not disappeared entirely.

By the late 1960s, EEC farm prices were high relative to those in other parts of the world, ranging from 131 percent of the world price for poultry to 175 percent for beef, 185 percent for wheat, 200 percent for oilseeds, 297 percent for butter, and 438 percent for white sugar. An estimate from 1999, when agriculture was a much smaller percentage of total economic output than in the 1960s, put the cost of the CAP to the British economy—combining the higher price to consumers of agricultural products and the cost to taxpayers of subsidies—of between 1 and 2 percent of GDP. Studies place macroeconomic cost of the CAP during the 1980s at between 0.5 and 3.5 percent of GDP. To put these estimated costs in context, the agriculture, mining, and utilities sectors each accounted for between 1 and 2 percent of total US output in 2010; construction accounted for about 3.5 percent. These costs were substantial but seen as necessary to achieve the greater goal of progress toward European unity.

The 1957 Treaty of Rome that established the EEC was largely silent on monetary matters. At the time of its signing, the Bretton Woods system of fixed exchange rates was in place, so there was little reason to be concerned about exchange rate fluctuations among EEC member countries. As the vulnerabilities of the Bretton Woods system became more obvious during the 1960s, a committee under the chairmanship of Luxembourg prime minister Pierre Werner was established to examine the possibility of closer monetary cooperation and more stable exchange rates among EEC countries. The committee reported in 1970 that achieving monetary union by the end of the decade was realistic, and that the next steps should include greater harmonization of economic policies (e.g., monetary, fiscal, budgetary, exchange), and a gradual removal of obstacles to the free flow of trade and capital within the community.

Why would countries want to share a currency? Economists have pondered the costs and benefits of such arrangements since the early 1960s, when Nobel laureate Robert Mundell advanced the notion of an "optimum currency area" (often rendered in subsequent literature as "optimal currency area"). The practical benefits of sharing a single currency are potent, particularly if the commercial ties between the countries are strong. One element of the practical advantages can be easily demonstrated with an example. By the time euro coins and notes were introduced in 2002, a total of 12 European countries (Austria, Belgium, Finland, France, Germany, Greece, Ireland, Italy, Luxembourg, the Netherlands, Portugal, and Spain) had adopted it. During the pre-euro era, if a tourist had started in one of these countries with one hundred German marks, Irish pounds, or Italian lira and then traveled to each of the 11 other eurozone countries doing nothing in each except exchange money into the local currency at each stop, and was charged, say, 3 percent per conversion, he or she would have spent about 28.5 percent of the original sum on commissions.

For firms that buy from foreign suppliers that invoice in another currency, exchange rate fluctuations turn fairly routine transactions into a trip to the casino. An unexpected change in the exchange rate could mean paying more for inputs and, ultimately, the difference between operating at a profit or at a loss. Should firms take such an existential risk? Or should they engage in costly exchange market transactions—such as purchasing futures contracts or foreign currency options—in order to minimize the risk? Thus, countries that engage in substantial cross-border transactions will, other things being equal, benefit from sharing a currency.

Other benefits are not quite so obvious but may be economically significant. If all goods and services are priced in one currency, price differentials between countries become more transparent. When prices are easily compared, firms and households are better able to buy from lower-cost sellers, leading to more cost-effective purchasing decisions which reward the most efficient producers. Smaller countries may also benefit from membership in a monetary union by paying lower interest rates on their debt. That is, because the bonds of smaller countries are no longer priced in the riskier (i.e., more likely to fluctuate) national currency, but instead in the more stable joint currency, investors are likely to lend to them on easier terms. Euro-denominated bonds will have a broader international appeal than those denominated in the Greek drachma or Portuguese escudo, since the euro is likely to be more stable than either of these two currencies. Benefits might also accrue to countries with reputations for irresponsible monetary policy, since joining a monetary union takes monetary authority out of the hands of national policy makers.

The main cost of joining a monetary union is the surrender of the national currency and the independent central bank. Since these are powerful national symbols, giving them up can be psychologically difficult. More importantly, joining a monetary union means yielding monetary sovereignty. Decisions on monetary policy, such as raising or lowering interest rates, are no longer made by domestic policy makers with the national interest in mind, but are instead made for the monetary union as a whole by an institution with a broader set of priorities. If one area of the monetary union is in recession and in need of a low interest rate policy while another area is operating at full capacity and would benefit from higher interest rates, it is impossible for the central authority to satisfy the needs of both regions. If the various parts of a monetary union are hit with different—or differently sized—macroeconomic shocks, the monetary union will experience adverse consequences unless there are regional adjustment mechanisms in place. Such adjustment mechanisms could include the migration of labor from high- to low-unemployment areas, a decline in relative prices and wages in high-unemployment areas, or regionally targeted fiscal policy to counterbalance a localized economic shock. For a number of reasons, including linguistic differences, labor market laws, and eurozone institutions, none of these adjustment mechanisms are feasible at present.

Examples of monetary unions, both historical and contemporary, abound. Catalogues of monetary unions distinguish two principal types: national and multinational. National monetary unions are established when previously independent regions are united into a single political unit. Such unifications occurred with the adoption of the Constitution in the United States in the eighteenth century, the national unifications of Germany and Italy in the nineteenth, and the reunification of Germany in the twentieth. In each of these cases, both the currency and the institutions responsible for monetary policy were established on a nationwide basis. These types of unions—when political unification precedes monetary unification—have proven to be quite durable.

Nineteenth-century multinational monetary unions included the Latin Monetary Union, established in 1865 by France, Belgium, Switzerland, and Italy, and the Scandinavian Monetary Union of Denmark, Norway, and Sweden, established in 1873. These unions were characterized primarily by the standardization of common coins, in terms of weight and specie content, which were allowed to circulate in all member countries. The Scandinavian Monetary

Union progressed even further toward a complete union by eventually allowing the notes of each country to circulate in the other member countries as well. Nonetheless, both of these monetary unions were less complete than the American, German, and Italian monetary unions, since even though Norway and Sweden shared a monarch and foreign policy between 1814 and 1905, they retained their own central banks and currencies. Neither the Latin nor the Scandinavian monetary union was durable: both eventually disintegrated under the inflationary pressures of World War I.

Several attempts were made during the 1970s to limit the extent of exchange rate fluctuations among European currencies. These plans carried such colorful names as "the snake" and "the snake in the tunnel," and were so named because a graphical representation of the exchange rates and the bands within which they were permitted to fluctuate resembled, well, a snake or a snake in a tunnel. Although exchange rates were allowed to vary by a few percentage points under these plans, macroeconomic fluctuations, particularly those associated with the oil shocks of 1973 and 1979, forced the arrangements to be abandoned. Instead, the Europeans concentrated on measures aimed at removing trade barriers between countries and strengthening the common market. In the late 1980s, a committee of European central bank governors meeting under the chairmanship of European Commission president Jacques Delors was appointed to consider how best to advance monetary unification. These deliberations were followed by directives aimed at allowing money to flow freely among European countries (such flows had previously been limited) and a decision to focus on establishing economic convergence, price stability, and budgetary discipline before irrevocably fixing the exchange rates among the countries to be joined in monetary union.

By the early 1990s, EEC governments had decided that the time for the next stage of European integration was ripe. The result was the Maastricht Treaty, formally, the "Treaty of the European Union," which came into force in 1993. The economic clauses of the treaty included a commitment to full economic and monetary union by the end of the decade. Among its provisions was the establishment of the European Monetary Institute, consisting of the member countries' national central banks, to facilitate the harmonization of monetary policies among the countries and to help prepare for the eventual creation of the European Central Bank (ECB). The treaty also set certain benchmarks that countries would have to meet before they could become full eurozone members. These "convergence criteria" mandated limits on inflation and long-term interest rates, and the maintenance of exchange rate stability for two years. Convergence criteria were also applied to government finance, limiting member country government debt and deficit as a percentage of GDP. In 1997, the heads of government of the member countries adopted the Stability and Growth Pact, which was aimed at enforcing fiscal discipline through a system of monitoring, warnings, and, ultimately, sanctions against offending members.

The ECB was established on June 1, 1998. On December 31, 1998, the currencies of Austria, Belgium, Finland, France, Germany, Ireland, Italy, the Netherlands, Portugal, and Spain were irrevocably fixed; the Greek drachma followed in June 2000. EEC members Denmark, Sweden, and the United Kingdom declined to join the euro and continued to maintain their own currencies. Starting on January 1, 1999, the euro was introduced for book transactions, including those on European securities exchanges. The union became complete on January 1, 2002, when euro coins and notes were introduced and the process of gradually retiring national currencies was begun.

The decision to adopt the euro was made more for political and ideological reasons than economic ones. At the time of the creation of the monetary union, Europe was not an optimal currency area— certainly not as much of an optimal currency area as the United States. For linguistic and other reasons, labor was not as mobile across European countries as it was across states in the United States or provinces in Canada. Europe had nothing like the fiscal federalism of the United States. And European economic shocks were larger and less correlated than those in the United States. European politicians took little note of academic opinion on the subject of monetary union, just as their predecessors had not been overly concerned about the costs of the CAP, and moved steadily— even precipitously—to irrevocable monetary union.

The euro was launched with great fanfare at the beginning of 1999, and the new notes, with even greater fanfare at the beginning of 2002. Despite a variety of missteps in the early days of the euro and the ECB, and criticisms leveled against the Europeans for failing to address labor and fiscal policy issues, the reaction to the euro during the early years was generally positive. Summing up the monetary record of the union in January 2005, one scholar wrote: "From many points of view, the first six years of the euro and the ECB have been uneventful. This is a happy observation, since in monetary policy 'uneventful' is all but synonymous with 'successful.'" At a conference held by the European Commission to celebrate tenth anniversary of monetary union, the commissioner responsible for economic and monetary affairs opened the proceedings by noting the consensus view that that euro had been a success. Research presented at the conference suggested that, in fact, even though Europe still had a ways to go in terms of satisfying the optimal currency area criteria, the score on that issue had improved. As one conference participant wrote: "There is greater resilience of the euro area as a whole, low actual and expected inflation, low interest rates and greater macroeconomic stability."

And then the subprime crisis hit.

The subprime crisis had its origins in the United States, stemming from loose monetary and fiscal policies combined with lax regulation and excessive risk taking made possible by the advent of new financial instruments. In contrast, fiscal and monetary policies in Europe prior to the subprime crisis had been more moderate.

Although Europe was not the prime instigator of the crisis, it was more than just an innocent bystander. European financial institutions had purchased substantial amounts of mortgage-backed and related derivative securities and took heavy losses when the prices of these plummeted. Further, European banks had borrowed relatively more than American banks, so when these losses were realized the financial distress in Europe was at least as severe as in the United States. And although much has been made of the run-up in US housing prices between 1999 and 2005, housing prices in some parts of Europe rose just as dramatically; in some cases, price increases exceeded their 30-year average by as much as 40 percent. The housing price rise was not uniform: although real estate markets were relatively sluggish in Austria and Germany, prices rose spectacularly in Spain, Ireland, Belgium, the Netherlands, and France. The collapse of the booms in these high-flying real estate markets led to further problems, both for financial institutions and for the national governments that bailed them out.

The crisis intensified in October 2009, when the newly elected Greek government revised its estimate of the government's budget deficit from 6.7 percent to 12.7 percent of GDP; the estimate was subsequently raised to 13.6 percent. Greece had been borrowing heavily for years. This process had been helped along by Greece's adoption of the euro, since as a eurozone member it could more cheaply and easily borrow on world markets than when its debt was denominated in drachmas. When the magnitude of Greece's fiscal woes became widely known, investors grew increasingly nervous about its ability to repay, leading to an increase in the interest rate that the Greek government was charged for new borrowing. How nervous were lenders? Consider the difference—in financial terms, the "spread"—between the yields on Greek debt and debt issued by Germany, considered at the time to be a model of fiscal sobriety. The spread between Greek and German 10-year bond yields, which had been a percent or less from the euro's inception in January 2000 through March 2009, jumped to nearly 3 percent at the beginning of 2010 and to 8 percent in August 2010. It would go on to exceed 30 percent in 2011 and 2012.

As Greece's situation—and the bond market's perception of it—deteriorated, European policy makers held a series of meetings to discuss the possibility of a bailout. Had Greece not joined the euro, it could have inflated its way out of the debt squeeze. To do this, the Bank of Greece would have increased the supply of drachmas. This, in turn, would have lowered the drachma's value via inflation and allowed the government to pay the interest due on its debt in a depreciated currency. The inflation would have caused a decline in the value of the drachma vis-à-vis its trading partners, which would have improved the market for Greek exports and encouraged more foreigners to visit—and spend money in—Greece. The cost of this policy would have been inflation, which would have eroded the value of savings and wages in Greece.

Given that Greece was using the euro instead of the drachma, short of an exit from the eurozone—a possibility discussed later—inflating away the problem was not an option. Instead, Greece sought a loan from the EU and the IMF so that it could service its euro-denominated debts. Taxpayers in the fiscally more sound European countries—particularly Germany—who were slated to bear much of the cost of the bailout, initially balked at the prospect of subsidizing Greece's fiscal irresponsibility. Because of the large amounts of Greek debt held by banks elsewhere in Europe, governments feared that a Greek default would lead to widespread bank failures across Europe, and so the EU and the IMF put together a rescue package for Greece. The deal, implemented in May 2010, provided €110 billion, enough euros for Greece to service its debts; a second bailout of about the same size was approved in July 2011. The Germans were not the only ones unhappy with these deals: the bailout was made conditional on the Greek government's agreement to implement severe austerity measures, including reducing the number of public sector workers and cutting wages. Austerity contributed a further substantial decline in Greek economic activity

and an increase in unemployment, which has led to widespread—
and sometimes violent—protests.

It soon became clear that other eurozone countries would
require bailouts. In Ireland, the collapse of a property bubble had
led the government to announce that it would guarantee the banks
that had financed the boom. By November 2010, the full extent of
the cost of that guarantee became known, and the Irish government
sought a bailout from the EU and the IMF. The resulting rescue
package amounted to €85 billion. In April 2011, Portugal, which had
unsustainably high levels of government and consumer debt, also
requested assistance and subsequently received a bailout package of
€78 billion. Cyprus followed with a €10 billion bailout in April 2013.

Although the crises in Greece, Ireland, and Portugal were
severe—and costly—these countries are among the smallest in the
EU. Greece, the largest of the three, constitutes less than 2 percent
of Europe's GDP and population. As European leaders scrambled to
come up with bailout agreements at a series of all-night summits and
to design mechanisms to provide emergency support to financial
institutions across the EU, observers worried that if troubles spread
to larger countries, requiring potentially larger bailouts, they would
not have the resources to come to the rescue. Italy, for example, is
the fourth-largest country in the EU and constitutes about 12 percent of EU GDP and population. European leaders feared that the
bankruptcy of Italy's bloated and inefficient state, which had been
run by a notoriously mercurial—and several-times convicted—
prime minister for the better part of the preceding decade, would
prove too much for the EU and IMF to handle. Under pressure from
European leaders, Italy installed a technocratic prime minister and
cabinet, which took office in late 2011 and subsequently undertook
substantial reforms through the end of its term in April 2013. Spain,
the EU's fifth-largest economy, suffered a devastating collapse of its
property bubble in 2008, eventually leading to a European bailout of
the country's largest real estate lender and several smaller financial
institutions in 2012.

There is no precedent for the European monetary union. At its inception, the eurozone consisted of a dozen countries; by early 2013 its membership had grown to seventeen, and a number of eastern European countries are slated to join in the near future. The members of the eurozone are among the world's most advanced industrialized nations and have a combined population and GDP approximately equal to that of the United States. In many ways, the euro has been a resounding success: a group of countries, nearly all of whom had fought on opposing sides in two devastating wars during the twentieth century, voluntarily surrendered their monetary sovereignty at the beginning of the twenty-first. In so doing, they yielded the right to issue their own currency and to control their own money supplies and interest rates to a supranational authority, the ECB. No other multinational monetary union has ever covered as large or as wealthy a region. And, in fact, the euro has brought substantial benefits by hastening the easing of barriers to the flow of goods, labor, and capital across Europe. Although these barriers might eventually have come down anyway, progress was no doubt hastened by politicians' desire to foster monetary union.

Despite these achievements, the euro has a fatal design flaw. In order for a one-size-fits-all monetary policy to work for the entire union, there must be a nonmonetary mechanism that enables the regions within the union to adjust to economic shocks. The European monetary union does not, as yet, have those mechanisms. Linguistic and other barriers prevent labor from easily migrating from high- to low-unemployment areas, removing one potential adjustment mechanism. The absence of fiscal federalism, government transfers from one area of the zone to another, removes another means of counterbalancing differential regional shocks. Without these mechanisms, the only major tool remaining to policy makers is region-specific monetary policy, which, in a monetary union, is impossible.

Even before the euro was launched, academics discussed scenarios under which it would break apart. As the euro crisis has unfolded, such speculation has become rampant—not just in the ivory towers of academia, but amongst journalists, policy makers, and the man and woman on the street. In the earliest days of the crisis, speculation focused on Greece and whether it would attempt to solve its fiscal and financial problems by exiting the euro—a "Grexit" for short—and reintroducing the drachma. As the crisis spread across the eurozone, the commitment of similarly fiscally weak countries to the euro was also questioned. And would the exit of one or two countries lead to a stampede?

As the cost of providing bailouts mounted, speculation arose that the more solvent countries, typified by Germany, would look for a way of disengaging from their struggling counterparts. Some suggested a two-tier currency system, in which the fiscally stronger nations of northern Europe retain the euro, while Greece and other fiscally troubled nations create a "southern euro." Others suggested that some countries might introduce a parallel currency that would circulate alongside the euro. And others suggested that instead of waiting for a Grexit, Greece should be expelled. Or perhaps that Germany and other northern European countries should leave the euro before the costs of propping it up became too much to bear. One British think tank, perhaps gloating over the fact that the United Kingdom did not join the euro in the first place, offered a prize of £250,000 for the plan that outlined the smoothest process by which a member state could exit the eurozone.

As the sovereign-debt crisis raged, editorial writers took emphatic positions on whether Greece could, should, or would leave the euro. Headlines typifying these positions ranged from "Greece must go" to "Greece is not leaving the eurozone, not now, not ever." The obstacles to leaving the euro are substantial. Legally, there is no formal mechanism for a country to exit the euro. A country that did decide to leave would have to cope with a whole host of technical and logistical issues. New notes and coins would have to be issued and distributed to banks and ATMs. Computers would have to be reprogrammed. Everything from vending machines to ticket-taking machines in parking garages would have to be changed over to the new currency. And all this would have to take place quickly, since once news emerged that the euro was to be replaced with a less valuable currency, euros would be hoarded.

The economic and political costs of leaving the euro would be substantial as well. Creditors of governments and firms in countries that exited from the euro would suffer a substantial capital loss as their euro-denominated claims would become worth only a fraction of their previous value. This would be catastrophic for financial institutions holding these claims on their balance sheets. One observer goes so far as to say that the breakup of the eurozone would trigger "the mother of all financial crises." Given that an exit would likely inflict havoc, countries that continued to use the euro might not be inclined favorably toward those that exited. For example, countries that abandoned the euro would probably not want to leave the nonmonetary arrangements of the EU, such as the single market's free movement of goods and services. Countries adversely affected by the exit from the eurozone might insist that countries that exit the euro also leave other European institutions.

Although the euro is likely to survive, it is still possible that it will collapse. The costs of the uncertainty surrounding the euro's survival are immense. Crédit Agricole, a French bank, sends the balances of its Greek subsidiary, Emporiki, electronically to Paris every evening and returns them in the morning. They engage in this unusual and relatively costly set of transactions just in case Greece abandons the euro overnight, which would leave any cash remaining in Emporiki overnight worth substantially less the following morning. Crédit Agricole and other French firms operating in Greece are poised to sell their Greek operations for a symbolic one euro, primarily to distance themselves from the cost of a possible Grexit.

A number of economists have suggested that the only way out of the euro mess is forward. They argue, convincingly, that short-term assistance from wealthier eurozone countries—with conditions attached—is necessary to stabilize the weaker eurozone countries,

allowing time for greater labor market integration and fiscal federalism to generate a more stable framework for Europe's future.
There are good reasons to think that governments—both north and
south—will support this plan. UBS, a Swiss bank, estimates suggest
that Grexit could cost the Greek economy between 40 and 50 percent of one year's aggregate output in the first year following the
exit, substantially worse than the declines Greece has witnessed in
the years following the eruption of the crisis. Responsible political leaders in Greece are not anxious to leave the euro. The radical
left-wing Syriza party, which pledged to turn down the bailout if
elected, argued that their goal was not to leave the eurozone, but
that their hard-line approach would enable them to negotiate easier
bailout terms.

On the other end of the north-south divide, Germany would also
suffer from the breakup of the euro. Much of Germany's prosperity in recent years has been based on its position as Europe's strongest exporter. If the euro collapsed or its weaker members exited,
Germany would be forced to face export markets with an expensive
new currency—either a new German mark or the euro consisting of
only the stronger members of the monetary union. In either case,
Germany would find itself priced out of export markets. Thus, if
the choice is between bailing out Greece and never selling another
Mercedes Benz outside Germany, responsible German leaders will
do their utmost to save the euro.

Despite the seemingly slow steps being taken toward rescuing
the euro, European politicians understand that the stakes are high
and that failure would be costly. Greece—after its second election
within six weeks—installed a pro-euro government. Germany and
the ECB have been leading the charge to save the euro, with ECB
president Mario Draghi going so far as to say that he will do whatever it takes to save the euro. Discussion among eurozone leaders
in late 2012 and early 2013 focused on initiatives to forge both a
fiscal union, to develop more federalism and discipline in member
state tax and spending decisions, and a banking union, to support

financial stability by establishing more uniform regulation and supervision in European banks.

The euro's benefits were demonstrated during its first half-dozen years. Its costs became more evident subsequently. If Europe's adjustment mechanism is made to work more smoothly, the euro can still be a policy success rather than the disaster it looks like 15 years after its establishment. As originally implemented, the euro was a failure; with a hard-headed practical approach, it may still become a success.

Chapter 11

What Have We Learned? Where Do We Go from Here?

"Tut, tut, child!" said the Duchess. "Everything's got a moral, if only you can find it."

LEWIS CARROLL
Alice in Wonderland, chapter 9

It would be tempting—and great for sales of this book—to conclude that the episodes sketched in the preceding chapters constitute a complete catalogue of the economic policy mistakes made during the last 200 years. Sadly, that is not the case. The period spanned by this book is littered with policy blunders; those discussed here represent a small, albeit elite minority. Nor can this book pretend to provide a comprehensive account of all the *types* of economic policy errors committed during the previous two centuries. The policy errors of the nineteenth and twentieth centuries are far too varied to be encompassed by just nine episodes. Any study of economic policy, modern or historical, must conclude that there is no "typical" economic policy mistake, just as there is no universal playbook for good economic policy.

Identifying the source of economic policy mistakes is difficult because the decisions to undertake them are rarely made solely on the basis of economic merits, assuming that economists could agree about the merits of a proposed policy, or in a vacuum. Rather, policies are usually the result of a complex web of interrelated—and sometimes conflicting—economic, political, and historical forces. For example, Britain's policy response to the Irish famine was dramatically transformed—for the worse—when the government of Sir Robert Peel was replaced by one led by Lord John Russell. The change in administration came about when Peel and his Conservative allies, backed by the opposition Whigs, engineered the repeal of the Corn Laws. The repeal of the Corn Laws, motivated in part by the desire to relieve Ireland's food shortage, cost Peel the support of enough members of his Conservative party to lead to his replacement by Russell; and his famine relief policy, by one that was far less constructive. The disastrous policy adopted by Japan's Ministry of Finance during the "lost decade" of the 1990s and, importantly, its ability to pursue such a policy without serious opposition, was a consequence of the ministry's long-held attitudes and unrivaled power within the Japanese government, both of which had evolved over decades. And the British did not institute the Navigation Acts in order to provoke their North American colonists into a revolutionary fervor; rather, the Acts were merely the latest in a centuries-long line of like-minded trade legislation enacted by Britain and many other colonial powers aimed at enriching the mother country at the expense of its rivals and, incidentally, its colonies.

In addition to these complicating factors, some misguided policies seem to have had accidental—almost random—causes. In March 1925, Chancellor of the Exchequer Winston Churchill hosted a small dinner to which he invited Sir Otto Niemeyer, Lord John Bradbury, Reginald McKenna, and John Maynard Keynes. Niemeyer and Bradbury, current and former Treasury civil servants, favored Britain's return to the gold standard; McKenna, who had been chancellor of the exchequer during World War I, and Keynes, the noted academic, pundit, and occasional policy advisor to the government, opposed it. It is not clear whether Churchill had already made up his mind that Britain would return to gold and wanted to know to what extent he would be skewered in the press by Keynes, or whether he was truly hoping for one last definitive debate on the gold standard's merits before making a final decision. Churchill's private secretary P. J. Grigg was present at the dinner and recalled in his autobiography that the opponents of the return to gold were not especially persuasive on that occasion. Grigg's account—the only surviving record of that evening—is not detailed enough for us to be absolutely certain of what transpired, but it is entirely possible that this economic policy mistake came about because John Maynard Keynes, one of the era's most articulate opponents of that policy had an "off night."

Despite the foregoing warnings against characterizing the typical economic policy mistake, some distinctive patterns stand out.

The policy missteps analyzed in this book resulted in large part from commitment to outdated or fundamentally flawed economic ideologies. Britain's return to the gold standard in 1925 is a case in point. The gold standard had been a cornerstone of the international financial order—and of British financial leadership—during the half century prior to World War I, and the return to gold had a strong emotional appeal for the British that made it politically difficult to resist. The policy was articulately—and very publicly—opposed by Keynes and Gustav Cassel, two of the most prominent and widely read economists of the day, so policy makers could not have been ignorant of the potential harmful effects of adopting the gold standard. Reginald McKenna, who also opposed the return to the gold standard, recognized the political reality of the situation. At the dinner described above, he told Churchill: "There is no escape; you have to go back; but it will be hell."

Ideology similarly played a destructive role in the British response to the Irish famine, when Lord John Russell's government exhibited a wrong-headed devotion to laissez-faire principles by refusing to interfere in the workings of food markets. This ideological commitment surely should have been trumped by the overriding need to alleviate suffering and save lives. George W. Bush's determination to lower taxes, despite the need for additional funding to fight two wars, can only be described as putting ideology above common-sense fiscal management. And the European drive toward a single currency despite the continent's disastrous history with the gold standard during the interwar period, not to mention the fact that Europe clearly was not an optimal currency area, suggests that the euro was, to paraphrase Oscar Wilde, the triumph of ideology over experience.

Another important source of policy mistakes has been the outsized influence of private interests. Although politicians typically embrace newly enacted economic policies with proclamations that they are being adopted in furtherance of the public good, these policies often also reflect the interests—and influence—of distinct groups within society. Thus, although the British decision to return to the gold standard was in large part a response to national sentiment, it was also backed by London's powerful financial industry, which received a boost in its international standing from the policy. Congressional votes on both the First and Second Bank of the United States were dominated by private interests: regions and classes that stood to benefit from the banks supported their establishment and continuation, as did their backers in the legislature; those that viewed the banks as unwelcome competitors opposed them. Similarly, the American financial industry was able to make its influence felt again and again in the run-up to the subprime crisis, as it encouraged legislators and regulators to ease up on the regulatory constraints under which it operated.

Policy mistakes often revolve around efforts to shift costs onto foreigners. If the motivation described in the preceding paragraph is accurately defined as "private interests," this type of cost-shifting effort can be thought of as "nationalistic interests." The domestic political appeal of such measures is obvious. The reparations imposed on Germany after World War I and the insistence that inter-Allied debts be fully discharged provide clear examples of this. The reparations themselves were an attempt to keep Germany both economically and militarily weak, and thereby strengthen the relative positions of the European allies, particularly France. The United States could have been a persuasive advocate in arguing for a reduction in reparations; however, this would have involved forgiving a portion of the inter-Allied debt, a cost it was not willing to bear. The implementation of the Smoot-Hawley tariff in the interwar period and the retaliatory responses it evoked from other countries provide further examples of attempts to shift costs to other countries—policies that eventually backfired.

A final element running through the episodes discussed here is that they were frequently compounded by excessive delay—either in the implementation of a beneficial policy or in the reversal of a policy mistake. The extraordinary efforts made by the Ministry of Finance to both conceal the severity of Japan's banking problems in the 1990s and postpone the day of reckoning substantially increased the eventual resolution cost—not to mention the economic cost—of that debacle. The interwar gold standard provides another example. Countries that left the gold standard earlier in the 1930s, including Britain, fared much better during the Great Depression than those that continued to cling to gold.

I argued in the introduction that although policy failures are depressing, we can learn valuable lessons by studying them. But have policy makers, in fact, learned anything? They have. The greatest advances have been made in the area of curbing nationalistic interests.

Among the most important lessons learned by policy makers have been those related to trade policy. Throughout the seventeenth and eighteenth centuries, and for much of the nineteenth, world commerce was conducted from behind massive tariff walls. Britain's repeal of the Corn Laws in 1846 marked the beginning of steady progress toward more open trade by the world's leading commercial and industrial powers. This trend was reversed during the interwar period, when the fall in world trade due to the declining incomes associated with the Great Depression was amplified by tariff hikes in many countries. After World War II, the General Agreement on Tariffs and Trade began a decades-long process of uninterrupted multilateral trade liberalization. Certainly, protectionist pressures have reared their heads now and then. During the 1992 American presidential campaign, H. Ross Perot argued that ratifying the North American Free Trade Agreement would lead to a "giant sucking sound" as US jobs migrated to Mexico and lowered the wages of American workers. And, even though many countries have recently introduced minor—and not so minor—impediments to the free flow of goods and services, the years since World War II have provided the longest sustained period of trade liberalization in history. This trend is particularly impressive given the recent subprime and euro crises: despite suffering the worst economic and financial setback since the Great Depression, policy makers seem genuinely disinclined to resort to tariff hikes, a distinct improvement over their predecessors during the interwar period.

Policy makers have also dramatically revised their thinking about reparations. From time immemorial harsh reparations were considered the right of the victors and the obligation of the vanquished. In the modern world, this tradition reached its apogee with the reparations imposed on Germany in the aftermath of World War I. The financial burdens of these reparations went far beyond those imposed after any other war in the nineteenth or twentieth century and are widely believed to have contributed to Germany's economic and political instability during the interwar period. Policy makers seemed to have learned the lesson of post–World War I reparations. Although the impulse to punish Germany and Japan after World War II was strong, policy makers wisely concluded that rebuilding these countries—at considerable cost—would promote prosperity at home and abroad and contribute to world peace.

Are there more lessons to be learned?

Yes.

The most important lesson is to reject policy proposals based primarily on ideology. Ideologically based policy comes about when policy makers grab hold of a key idea and use it as their main guide to making policy decisions. Sometimes, this key idea becomes embedded as "conventional wisdom," perhaps because "we have always done it that way." Habit—or is it complacency?—often blinds us to the fact that past policy prescriptions may have out-lived their usefulness. Britain had adhered to the gold standard continuously for over 90 years—longer than any other country—before World War I forced it and the rest of the industrialized world to abandon gold. During the pre–World War I gold standard years, Britain became one of the greatest military, industrial, commercial, and financial empires the world had ever known. It may not have been unreasonable for the public and policy makers to associate Britain's imperial greatness with adherence to the gold standard. Nonetheless, the warnings of Keynes and others should have led policy makers to question the conventional wisdom of returning to the gold standard.

Economic policy based on conventional wisdom is not just a relic of the distant past. During the past half century, a dominant para-digm among economists and policy makers has been deregulation. Nowhere has this been more evident than in the realm of finance. In the aftermath of the Great Depression of the 1930s, governments imposed strict regulation on all aspects of banking and finance—a sort of financial lockdown. This severe regulatory regime both stunted financial innovation and was a drag on economic growth, but kept the industrialized world crisis free. Starting in the 1960s, policy makers, egged on by the economics profession, began to roll back the financial lockdown, a trend that continued uninterrupted until the subprime crisis blew up in 2008. Deregulation persisted even as improvements in communications and technology made the financial industry more complex, harder to monitor, and more adept at taking risks. Thus, at the very time when the financial system was growing more crisis prone and in need of more sophisticated regula-tion, the conventional wisdom of deregulation held sway.

Economic ideologies also may become entrenched because policy makers and institutions become trapped in a "groupthink" mentality. Two independent expert reviews of the Bank of England published in late 2012 found just such a problem. One commented that although Bank of England staff members are often willing to challenge their superiors, they tend to "filter" their advice to make it more palatable to the higher-ups. Another reviewer observed that the financial crisis highlighted just how wrong the consensus view was and suggested that the Bank of England would benefit by considering divergent views. Thus, it is not surprising that weeks after these reports were released, the British government decided to appoint the first foreigner—a Canadian—to ever lead the Bank of England in its 300-plus year history.

The danger of following the conventional wisdom highlights an important strength of the American central bank. Established in 1913–14, the US Federal Reserve system consists of 12 regional reserve banks and the Board of Governors in Washington. Initially, the reserve banks had considerable autonomy; however, following the Great Depression their independence was seen as an impediment to coherent monetary policy making and was curtailed, leaving them with only a consultative role in the policy-making process. One artifact of the Fed's original organizational structure is that the reserve banks have their own research departments, each with distinctive views on economic policy. The benefits of the Fed's structure is underscored by a story told to me by a Federal Reserve economist from one of the regional reserve banks who had just returned from presenting some research at the Bank of Canada. The economist noted that when he attended conferences that assembled economists from the Board of Governors and the reserve banks, he typically encountered a wide-ranging set of policy views. This, he said, was in stark contrast to his visit to Ottawa, where he sensed that there was a "Bank of Canada view," and not as much diversity of opinion.

Thus, an important tactic in avoiding policy that relies wholly on ideology or conventional wisdom is to insure that diverse views are taken into consideration during the policy-making process. Of course, institutions of the size and geographic spread of the Federal Reserve are rare. Nonetheless, diversity of opinion in policy making can be bolstered by establishing committees of outside experts or commissioning regular external reviews of policy and the policy making process. At present, such reviews typically only take place after a crisis—when it is already too late.

Policy based on ideology can also be implemented because those with influence in the process hold fast to a particular point of view— either from conviction or because of electoral concerns—whether sober analysis supports it or not. For these ideologues, the only cure is cold, hard economic analysis. This does not mean that all foundational beliefs in economics have to be challenged on a daily basis. Most economists—myself included—believe that the market-based economic systems that characterize the industrialized world today perform far better than the Soviet-style command economies in existence prior to the fall of the Berlin Wall; that setting all personal income tax rates at 95 percent will choke off work effort, and setting them at 5 percent will not generate enough tax revenue to allow the government to perform its core functions; that relatively free and unfettered trade leads to a higher standard of living than the high-barriers-to-trade alternative. Within these broad guidelines, there is considerable room for disagreement and debate. Nonetheless, we should be suspicious of those who constantly push toward an extreme ideological agenda no matter what the circumstances.

One of the best examples of ideologically based policy initiatives is the "no new tax pledge," popularized by Grover Norquist's Americans for Tax Reform, taken up by the Tea Party movement, and signed by almost all the Republican members of the 112th Congress. We should be wary of politicians who proclaim that they have never supported any type of tax increase—and never will!—because they are driven by ideology, a desire to get (re)elected, or both. This is a far cry from politicians who prefer—and advocate for—lower taxes but recognize that sometimes tax increases are necessary. With the United States facing a host of critical short- and long-term budget issues, plus looming debt-ceiling and deficit-reduction deadlines, it is hard to imagine how the anti-tax ideologues can face the harsh fiscal reality without blinking.

Policy makers must be willing to reconsider long-held beliefs and prepared to work outside their ideological comfort zones. But how? After all, in economics, as in many other disciplines, it can take years for new ideas to surface and gain acceptance. How can policy makers know when economic ideas have become outdated? Or when changes in circumstances render a previously sound economic ideology obsolete? In short, how are policy makers—and the citizens who sit in judgment of them—to know whether a proposed policy or policy change constitutes a bold new initiative or a foolhardy leap into the abyss?

The short answer is that we can't *know*. However, economics does have a number of analytical tools that can provide guidance. Theoretical and empirical models combine current understanding about the interrelationships between various elements in the economy and can help predict the consequences of proposed policies. Cost-benefit analysis weighs the hypothesized expenditures associated with a policy against its anticipated payoff. And historical and comparative studies can provide useful analogies, analyzing the consequences of similar policies adopted at other times and in other places. These tools have proven their worth, although none is perfect. Theoretical and empirical models can be misspecified and are subject to data limitations, cost-benefit analyses often rely on a host of unknown variables, and historical and comparative studies assume—not always correctly—that economic relationships are stable across both time and space. Despite their many shortcomings, they are among the most powerful weapons in the policy maker's arsenal. Using these tools to subject proposed initiatives to rigorous testing is far more likely to yield sensible policy prescriptions than blind adherence to ideology or precedent.

Policy makers must also be wary of the influence of both private interests and nationalistic interests. As I noted in the introduction, most economic policies have distributional consequences. And those who are affected by government policy will strive to protect their interests, be they securing a piece of government largesse or avoiding a government-imposed regulatory burden. The battles between the regulators and the regulated are likely to be particularly fierce in the coming years as the US Consumer Financial Protection Bureau, established under the Dodd-Frank Wall Street Reform and Consumer Protection Act, designs new rules for the financial marketplace. The pursuit of self-interest is as old as mankind itself. Individuals, corporations, and all sorts of coalitions of similarly interested people will band together to attempt to influence policy. They cannot—and in a free society, should not—be barred from advocating for their interests. Nonetheless, rules should be enacted and maintained that prevent excessive influence by any one sector of society over policy. This can be best enforced by promoting as much transparency in the policy-making process as possible, so that excessive influence of private interests is exposed to public scrutiny. As the American Supreme Court Justice Louis Brandeis said, "Sunshine is the best disinfectant."

Finally, it is vital that bad policies be recognized and reversed as soon as possible. This prescription also has pitfalls, since those who favor a new policy, or the cancellation of an old one, often argue that the sky will fall if their prescription is not adopted immediately. Such pressures are greatest in the wake of crises, when dire predictions and scare-mongering can work to subvert reasoned debate. And in a crisis-induced rush to repeal an old policy or adopt a new one, no end of mischief can occur as various private interests enter the legislative and regulatory fray. There is a trade-off between deliberateness and speed, which is made more complicated by the fact that a favorite tactic among politicians and private interests hoping to avoid the sting of a new rule or law is to delay implementation by sending the new measure out for further study.

Economic policy must be subjected to rigorous analysis. This may, on occasion, lead to the reversal of previously held positions and put politicians in the uncomfortable position of having to "flip-flop" on an issue. I often think that we should give one or two "get out of the political doghouse free" passes to public officials who say, "When I voted in favor of this policy I thought it was the right policy, but now I see that I was wrong. And I am prepared to vote against a measure that I once supported." Given political realities, I don't expect this anytime soon. I would welcome the day when a politician attacked for changing his or her position replies with the words of John Maynard Keynes when similarly challenged: "When I am wrong, I change my mind—what do you do?"

NOTES

page vii. "The problem with any ideology": "Bill Clinton Extended Interview Pt. 1," *The Daily Show with Jon Stewart*, September 20, 2012, http://www.thedailyshow.com/watch/thu-september-20-2012/exclusive---bill-clinton-extended-interview-pt--1.

page xiv. "The day after Lehman's bankruptcy": The US Treasury subsequently participated in the bailout by taking an equity stake in the firm. In December 2012, the Treasury sold off its last remaining common shares in AIG and in March 2013, AIG repurchased the last warrants issued to the Treasury, ending the US government's direct financial interest in AIG. The Treasury's participation in the AIG bailout netted the taxpayer a profit of more than $20 billion.

pages xiv–xv. "The previous government had increased spending": Greece would later be condemned by the European Commission for falsifying public finance data. See "The Politics of Deficits and Economic Statistics," *The Economist* online, November 19, 2009, http://www.economist.com/node/14921406 on Greece's fiscal woes and Paul Shirley, "Greece's Double Dribble," *Wall Street Journal* online, June 22, 2012, http://online.wsj.com/article/SB10001424052702304765304577480473311092932.html for an amusing discussion of Greek attitudes toward paying debts.

Chapter 1: Introduction

page 1. "Hospitals large and small": Orlander and Fincke (2003).

page 2. "During the past two centuries": Maddison (2009).

page 2. "Does it arise from": Hamada and Nogouchi (2005).

page 4. "The subprime crisis that marked": Grossman (2010a).

page 4. "Within the last sixty years": Evans (1859 [1969]: 1).

page 5. "If it has 'always been done this way,'": Janis (1983).

pages 13–14. "For example, if the government imposes a tax on bread": Subsidies also generate deadweight loss. By paying sellers to produce something that they would not (or that they would not in the same quantity) in the absence of the subsidy, the cost to the government exceeds the combined benefit to producers and consumers.

page 14. "The 2008 farm bill": Goodwin, Mishra, and Ortalo-Magné (2011).

pages 14–15. "When you look at what happened": "Senator Klobuchar Pushes for Progress on Farm Bill," Senator Amy Klobuchar website, Events, Speeches and Floor Statements, December 12, 2007, http://klobuchar.senate.gov/multimediagallery_detail.cfm?id=288915&. Retrieved December 13, 2012.

Chapter 2: How to Lose an Empire without Really Trying

page 18. "From the time they get up": "Notable Quotes from Gov. Arnold Schwarzenegger," *Sacramento Bee* online, http://www.sacbee.com/2008/10/03/1286975/notable-quotes-from-gov-arnold.html, October 3, 2010. Retrieved December 13, 2012.

pages 18–19. "The enduring Roman influence": Reid and Stanfield (1997). The concluding statement is not completely accurate, since some of the words are a step or two removed from Latin. Nonetheless, the point is apt.

page 19. "Although history provides many examples": Davis and Huttenback (1986: chapter 1); Ferguson (2005: 11).

page 19. "During Leopold's rule": Hochschild (1989).

page 19. "For the four western European powers": I omit Russia's colonization of Alaska. There were some 600 Russians in Alaska at the time it was purchased by the United States in 1862. I also omit Sweden's brief attempt at colonization, centered on the borders of Delaware, New Jersey, and Pennsylvania.

page 20. "By the outbreak of World War I": Bryson (2010: 195); David and Wright (1997: 203).

page 20. "During their rule of the colonies": In this chapter, I use the terms "English" and "British" interchangeably, which is not, strictly speaking, accurate. Between 1603 and the 1707 Act of Union, England and Scotland had a common monarch but remained distinct countries, each with its own parliament. Hence, the colonial power prior to 1707 was properly "England." Following the Act of Union, England and Scotland became the United Kingdom of Great Britain, making "Britain" the more appropriate proper name.

page 20. "To understand British imperial policy": Classic works on mercantilism include those by Schmoller (1897) and Heckscher (1935). Heckscher (1935 I: 19) suggests that an exact definition of mercantilism is difficult to pin down: "Mercantilism never existed in the sense that Colbert or Cromwell existed. It is only an instrumental concept which, if aptly chosen, should enable us to understand a particular historical period more clearly than we otherwise might."

page 21. "Although these feudal lords often owed": Kohn (2005: 2–3).

page 21. "Such rules included standardizing weights": It is not clear how successful these measures were at fostering national unification. Heaton (1937: 374).

page 21. "Selling monopolies": Ekelund and Tollison (1981; 1997).

page 22. "Imperial governments managed": Frieden (2012).

page 22. "Mercantilism was the prevailing": Irwin (1993; 1996).

page 22. "Because of this, trade policy often consisted": The consequence of tariffs for domestic producers and consumers is described in more detail in chapter 7.

page 22. "In one instance, the British East India Company": Although the rebellion had many causes, it appears to have been set off by the fact that the cartridges for the new Lee Enfield rifles, which soldiers had to rip with their teeth in order to load, were greased with either cow or pig fat. This infuriated both Hindu and Muslim soldiers.

page 23. "But what have we gained": Irwin (1993: 92).

page 23. "The cessation of hostilities": Israel (1989: 197; 1997: 306).

page 24. "Although some of these were completely new": Beer (1912: 59ff.).

page 24. "Some of these were to the detriment": For details of the regulations discussed here, see Beer (1912: 60, 85ff.); Van Tyne (1951: 64ff.); Nettels (1952: 108ff.); Thomas (1965: 619ff.); and Harper (1939a, 1942).

page 24. "In theory, this regulation should have benefited": Harper (1942: 4) argues that British dominance of shipping was due to "other clauses of the Navigation Acts." See Harper (1939b: 63ff.). This view is not universally held. See, for example, Nettels (1952: 110ff.).

page 25. "Transshipping £100's worth of tobacco": McClelland (1969: 377–380).

page 26. "The philosophy behind England's imperial policy": Bryson (2010: 298).

page 26. "The British statesman William Pitt the Elder": Van Tyne (1951: 65).

page 26. "One prominent customer": Dalzell and Dalzell (1988: 56).

page 28. "Bancroft's *History of the United States*": Dickerson (1951: 302ff.).

page 28. "Among the benefits": Beer (1912: 58–127).

page 28. "No case can be made": Dickerson (1951: 55).

page 28. "In its total effect, British policy": Nettels (1952: 113–114).

page 29. "The higher estimate, over the course of 1790–1801": Harper (1939a; 1939b; 1942: 3, 6).

page 29. "The ensuing decade": Thomas (1965); McClelland (1969; 1973); Walton (1971; 1973); Hughes and Krooss (1969); Reid (1970; 1978).

page 29. "And, in fact, that remains the consensus": Whaples (1995).

page 29. "If the burden of the Navigation Acts": Some have argued that, in fact, the colonists *did not* emphasize the Navigation Acts—or economic restrictions more generally—in their complaints against the British. Of the two dozen grievances listed in the Declaration of Independence, only two (both quoted in the text) cited economic issues (i.e., trade and taxation). However, this may have been because the revolutionaries wanted to cast their struggle as primarily ideological rather than economic. According to Sawers (1992: 278): "Thomas Jefferson, in his summary of the patriots' grievances that was to serve as the basis for the Declaration of Independence, presented an extended critique of the economic injustices imposed by the British. The final version, however, mentions only taxation without representation and the inability to ship to non-British ports."

page 29. "Those that suffered the most": Ransom (1968); Thomas (1968); Sawers (1992).

page 30. "Previously, English exporters": Egnal and Ernst (1972: 15–16).

Chapter 3: Establish, Disestablish, Repeat

page 34. "Virtually every country in the world": Some countries have currency boards or other monetary authorities instead of a central bank. In central Africa, western Africa, and the eastern Caribbean, one institution serves as the monetary authority for several countries. In Andorra, Liechtenstein, Micronesia, San Marino, Tuvalu, and Vatican City, the monetary authority rests with the central bank of a larger entity.

page 34. "The Bank of England is only slightly younger": Cobbett (1814, xxii: 519).

pages 34–35. "The central banks of Austria": The German central bank, the Bundesbank, was established in 1957 but can trace its origins to the Prussian State Bank (1846) and even to the Royal Giro and Loan Bank established by Frederick the Great (1765). The Bank of Italy (1893) was created by the merger of several government note-issuing banks that predate the unification of Italy in 1861. Capie et al. (1994: appendix B).

page 35. "From the demise of the second of these institutions": Other exceptions include Australia and Canada, which also established central banks in the twentieth century.

page 35. "Historically, central banks": Although this chapter uses the term "central bank" exclusively, a more appropriate term for their early incarnations is really "government bank," that is, a private bank with certain public obligations. As these institutions morph into the quasi-public institutions we know today—sometime in the late nineteenth and early twentieth centuries—the term "central bank" becomes more appropriate.

page 35. "As one nineteenth-century observer noted": The unpopular king was William III. Thomas (1934: 4). See, however, Capie et al. (1994: 126).

page 36. "Charter renewals": Broz and Grossman (2004). Charter renewals also took place when the bank appeared to be too profitable and the government attempted to renegotiate the contract on more favorable terms.

page 36. "Many modern central banks": It is not universal practice for central banks to take part in banking supervision. During the last 25 years, several countries have combined regulatory authority over banks, securities markets, and insurance companies in a single authority that stands apart from the central bank. Norway was the first country to adopt this model, in 1986 (Grossman 2010b). Central banks that are responsible for both monetary policy (discussed below) and banking supervision may find these two goals in conflict. Goodhart and Schoenmaker (1995). In the aftermath of the subprime crisis and the European sovereign-debt crisis, policy makers are moving toward granting greater supervisory responsibilities to the Federal Reserve and the European Central Bank.

page 37. "They alter the level of reserves": The US Federal Reserve System has an explicit mandate to promote employment and price stability. The mandates of the European Central Bank and Bank of Japan extend only to maintaining price stability. The Bank of England's primary goal is price stability, although its secondary policy aims include growth, employment, and financial stability. "Japan Lawmakers Push to Curb Central Bank," *Wall Street Journal* online, June 4, 2012, http://online.wsj.com/article/SB100014240527023033956045774317807766802566.html.

page 37. "In earlier times, the main component of demand liabilities": The sums of the assets and liabilities will, by definition, be equal. To the extent that assets exceed liabilities, institutions will have a positive net worth, which is, by convention, listed on the liabilities side of the bank balance sheet.

page 38. "An increase in reserves": This presupposes that banks *want* to lend money. During times of economic uncertainty when loans may carry more risk, such as in the wake of the subprime crisis, banks may be reluctant to make new loans, which can reduce the effectiveness of monetary policy to stimulate the economy. The use of expansionary monetary policy in such situations is sometimes compared with "pushing on a string."

page 38. "This is something that commercial banks": In the nineteenth and early twentieth centuries, private clearing houses often played this role during banking panics in the United States. Cannon (1910). And J. P. Morgan famously acted as lender of last resort during the financial crisis of 1907. Today, the lender of last resort is most often a central bank.

page 39. "During the nineteenth century, bank reserves": For complicated reasons, silver was the main circulating monetary metal in the United States prior to 1834; gold became the de facto standard from 1834 to the beginning of the Civil War.

page 41. "Not worth a Continental": Dewey (1934: 56); Sylla (2011: 67); Grubb (2008).

page 41. "Securities markets had emerged": Sylla (2011: 59–60).

page 42. "The Bank of the United States (BUS)": The following paragraphs draw heavily on Grossman (2010a: 222–229). See also Holdsworth and Dewey (1910) ; Myers (1970); Hammond (1957).

pages 45–46. "Albert Gallatin": Gallatin (1879, III: 285). See Fenstermaker and Filer (1986); and Cowen (2000) for alternative views of the consequences of BUS; and Schweikart (1991) for a review of the literature.

page 46. "According to one observer": Hammond (1957: 243).

page 46. "If bankers feared": Hammond (1957).

page 47. "Jones's successor was": Catterall (1903); Perkins (1983); Dewey (1934); Hammond (1957); Federal Reserve Bank of Philadelphia (2010).

page 47. "Cheves was naturally conservative": Perkins (1983: 455).

page 47. "One critic characterized Cheves's performance": Ibid.

page 48. "The bank's lender-of-last-resort operations": Davies (2008); Knodell (1998); Hammond (1957).

page 49. "Both the constitutionality and expediency of the law": Clarke and Hall (1832 [1967]: 734).

page 50. "Still others ascribe 2BUS's downfall": Hammond (1957: 443–444); Holdsworth and Dewey (1910: 248ff.); Gatell (1966); Temin (1968).

page 50. "These boom-bust panics": Temin (1968); Timberlake (1978).

27. page 51. "Easy access to the note-issuing franchise": Rolnick and Weber (1983). See, however, Rockoff (1985).

page 51. "Failures were often blamed on 'wildcat banks'": Dwyer (1996: 1).

page 52. "The national banking era was beset by financial turbulence": Sprague (1910).

page 53. "Once the Federal Reserve was established": Miron (1986).

Chapter 4: The Great Hunger

page 54. "John Mitchel": Quoted in Ó Gráda (1999: 6).

page 54. "The Irish famine": O'Rourke (1994: 309); Guinnane (1994: 303). Famine death tolls are typically presented by scholars in terms of "excess mortality," that is, the number of people who died from the famine in excess of the number that would have died in its absence.

page 54. "The Great Hunger": See McHugh (1957) and Ó Gráda (1999) on the oral tradition of the famine. The books referred to are by Gallagher (1982); Kinealy (1994); Mokyr (1983).

pages 54–55. "She further wrote that": Quoted in Ó Gráda (1999: 4).

page 55. "The Egyptian famine": Hertz (1960: 1052); Ó Gráda (2009: 13).

page 55. "Another researcher, writing in the 1920s": Mallory (1926: 1).

page 55. "Famines were known": Garnsey (1988); Ó Gráda (2009).

pages 55–56. "Being aware that I should have to witness": Woodham-Smith (1962: 162).

page 56. "All these famines, however": The quote about the Great Leap Forward is from Ó Gráda (1999: 5). Comparative famine data are from Ó Gráda (2007: 20). Peng (1987: 648–49), who estimates 23 million deaths as a result of the famine associated with the Great Leap Forward, cites alternative estimates ranging from 16.5 to 29.5 million people. According to these data, the only famine deadlier by this measure was Ireland's 1740–41 famine, which killed 13 percent of the population (about 300,000 people).

page 57. "Whoever says 'Irish famine'": Ó Gráda (1999: 13).

page 57. "During the early 1840s": Ó Gráda (1989: 22; 1999: 17–18) does not provide dates for the estimates for Holland or Alsace.

pages 57–58. "As a crop, the potato flourished": Mokyr (1981); Bourke (1993); Nunn and Qian (2011).

page 58. "Assessing pre-famine Irish diets": Clarkson and Crawford (1988: 191).

page 58. "To be convinced that potatoes are as nutritious": Ó Gráda (1999: 15). Because "corn" is the generic term for "grain" in British English, "corn bread" refers to any grain-based bread.

page 59. "The spores of the fungus spread": Woodham-Smith (1962: 94ff.); Kinealy (1994: 31).

page 59. "The blight returned in 1849": Ó Gráda (1999: 40); Bourke (1959/1960: 11).

page 60. "The objective of the imports": O'Neill (1957: 215); Donnelly (2001: 49).

page 61. "According to a report in the *Economist* on January 2, 1847": Quotes are from Ó Gráda (1999: 50–51).

page 61. "As a practical matter, prohibiting grain exports": Irish grain exports during this amounted to 430,000 tons. Ó Gráda (1999: 124).

page 61. "I have no confidence in such remedies": Kinealy (1994: 37).

page 62. "The law was popular with British and Irish landholders": Atkin (1992: 17).

page 62. "These measures were, to a large extent, based on successful policies": Kinealy (1994: 38).

pages 62–63. "The limited distress": O'Neill (1957: 222).

page 63. "The situations they encountered were of completely different magnitudes": Ibid.: 256.

pages 63–64. "In the first place, I think that the supply of Indian corn": *Hansard* (88: 771–72).

page 64. "It must be thoroughly understood": Gooch (1925, I: 151).

page 64. "The fetish of free trade" O'Neill (1957: 257).

page 64. "With respect to many of the public works": *Hansard* (88: 772).

page 65. "In the words of English politicians and civil servants": Donnelly (2001: 70).

page 65. "Workers were paid less than a subsistence wage": Ó Gráda (1989: 45).

page 66. "Yet another appended a rider": Gallagher (1982: 76–77).

page 66. "Various authorities place the date": Ó Gráda (1999: 41).

Chapter 5: The Krauts Will Pay

page 68. "Following the First Punic War": The indemnity was to be paid over the course of the subsequent decade. Polybius (1922:169–171). The sum was the equivalent of slightly less than 200,000 pounds (90,000 kilograms) of silver.

page 68. "Following the Second Punic War": The indemnity was to be paid over the course of the subsequent 50 years. Livy (1921: 287).

page 69. "About 8.5 million military personnel": O'Brien (1994).

page 69. "To get a sense of the magnitude of the carnage": The Correlates of War database contains data on military deaths in interstate (from 1823) and civil (from 1816) wars. Sarkees (2000); Sarkees and Wayman (2010).

page 70. "The Treaty of Versailles": Sources on the treaty—and reparations more generally—include Keynes (1920; 1922; 1932); Mantoux (1946); Bergmann (1927); Schacht (1931); Moulton and Pasvolsky (1932); Felix (1971); Maier (1975); Silverman (1982); Schuker (1988); Feldman (1993).

page 71. "These included a proportion of German's existing merchant ships": Germany was required to turn over all merchant ships of 1600 gross tons and above, half of all ships between 1000 and 1600 gross tons, one-quarter of all steam trawlers and other fishing boats, and up to 20 percent of its river fleet.

page 71. "These meetings took place": Keynes (1920: 226).

page 72. "France's resolve can be traced to three factors": Keynes (1920: 33–34).

page 72. "This limited the Americans' ability": Eichengreen (1992: 131).

page 72. "Under the London Schedule of Payments": Bergmann (1927: 57); Keynes (1920: 147); Eichengreen (1992: 131).

page 72. "The London Schedule of Payments can be put into historical perspective": White (2001: 351).

page 73. "Similarly, the French were owed": Moulton and Pasvolsky (1932: 426); Silverman (1982: 145).

page 73. "Proposals to negotiate a reduction": Lutz (1930).

page 74. "Furthermore, the cost of the maintenance": Trouton (1921).

page 74. "Clearly, German officials had every incentive": Feldman (1993).

page 74. "They also took a toll": In addition to the problem of extracting sufficient resources from the German economy to pay reparations, there was a "transfer problem," since converting reparations resources into foreign currencies would lead to a depreciation of the German mark. Keynes (1929).

page 75. "The resulting increase in the currency supply": Although the increase in the currency supply was impressive, the increase in the price level during the same period was far more dramatic, increasing to more than 30 billion times its January 1921 level by December 1924. The increase highlights to role of inflationary expectations in hyperinflations. Sargent (1982).

page 76. "Notes in the trillions": Pick (1977: 267–72).

page 76. "A law passed in August 1924": Goodman (1992: 33).

page 77. "The plan was considered a success": Eichengreen (1992: 150); Kent (1989: 245ff.); Kuczynski (1926); Schuker (1988).

page 78. "The Young Committee": Guinnane (2004: 14).

page 78. "The Young Plan included": Moulton and Pasvolsky (1932: 187ff.). The plan also established the Bank for International Settlements in Basel to take over the collection, administration, and distribution of reparations payments previously handled by the agent general in Berlin and made slight adjustments to the distribution of reparations among the Allies.

page 78. "When the one-year moratorium expired": Ritschl (1996); Kent (1989: 372).

page 79. "I ought to let you know": Cited in Skidelsky (1986: 375).

page 79. "Less than six months later, Keynes": Keynes resigned from the British delegation on June 7, 1919. The treaty was signed on June 28. The foreword in the American edition of *The Economic Consequences of the Peace* (published 1920) is dated November 1919.

page 79. "Germany was 'broke'": Schuker (1988: 14).

page 80. "A number of scholars have argued": See, for example, Schuker (1988: 16) and Guinnane (2004: 14). See also Étienne Mantoux's (1946) rebuttal of Keynes in *The Carthaginian Peace; or The Economic Consequences of Mr. Keynes*.

page 80. "The Young Plan": Guinnane (2004: 14).

page 81. "Hitler attracted his first crowds": Felix (1971: 175–76).

page 81. "Have policy makers learned": See chapter 10 for a more detailed discussion of the treatment of Germany after World War II.

Chapter 6: Shackled with Golden Fetters

page 82. "To understand the Great Depression": Bernanke (1995: 1).

page 83. "A key development in that progress": Eichengreen (1992; 2004).

page 83. "Third, precious metals can be weighed and measured": In fact, the process of determining the gold or silver content of coins is not nearly so straightforward. Because gold and silver coins are almost always composed of a combination of both precious and nonprecious metals, determining the precise value of any given coin is impossible without melting it down. This is both costly and, of course, destroys the coin. Gandal and Sussman (1997) argue that less precise (and less destructive) techniques for determining the gold content of coins led mint masters in medieval France to "cheat," that is, to issue coins with slightly less gold than promised on their face.

page 84. "By minting coins containing less precious metal": Sussman (1993).

page 84. "Until the middle of the nineteenth century": Friedman (1990: 1169). The gold-silver price ratio was lower in medieval Europe and Asia. Munro (1983); von Glahn (1996). Gold coins were used in ancient Rome and in the medieval commercial centers of Venice and Florence, where they were useful for high-value international transactions. Eichengreen (1996: 8ff.).

page 84. "This system rendered large-scale transactions all but impossible": Heckscher (1954: 89).

page 85. "By setting a too low price for the coin": Feavearyear (1963: 153ff.).

page 85. "The market price of gold": Gold coins issued by Japan, the United Kingdom, and other countries similarly carry a low face value relative to their gold content.

page 85. "Although such a situation seems fanciful": "United States Mint Moves to Limit Exportation and Melting of Coins," press release,

United States Mint online, December 14, 2006, http://www.usmint. gov/pressroom/index.cfm?action=press_release&ID=724.

page 86. "One reason for the persistence of bimetallism": Redish (1990).

page 86. "Second, highly indebted sectors": Eichengreen (1996).

page 87. "The addition of this rising industrial power": Oppers (1996); Meissner (2005). The US law re-establishing the gold standard was enacted in 1875.

page 88. "Thus, the gold standard": Frieden (2006: 6–7). According to Gregory (1932: 10), "There can be no question that the development of an international gold standard in the second half of the nineteenth century and the enormous growth of international trade and investment which then took place are no mere coincidences."

pages 89–90. "[I]n our opinion, it is imperative": Committee on Currency and Foreign Exchange after the War (Cunliffe Committee), *First Interim Report*, 1918.

page 90. "To a world which was seeking to recreate that stability": Youngson (1960: 31).

page 90. "A French observer noted": Yeager (1966: 225). Alfred Sauvy, cited by Kindleberger (1986: 28).

pages 90–91. "A. C. Pigou": UK Public Record Office T160/197/ F7528/01/2.

page 91. "Something of a recluse": Ahamed (2009).

page 91. "The friendship lasted": Ibid.

page 91. "In a letter to Strong dated October 8, 1923": Strong papers, Federal Reserve Bank of New York Archives, handwritten letter from Norman to Strong, dated October 8, 1923, marked personal.

pages 91–92. "He accomplished this by maintaining high interest rates": Gregory (1957).

page 92. "The achievement was applauded": Strong papers, Federal Reserve Bank of New York Archives, cable from Strong to Norman, dated April 29, 1925.

page 93. "By the end of the decade": Eichengreen (1996: 46ff.).

page 93. "Although Churchill's announcement was welcome in financial circles": Cassel (1920); Irwin (2011b).

page 94. "By what *modus operandi*": Keynes (1925: 17).

pages 95–96. "However, the bank was also concerned": Eichengreen, Watson, and Grossman (1985).

page 96. "An examination of public statements and private correspondence": Eichengreen (1992: 391) argues that central bank governors, who had been mostly insulated from the consequences of their decisions on domestic economic conditions during the pre–World War I period, were subject to much more political and popular pressure during the interwar period.

page 96. "Each time the bank raised interest rates": Moggridge (1972: 161).

page 96. "The reduction in your rate": This quote and the subsequent one are taken from the Benjamin Strong papers in the archives of the Federal Reserve Bank of New York.

page 96. "The interwar gold standard": Eichengreen (1996: 48).

pages 96–97. "This put policy makers in the politically uncomfortable position": Cairncross and Eichengreen (1983: 46).

page 97. "By absorbing the troubled Boden Credit Anstalt": Eichengreen (1996: 78).

page 98. "Countries that departed from gold early": Eichengreen and Sachs (1985); Grossman (1994).

page 99. "Britain's decision to return to the gold standard": Eichengreen and Temin (2000).

page 100. "Yes I have made mistakes also": Moggridge (1972: 14–15).

Chapter 7: Trading Down

page 101. "The history of the American tariff": Schattschneider (1935: 283).

page 101. "If there were an Economist's Creed": Krugman (1987: 131).

page 101. "These policies and others": Free trade does not necessarily imply a complete absence of tariffs or other trade barriers. Countries frequently impose sales or value added taxes on domestic consumption; assessing a tariff that is roughly equivalent to such common domestic taxes does not violate the principle of free trade. Similarly, free trade does not mean that countries must abandon any restrictions on imports arising from health or safety concerns.

page 105. "A more modern argument": Baldwin (1992); Bhagwati (2002).

page 105. "Despite the various intellectual challenges": Whaples (2006).

page 105. "Nearly all European states": Irwin (1993: 92–98).

page 106. "The many states that would later become Germany": Ashley (1920: 3).

page 106. "A ship carrying cargo": Henderson (1939: 21–22).

page 106. "Aside from a short-lived accord": Irwin (1993: 93).

pages 106–107. "One of the first major breakthroughs": Schonhardt-Bailey (1996; 2006). The quote below is from Schonhardt-Bailey (2006: 9).

page 107. "The Corn Laws were phased out": The repeal law was passed in 1846, but the tariff was not completely eliminated until 1849.

page 108. "Wearied by our long and unavailing efforts": Quoted in Irwin (1993: 94).

page 108. "A second major push toward free trade": Ashley (1920: 297ff.); Irwin (1993: 96–98).

page 108. "The French subsequently concluded treaties": Ashley (1920: 301–302).

page 110. "Even Britain, the most free-trade country in Europe": Williamson (2006).

page 110. "US tariffs had not been uniformly protectionist": Ashley (1920); Taussig (1931 [1966]).

page 110. "Hamilton's *Report on Manufactures*": Irwin (2004).

page 110. "With the increase in imports": Stanwood (1903, I: 202) wrote: "It may be said without reservation that the sole object of [the 1824 act] in the minds of its friends was the protection of manufacturers ... it was not merely the chief, but the only aim of the promoters of the bill."

page 111. "From that time through the war's end": Taussig (1931 [1966]: 160).

page 112. "Justification for tariff increases": Kindleberger (1986: 61). The last of these was known as "exchange dumping."

page 112. "Further, the extensive reparations imposed on Germany": Friedman (1974: 10).

page 112. "Germany had been required": Kindleberger (1989: 162–163).

page 113. "International conferences": Kaplan (1996: 14); Stowell (1930); Kindleberger (1986: 63–64).

page 113. "The session lasted 14 months": Eichengreen (1989); Callahan, McDonald, and O'Brien (1994: 683–684).

page 114. "Although the increase was substantial": Irwin (2011a: 101ff.).

page 114. "Put more succinctly": Schattschneider (1935: 127–128).

pages 114–115. "Further evidence suggests that the measure passed": Pastor (1980); Eichengreen (1989); Callahan, McDonald, and O'Brien (1994); Irwin and Kroszner (1996).

page 115. "The academics had little impact": Cited in Kaplan (1996: 37–38).

page 115. "Shortbridge, it should be noted": Biographical Directory of the United States Congress website, http://bioguide.congress.gov/scripts/biodisplay.pl?index=S000380.

page 115. "The League of Nations saw it": League of Nations (1933).

page 115. "As a score of writers have pointed out": Jones (1934: 2).

page 115. "Even those who argue that Smoot-Hawley was not a major factor": Irwin and Kroszner (1996: 173).

page 115. "Other modern observers": Callahan, McDonald, and O'Brien (1994: 683).

page 116. "Although some modern authorities maintain": Meltzer (1976) and Crucini and Kahn (1996) argue that the consequences of Smoot-Hawley were substantial. Dornbusch and Fischer (1986: 466–470), Eichengreen (1989), and Irwin (1998a, 2011) suggest that the consequences were more modest.

page 116. "Further, Smoot-Hawley was the epitome": Irwin (2011a: 218).

page 116. "However, a substantial portion of the reduction": Eichengreen and Irwin (2010) find that countries remaining on the gold standard were more likely to adopt tariffs in an attempt to reduce spending on imports.

page 117. "Extensive increases in duties": League of Nations (1933: 194).

page 117. "Switzerland boycotted": Jones (1934).

page 117. "How many tens of thousands of American workmen": McDonald, O'Brien, and Callahan (1997).

page 118. "Some scholars suggest that Smoot-Hawley": Eichengreen (2012: 291).

page 118. "Not only did world trade decline": Irwin (2012a).

page 118. "The RTAA was renewed": Irwin (1993: 113).

page 118. "The WTO now has 159 members": Clemens and Williamson (2004); "The GATT Years: From Havana to Marrakesh," World Trade Organization website, http://www.wto.org/english/thewto_e/whatis_e/tif_e/fact4_e.htm.

page 119. "In fact, the only hate mail": See Charles Schumer and Paul Craig Roberts, "Second Thoughts on Free Trade," Opinion, *New York Times* online, January 6, 2004, http://www.nytimes.com/2004/01/06/opinion/second-thoughts-on-free-trade.html and Richard S. Grossman, letter to the editor, *New York Times,* January 6, 2004, http://www.nytimes.com/2004/01/11/opinion/l-free-trade-winners-and-losers-923230.html. Retrieved December 13, 2012.

page 119. "But despite these and other real challenges": Grossman and Meissner (2010). See, however, Irwin (2012b) on the worrisome rise of a variety of trade restrictions, as well as the Global Trade Alert website, http://wwwGlobalTradeAlert.org.

Chapter 8: Why Didn't Anyone Pull the Andon Cord?

page 121. "[Calvin Coolidge's] characteristic way": Mencken (2006: 128).

page 121. "Only yesterday, it seems": Krugman (1999: 60).

page 121. "The Toyota Motor Corporation": Michiyo Nakamoto, "Toyota reclaims global top spot," *Financial Times* online, January 28, 2013, http://www.ft.com/intl/cms/s/0/48a73f60-6928-11e2-b254-00144feab49a.html#axzz2LNbtkfMA.

page 121. "Toyota's Total Production System (TPS)": See, for example, *Harvard Business Review* (2009); Hino (2006); Liker (2004); Osono et al. (2008).

page 121. "When assembly line workers spot a problem": *Andon* is a traditional Japanese paper lantern.

pages 121–122. "Pulling the andon cord": For a picture and description of Toyota's andon signboard, see Stephen Williams, "Toyota Quality Control Includes 'Popeye' and 'Greensleeves,'" *New York Times* Wheels blog, September 4, 2009, http://wheels.blogs.nytimes.com/2009/09/04/toyota-quality-control-includes-greensleeves-and-popeye/.

page 122. "Production continues unimpeded": Edmondson (2011: 50).

page 124. "Banks that found themselves in trouble": Hoshi (2002).

page 124. "Overseeing the Japanese financial system": Hartcher (1998: 2–3).

page 125. "It was the lead regulator and supervisor": Amyx (2004: 43–44).

page 125. "The relationship between the MoF and the banking sector": Amyx (2004: 257).

page 125. "The banks are believed to have bought": Bird (2002: 5).

page 125. "Other examples include MoF suggestions": Hartcher (1998: 57–58).

page 125. "After Daiwa Bank ignored MoF suggestions": Vogel (1996: 171).

page 126. "Ties between the ministry and the Diet": Amyx (2004: 61).

16. page 127. "Obtaining the inspection dates": Amyx (2004: 118).

page 129. "The boom in real estate and equities": Caballero et al. (2008: 1493).

page 130. "Responses to the banking problems": Dziobek and Pazarbaşioğlu (1997).

page 131. "Rather than confronting the financial distress": Cargill et al. (2000: 42ff.).

page 131. "The mandarins of Japan's Ministry of Finance": *Economist* (June 10, 1995: 96).

page 131. "This path was followed despite the October 1994 statement of Yasushi Mieno": Nakaso (2001: 4).

page 133. "For its role in the cover-up": The accounts are from Hartcher (1998: 156–157) and Brown (1999: 117ff.).

page 133. "A proposal to secure public funding": Packer (2000).

pages 133–134. "The eventual consequences of these efforts": Hoshi and Kashyap (2009: 16).

page 135. "The plan injected": Center on Japanese Economy and Business (2008).

page 135. "The Bank of Japan": Cargill (2005); Mora (2008).

Chapter 9: Worst Financial Crisis since the Great Depression

page 137. "I've had it up to my keister": According to Sen. Bob Dole, quoted in the *New York Times*, March 23, 1983, p. A16.

page 137. "When Romer herself later asked": "Romer Offers Young Academics Solace, Sense and Secrets," UC Berkeley News Center website, October 11, 2011, http://newscenter.berkeley.edu/2011/10/11/romer-talk-offers-young-academics-solace-sense-and-secrets/.

page 138. "Banking crises were common": Grossman (2010a: 297–313). Other catalogues of banking and financial crises, both historical and contemporary, include those of Kindleberger (1978); Lindgren, Garcia, and Saal (1996); and Bordo, Eichengreen, Klingebiel, and Martinez-Peria (2001); Caprio and Klingebiel (2003).

pages 138–139. "Boom-bust crises occur": Grossman (2010a: 62); Schularick and Taylor (2012).

page 139. "Boom-bust crises play a central role": The key works are Fisher (1932; 1933). See Minsky (1970; 1982) for a more modern mathematical approach that has spawned a huge theoretical literature. Kindleberger (1978: 15) finds antecedents to Fisher in the work of the late nineteenth- and early twentieth-century economists John Stuart Mill, Alfred Marshall, and Knut Wicksell.

page 139. "Fisher laments this excessive buildup": Fisher (1932: 43).

page 139. "The contraction in the availability of loans": Bernanke (1983).

page 139. "Two other distinctive features": Kindleberger (1978).

page 140. "This often occurs when the central bank follows": Gold imports would have resulted from a balance of payments surplus. For example, a country experiencing several consecutive years of abundant harvests would have exported much of the crop and accumulated gold as foreign buyers paid with gold.

page 140. "During the weeks following the outbreak of a panic": Kindleberger (1978: 127).

page 141. "Today, our high taxes fund a surplus": George W. Bush, "Address Accepting the Presidential Nomination at the Republican National Convention in Philadelphia," August 3, 2000, online by Gerhard Peters and John T. Woolley, *The American Presidency Project*, http://www.presidency.ucsb.edu/ws/?pid=25954.

pages 141–142. "Supported by a Republican majority": The Senate that convened on January 3, 2000, was evenly divided between Republicans and Democrats. Because Vice President Al Gore held the tie-breaking vote until January 20 of that year, Democrats were the majority party. When Dick Cheney became vice president on January 20, the majority shifted to the Republicans. When Republican senator James Jeffords of Vermont decided to caucus with the Democrats from June 6, 2001, Democrats again held the majority, which they retained until the 2002 elections returned the Republicans to a majority in January 2003.

page 142. "Some of the tax cuts, which were to be phased in": Congressional Budget Office, "Effective Tax Rates under Current Law, 2001 to 2014," August 2004, pp. 1–2, http://www.cbo.gov/publication/15919.

page 142. "The war led to the deployment": Belasco (2009). These figures exclude as many as 100,000 personnel deployed elsewhere in the Middle East to support US forces in Afghanistan and Iraq.

page 142. "By 2008, annual military spending": The budget data (Department of Defense—Military Programs) are nominal, that is, not corrected for inflation. http://www.whitehouse.gov/sites/default/files/omb/budget/fy2012/assets/hist04z1.xls. Retrieved December 22, 2011.

page 142. "The net effect of the tax cuts": The data are not adjusted for inflation. http://www.whitehouse.gov/sites/default/files/omb/budget/fy2012/assets/hist01z1.xls. Retrieved December 22, 2011.

page 142. "This fiscal stimulus encouraged more spending": The economic boom was also fueled by substantial inflows of capital from abroad. Chinn and Frieden (2011).

page 143. "Second, Fed policy makers were concerned": Gourinchas (2010: 7).

page 143. "Whatever the reason for the prolonged monetary easing": Porter (2004); Hartcher (2006: 101ff.); Chinn and Frieden (2011); Bernanke (2009).

page 144. "When interest rates increased during the mid-1990s": Chomsisengphet and Pennington-Cross (2006: 38).

pages 144–145. "And even if I appear to be good credit risk": These would include going to court to commence potentially long and expensive foreclosure proceedings. Once the foreclosure was complete, the property would have to be resold, another expensive and time-consuming process.

page 145. "These policy actions gave a boost to the subprime market": Alt-A loans, which had some of the same less-creditworthy characteristics as subprime loans, grew to become a similarly sized share of the MBS market by 2006.

page 145. "More than 80 percent of all new subprime loans": Gorton (2008).

page 146. "As a managing director of Moody's": Gretchen Morgenstern, "Debt Watchdogs: Tamed or Caught Napping?" *New York Times*, December 6, 2008. http://www.nytimes.com/2008/12/07/business/07rating.html. Downloaded December 26, 2011.

page 146. "CDSs involve no such pooling of risk": Nomura Fixed Income Research (2004).

page 147. "My mortgage company hadn't cared": Andrews (2009: 6).

page 148. "Thus, holding CDSs for which the protection seller": Tett (2009: 49); Levine (2010: 202–204).

page 149. "Although the SEC announced its determination to hire": "The Day the SEC Changed the Game," *New York Times*, September 28, 2008, http://topics.nytimes.com/topics/news/business/series/the_reckoning/index.html. Levine (2010) argues that a 2004 ruling bringing these five investment banks under SEC supervision was problematic because the SEC did not have the necessary staff or expertise to carry out this function.

page 149. "Efforts to increase disclosure": Levine (2010).

page 151. "Nobody duped me": Andrews (2009: x).

Chapter 10: I'm OK. Euro Not OK?

page 152. "It can't happen." Cited in Jonung and Drea (1992).

page 152. "After all, as the quote by Rudiger Dornbusch demonstrates": Feldstein (1992).

page 153. "In December 2011, the ratings agency Standard and Poor's": In fact, S&P's only put 15 of the 17 eurozone countries on its "credit watch with negative implications" list on December 5, 2011. Greece and Cyprus had been put on the list earlier. See "Standard &

Poor's Puts Ratings on Eurozone Sovereigns on Credit Watch with Negative Implications," Standard and Poor's Global Portal, Ratings Direct, http://www.standardandpoors.com/ratings/articles/en/us/?articleType=PDF&assetID=1245325261088.

page 153. "During the same month, 50 percent of Dutch people": Matt Steinglass, "Guilder Revived as Dutch Make Monkey out of Euro," *Financial Times*, December 18, 2011, http://www.ft.com/cms/s/0/d15c794e-2593-11e1-9cb0-00144feabdc0.html.

page 154. "Schemes for peaceful political and economic cooperation": See Cruce's *Le Nouveau Cynée* and Penn's "Essays Towards the Present and Future Peace of Europe." It is not clear if the Grand Design of Henry IV was a utopian peace plan, as described in the memoirs of his superintendant of finance, Maximilien de Béthune, Duke of Sully, or merely a scheme for a military alliance. Ogg (1921); Urwin (1991: 2).

page 154. "Philosophers Jean Jacques Rousseau": Tryon (1911).

page 154. "Not all early plans for greater international cooperation": The Zollverein was an outgrowth of the 1818 Prussian customs union.

page 155. "The International Telegraph Union": Molle (2001). These have subsequently been renamed the International Telecommunications Union and the International Postal Union.

page 155. "Other practical international agreements": Erzberger (1919).

page 156. "According to Morganthau, these harsh terms": Morganthau (1947).

page 157. "I want to say that I am not interested": Ibid.

page 157. "This stricture was eased": Dorn (1957); Kindleberger (1968).

page 157. "Despite the softening of the attitude toward Germany": The Saar was administered by the French from 1947 and was returned to Germany in 1957. The administration of the Ruhr's coal and steel output was transferred to the European Coal and Steel Community in 1952.

page 157. "As compensation for this territorial imposition": Yoder (1955).

page 158. "According to the treaty, the ECSC": Merry (1955); Adler (1970).

page 159. "This is a drop in the bucket next to the 1.23 million tons of butter": Stephen Castle, "The EU's butter mountain is back," *New York*

Times, February 2, 2009, http://www.nytimes.com/2009/01/22/world/europe/22iht-union.4.19606951.html?_r=0.

page 159. "Studies place macroeconomic cost of the CAP": Howarth (2000: 5); Gylfason (1995).

page 159. "To put these estimated costs in context": Bureau of Economic Analysis, US Department of Commerce, "2010 Economic Recovery Led by Durable Goods Manufacturing: Revised Statistics of Gross Domestic Product by Industry for 2003-2010," news release, December 13, 2011, http://www.bea.gov/newsreleases/industry/gdpindustry/2011/pdf/gdpind10_rev.pdf.

page 160. "Economists have pondered the costs and benefits": Mundell (1961).

page 160. "During the pre-euro era, if a tourist had started": The moneys of Luxembourg and Belgium could be used for transactions in both countries, so only 10 conversions would be necessary if the traveler followed his/her sojourn in Belgium with one in Luxembourg, or vice versa. Nonetheless, even 10 conversions would have cost the traveler more than 26 percent of the original sum.

page 162. "These types of unions": Bordo and Jonung (2003); Bordo and James (2008).

page 164. "On December 31, 1998, the currencies of Austria": The currency of Luxembourg (interchangeable with that of Belgium), of Monaco (interchangeable with that of France), of San Marino, and of Vatican City (interchangeable with that of Italy) were fixed at the same time as those of the Belgium, France, and Italy.

page 165. "And European economic shocks were larger": Eichengreen (1997).

page 164. "European politicians took little note of academic opinion": Wyplosz (2006).

page 165. "This is a happy observation": Eichengreen (2005: 19).

page 165. "At a conference held by the European Commission": Martins (2008).

page 165. "As one conference participant wrote": Mongelli (2008: 52).

page 166. "Further, European banks had borrowed relatively more": Eichengreen (2009).

page 166. "The collapse of the booms in these high-flying real estate markets": Eichengreen (2009); Gros (2006); Hilbers et al. (2008).

page 166. "The crisis intensified in October 2009": Nelson et al. (2010).

page 166. "This process had been helped along": Chinn and Frieden (2011).

page 169. "Even before the euro was launched": Garber (1998); Scott (1998).

page 170. "Others suggested that some countries might introduce a parallel currency": Bootle (2012); Tett (2012).

page 170. "Headlines typifying these positions": Roubini (2012); Bremmer (2011).

page 171. "And all this would have to take place quickly": Eichengreen (2007b). Such hoarding is an example of Gresham's Law (see chapter 6).

page 171. "One observer goes so far as to say that the breakup": Eichengreen (2007a).

page 171. "They engage in this unusual and relatively costly set of transactions": "Iron Enters the Soul," *Economist*, October 6, 2012, http://www.economist.com/node/21564237.

page 171. "A number of economists have suggested": Eichengreen (2010a); Krugman (2010); Gros and Mayer (2010).

page 172. "There are good reasons to think that governments": "Cutting Up Rough," *Economist*, May 16, 2012, http://www.economist.com/node/21555923.

Chapter 11: What Have We Learned?

page 176. "Grigg's account": Grigg (1948: 182ff.).

pages 178–179. "During the 1992 American presidential campaign": http://www.youtube.com/watch?v=Rkgx1C_S6ls.

page 179. "And, even though many countries have recently introduced": For a discussion of recent trends in trade restrictions, see World Trade Organization (2012).

page 179. "This trend is particularly impressive": Grossman and Meissner (2010).

page 180. "Nonetheless, the warnings of Keynes and others": Eichengreen and Temin (2000).

page 180. "Thus, at the very time when the financial system was growing more crisis prone": Turner (2010: 2); Rajan (2005).

page 180. "Economic ideologies also may become entrenched": Janis (1983).

page 181. "Another reviewer observed": Winters (2012: 13); Stockton (2012:7). See also Ball (2012).

page 182. "One of the best examples of ideologically based policy initiatives": The Americans for Tax Reform website, http://s3.amazonaws.com/atrfiles/files/files/081012-federalpledgesigners.pdf, reports that 236 Republican House members of the 112th Congress signed the pledge, while six did not. The number of Republican signers in the Senate was less overwhelming: 40 signed and seven did not. Only two Democratic congressmen and one Democratic senator signed.

page 183. "And historical and comparative studies": Eichengreen (2012).

page 183. "Theoretical and empirical models can be misspecified": See, for example, Esther Bintliff, "Reinhart and Rogoff: your essential reading list," *Financial Times* "The World" blog, April 17, 2013, http://blogs.ft.com/the-world/2013/04/reinhart-and-rogoff-your-essential-reading-list/.

BIBLIOGRAPHY

Adler, Michael (1970). "Specialization in the European Coal and Steel Community." *Journal of Common Market Studies* **8**(3): 175.

Ahamed, Liaquat (2009). *Lords of Finance: The Bankers Who Broke the World*. New York: Penguin Press.

Amyx, Jennifer Ann (2004). *Japan's Financial Crisis: Institutional Rigidity and Reluctant Change*. Princeton, NJ: Princeton University Press.

Andrews, Edmund L. (2009). *Busted: Life Inside the Great Mortgage Meltdown*. New York: W.W. Norton.

Ashley, Percy (1920). *Modern Tariff History: Germany-United States-France*. New York: E. P. Dutton.

Atkin, Michael (1992). *The International Grain Trade*. Cambridge: Woodhead.

Bagehot, Walter (1924). *Lombard Street*. London: J. Murray.

Baldwin, Robert E. (1992). "Are Economists' Traditional Trade Policy Views Still Valid?" *Journal of Economic Literature* **30**(2): 804–829.

Ball, Lawrence (2012). "Ben Bernanke and the Zero Bound." National Bureau of Economic Research (NBER) Working Paper 17836.

Baring, Francis (1797 [1993]). *Observations on the Establishment of the Bank of England, and on the Paper Circulation of the Country*. London: Minerva Press.

Bebr, Gerhard (1953). "The European Coal and Steel Community: A Political and Legal Innovation." *Yale Law Journal* **63**(1): 1–43.

Beer, George L. (1912). *The Old Colonial System, 1660–1754*. New York: Macmillan.

Belasco, Amy (2009). "Troop Levels in the Afghan and Iraq Wars, FY2001-FY2012: Cost and Other Potential Issues." Washington, DC: Congressional Research Service Report R40682. July 2, 2009.

Berglund, Abraham (1923). "The Tariff Act of 1922." *American Economic Review* **13**(1): 14–33.

Berglund, Abraham (1933). "Tariff Walls and Commercial Policy." *Annals of the American Academy of Political and Social Science* **170**(1): 146–151.

Bergmann, Carl (1927). *The History of Reparations*. Boston and New York: Houghton Mifflin.

Bergmann, Carl (1930). "Germany and the Young Plan." *Foreign Affairs* **8**(4): 583–597.

Bernanke, Ben S. (1983). "Nonmonetary Effects of the Financial Crisis in Propagation of the Great Depression." *American Economic Review* **73**(3): 257–276.

Bernanke, Ben S. (1995). "The Macroeconomics of the Great Depression: A Comparative Approach." *Journal of Money, Credit and Banking* **27**(1): 1–28.

Bernanke, Ben S. (2009). "Four Questions about the Financial Crisis." Speech at Morehouse College, Atlanta, Georgia. http://www.federalreserve.gov/newsevents/speech/bernanke20090414a.htm. Retrieved December 13, 2012.

Bhagwati, Jagdish (2002). *Free Trade Today*. Princeton, NJ: Princeton University Press.

Bird, Alan. (2002). *Encyclopedia of Japanese Business and Management*. New York: Routledge.

Board of Governors of the Federal Reserve System (2005). *The Federal Reserve System: Purposes and Functions*. Washington, DC: Board of Governors of the Federal Reserve System.

Bogart, Ernest Ludlow (1920). *Direct and Indirect Costs of the Great World War*. New York: Oxford University Press.

Bootle, Roger (2012). "Euro Break-up: Let Germany Lead the Northern Core and France the Rest." *Telegraph* online. July 5, 2012. http://www.telegraph.co.uk/finance/comment/9378302/Euro-break-up-Let-Germany-lead-the-northern-core-and-France-the-rest.html.

Bordo, Michael D. (1996). "Log-rolling, Partisanship, and Economic Interest in the Passage of the Hawley-Smoot Tariff: A Comment." *Carnegie-Rochester Conference Series on Public Policy* **45**: 201–205.

Bordo, Michael D., Ehsan U. Choudhri, and Anna J. Schwartz (2002). "Was Expansionary Monetary Policy Feasible during the Great Contraction? An Examination of the Gold Standard Constraint." *Explorations in Economic History* **39**(1): 1–28.

Bordo, Michael D., Barry Eichengreen, Daniela Klingebiel, and Maria Soledad Martinez-Peria (2001). "Is the Crisis Problem Growing More Severe?" *Economic Policy* **32**: 53–82.

Bordo, Michael D. and Harold James (2008). "A Long Term Perspective on the Euro." Workshop EMU@10: Achievements and Challenges. Brussels: European Commission, Directorate-General for Economic and Financial Affairs.

Bordo, Michael D. and Lars Jonung (2003). "The Future of EMU: What Does the History of Monetary Unions Tell Us?" In *Monetary Unions*. Edited by Forrest Capie and Geoffrey Wood. London: MacMillan, 42–69.

Borrell, Brent and Lionel Hubbard (2000). "Global Economic Effects of the EU Common Agricultural Policy." *Economic Affairs* **20**(2): 18–26.

Bourke, Austin (1993). *The Visitation of God? The Potato and the Great Irish Famine*. Dublin: Lilliput Press.

Bourke, P. M. Austin. (1959/1960). "The Extent of the Potato Crop in Ireland at the Time of the Famine." *Journal of the Statistical and Social Inquiry Society of Ireland* **20**(3): 1–35.

Bremmer, Ian. (2011). "Greece Is Not Leaving the Eurozone, Not Now, Not Ever." *Financal Times*, September 28, 2011, http://blogs.ft.com/the-a-list/2011/09/28/greece-is-not-leaving-the-eurozone-not-now-not-ever/#axzz1bkwS8kFj.

Broadberry, Stephen and Mark Harrison (2005). "The Economics of World War I: An Overview." In *The Economics of World War I*. Edited by Stephen Broadberry and Mark Harrison. Cambridge: Cambridge University Press, 3–40.

Brown, J. Robert (1999). *The Ministry of Finance: Bureaucratic Practices and the Transformation of the Japanese Economy*. Westport, CT: Quorum Books.

Brown, William Adams (1940). *The International Gold Standard Reinterpreted, 1914-1934*. New York: National Bureau of Economic Research.

Broz, J. Lawrence and Richard S. Grossman (2004). "Paying for Privilege: The Political Economy of Bank of England Charters, 1694-1844." *Explorations in Economic History* **41**(1): 48–72.

Brunnermeier, Markus K. (2009). "Deciphering the Liquidity and Credit Crunch 2007-2008." *Journal of Economic Perspectives* **23**(1): 77–100.

Bryson, Bill (2010). *At Home: A Short History of Private Life*. New York: Doubleday.

Burns, Arthur F. (1988). *The Ongoing Revolution in American Banking*. Washington, DC: American Enterprise Institute.

Caballero, Ricardo J., Takeo Hoshi, and Anil K. Kashyap (2008). "Zombie Lending and Depressed Restructuring in Japan." *American Economic Review* **98**(5): 1943–1977.

Cairncross, Alec (1986). *The Price of War: British Policy on German Reparations, 1941–1949*. New York: Blackwell.

Cairncross, Alec and Barry Eichengreen (1983). *Sterling in Decline: The Devaluations of 1931, 1949, and 1967*. Oxford: Blackwell.

Callahan, Colleen M., Judith A. McDonald, and Anthony Patrick O'Brien (1994). "Who Voted for Smoot-Hawley?" *Journal of Economic History* **54**(3): 683–690.

Cannon, James G. (1910). *Clearing Houses*. Washington, DC: Government Printing Office.

Capie, Forrest (1981). "Shaping the British Tariff Structure in the 1930s." *Explorations in Economic History* **18**(2): 155–173.

Capie, Forrest, Charles Goodhart, Stanley Fischer, and Norbert Schnadt (1994). *The Future of Central Banking: The Tercentenary Symposium of the Bank of England*. Cambridge: Cambridge University Press.

Caprio, Gerard Jr. and Daniela Klingebiel (2003). "Episodes of Systemic and Borderline Financial Crises." World Bank Working Paper. http://econ.worldbank.org/WBSITE/EXTERNAL/EXTDEC/ EXTRESEARCH/0,,contentMDK:20699588~pagePK:64214825~ piPK:64214943~theSitePK:469382,00.html.

Cargill, Thomas F. (2000). "What Caused Japan's Banking Crisis?" In *Crisis and Change in the Japanese Financial System*. Edited by Takeo Hoshi and Hugh Patrick. Boston; Dordrecht, and London: Kluwer Academic, 37–58.

Cargill, Thomas F. (2005). "Is the Bank of Japan's Financial Structure an Obstacle to Policy?" *IMF Staff Papers* **52**(2): 311–334.

Cargill, Thomas F., Michael M. Hutchison, and Takatoshi Ito (1997). *The Political Economy of Japanese Monetary Policy*. Cambridge, MA: MIT Press.

Cargill, Thomas F., Michael M. Hutchison, and Takatoshi Ito (2000). *Financial Policy and Central Banking in Japan*. Cambridge, MA: MIT Press.

Cassel, Gustav (1920). "Further Observations on the World's Monetary Problem." *Economic Journal* **30**(117): 39–45.

Catterall, Ralph C. H. (1903). *The Second Bank of the United States*. Chicago: University of Chicago Press.

Center on Japanese Economy and Business (2008). "Symposium Summary Report: Lessons from the Japanese Bubble for the U.S." New York: Columbia University, November 19, 2008. http://ajadvisers.com/risingsunblog/wp-content/uploads/ 2009/02/cjeb-111908-report_lessons-from-the-japanese-bubble-for-the-us.pdf. Accessed December 13, 2012.

Chandler, Lester Vernon (1958). *Benjamin Strong, Central Banker*. Washington, DC: Brookings Institution.

Chase, John L. (1954). "The Development of the Morgenthau Plan through the Quebec Conference." *Journal of Politics* **16**(2): 324–359.

Chinn, Menzie D. and Jeffrey A. Frieden (2011). *Lost Decades: The Making of America's Debt Crisis and the Long Recovery*. New York: W. W. Norton.

Chomsisengphet, Souphala and Anthony Pennington-Cross (2006). "The Evolution of the Subprime Mortgage Market." *Federal Reserve Bank of St. Louis Review* **88**(1): 31–56.

Clapham, J. H. (1921). *The Economic Development of France and Germany, 1815-1914*. Cambridge: Cambridge University Press.

Clarke, M. St. Clair and D. A. Hall (1832 [1967]). *Legislative and Documentary History of the Bank of the United States, Including the Original Bank of North America*. New York: A. M. Kelley.

Clarke, Stephen V. O. (1967). *Central Bank Cooperation: 1924-31*. New York: Federal Reserve Bank of New York.

Clarkson, L. A. and E. M. Crawford (1988). "Dietary Directions: A Topographical Survey of Irish Diet, 1836." In *Economy and Society in Scotland and Ireland, 1500-1939*. Edited by R. Mitchison and P. Roebuck. Edinburgh: J. Donald, 171–192.

Clay, Henry (1957). *Lord Norman*. London: Macmillian.

Clemens, Michael A. and Jeffrey G. Williamson (2004). "Why Did the Tariff-Growth Correlation Change after 1950?" *Journal of Economic Growth* **9**(1): 5–46.

Cobbett, William (1814). *The Parliamentary History of England.* London: T. C. Hansard.

Conant, Charles A. (1896). *A History of Modern Banks of Issue.* New York: G. P. Putnam's Sons.

Congressional Budget Office (2004). "Effective Tax Rates under Current Law, 2001 to 2014," August 2004. http://www.cbo.gov/publication/15919.

Congressional Budget Office (2009). "Data on the Distribution of Federal Taxes and Household Income." http://www.cbo.gov/publications/collections/taxdistribution.cfm, Retrieved April 26, 2010.

Cowen, David J. (2000). "The First Bank of the United States and the Securities Market Crash of 1792." *Journal of Economic History* **60**(4): 1041–1060.

Craig, Valentine V. (1998). "Japanese Banking: A Time of Crisis." *FDIC Banking Review* **11**(2): 9–17.

Crucini, Mario J. and James Kahn (1996). "Tariffs and Aggregate Economic Activity: Lessons from the Great Depression." *Journal of Monetary Economics* **38**(3): 427–467.

Dalzell, Robert F. and Lee Baldwin Dalzell (1998). *George Washington's Mount Vernon: At Home in Revolutionary America.* New York: Oxford University Press.

Danker, Deborah J. and Matthew M. Luecke (2005). "Background on FOMC Meeting Minutes." *Federal Reserve Bulletin* **91**: 175–179.

David, Paul and Gavin Wright (1997). "Increasing Returns and the Genesis of American Resource Abundance." *Industrial and Corporate Change* **6**(2): 203–245.

Davies, Phil (2008). "The 'Monster' of Chestnut Street." *Federal Reserve Bank of Minneapolis Region* **22**(3): 8–11, 40–46.

Davis, Lance E. and Robert A. Huttenback (1986). *Mammon and the Pursuit of Empire: The Political Economy of British Imperialism, 1860-1912.* Cambridge: Cambridge University Press.

Dawes, Rufus C. (1925). *The Dawes Plan in the Making.* Indianapolis: Bobbs-Merrill.

Dewald, William G. (1972). "The National Monetary Commission: A Look Back." *Journal of Money, Credit and Banking* **4**(4): 930–956.

Dewey, Davis R. (1934). *Financial History of the United States.* New York: Longmans, Green and Co.

Dickerson, Oliver Morton (1951). *The Navigation Acts and the American Revolution*. Philadelphia: University of Pennsylvania Press.

Donnelly, J. S. (2001). *The Great Irish Potato Famine*. Phoenix Mill, Gloucestershire: Sutton Publishing.

Dorn, Walter L. (1957). "The Debate over American Occupation Policy in Germany in 1944-1945." *Political Science Quarterly* **72**(4): 481–501.

Dornbusch, Rudiger and Stanley Fischer (1986). "The Open Economy: Implications for Monetary and Fiscal Policy." In *The American Business Cycle: Continuity and Change*. Edited by Robert J. Gordon. Chicago: University of Chicago Press, 459–516.

Duncker, Max (1882). *The History of Antiquity*. London: Richard Bentley and Son.

Dwyer, Gerald P. Jr. (1996). "Wildcat Banking, Banking Panics, and Free Banking in the United States." *Federal Reserve Bank of Atlanta Economic Review* **81**(3–6): 1–20.

Dziobek, Claudia and Ceyla Pazarbaştioğlu (1997). "Lessons and Elements of Best Practice." In *Systemic Bank Restructuring and Macroeconomic Policy*. Edited by William E. Alexander, Jeffrey M. Davis, Liam P. Ebrill, and Carl-Johan Lindgren. Washington, DC: IMF, 75–144.

Edmondson, Amy C. (2011). "Strategies for Learning from Failure." *Harvard Business Review* **89**(4): 42–54.

Edwards, R. Dudley and T. Desmond Williams. (1957). *The Great Famine: Studies in Irish History, 1845-52*. New York: New York University Press.

Edwards, Sebastian (2009). "Protectionism and Latin America's Historical Economic Decline." *Journal of Policy Modeling* **31**(4): 573–584.

Egnal, Marc and Joseph A. Ernst (1972). "An Economic Interpretation of the American Revolution." *William and Mary Quarterly* **29**(1): 4–32.

Eichengreen, Barry (1989). "The Political Economy of the Smoot-Hawley Tariff." *Research in Economic History* **12**: 1–43.

Eichengreen, Barry (1992). *Golden Fetters: The Gold Standard and the Great Depression, 1919-1939*. New York: Oxford University Press.

Eichengreen, Barry (1996). *Globalizing Capital*. Princeton, NJ: Princeton University Press.

Eichengreen, Barry (1997). *European Monetary Unification: Theory, Practice, and Analysis.* Cambridge, MA: MIT Press.

Eichengreen, Barry (2004). "Viewpoint: Understanding the Great Depression." *Canadian Journal of Economics / Revue canadienne d'Economique* **37**(1): 1–27.

Eichengreen, Barry (2005). "Europe, the Euro and the ECB: Monetary Success, Fiscal Failure." *Journal of Policy Modeling* **27**(4): 427-439.

Eichengreen, Barry (2007a). "The Euro: Love It or Leave It?" Vox EU online. http://www.voxeu.org/index.php?q=node/729. Retrieved February 25, 2010.

Eichengreen, Barry (2007b). "The Breakup of the Euro Area." NBER Working Paper 13393.

Eichengreen, Barry (2009). "The Crisis and the Euro." Unpublished working paper, http://emlab.berkeley.edu/~eichengr/crisis_euro_5-1-09.pdf.

Eichengreen, Barry (2010a). "Europe's Trojan Horse." http: www. project-syndicate.org/commentary/eichengreen14/English. Retrieved February 25, 2010.

Eichengreen, Barry (2010b). "The Breakup of the Euro Area." In *Europe and the Euro.* Edited by Alberto Alesina and Francesco Giavazzi. Chicago: University of Chicago Press, 11–57.

Eichengreen, Barry (2010c). *Exorbitant Privilege: The Decline of the Dollar and the Future of the International Monetary System.* New York: Oxford University Press.

Eichengreen, Barry (2012). "Economic History and Economic Policy." *Journal of Economic History* **72**(2): 289–307.

Eichengreen, Barry and Marc Flandreau (1994). "The Geography of the Gold Standard." Centre for Economic Policy Research (CEPR) Discussion Paper 1050.

Eichengreen, Barry and Douglas A. Irwin (1995). "Trade Blocs, Currency Blocs and the Reorientation of World Trade in the 1930s." *Journal of International Economics* **38**(1–2): 1–24.

Eichengreen, Barry and Douglas A. Irwin (2010). "The Slide to Protectionism in the Great Depression: Who Succumbed and Why?" *Journal of Economic History* **70**(4): 871–897.

Eichengreen, Barry and Jeffrey Sachs (1985). "Exchange Rates and Economic Recovery in the 1930s." *Journal of Economic History* **45**(4): 925–946.

Eichengreen, Barry and Peter Temin (2000). "The Gold Standard and the Great Depression." *Contemporary European History* 9(2): 183–207.

Eichengreen, Barry, Marc Uzan, Nicholas Crafts, and Martin Hellwig (1992). "The Marshall Plan: Economic Effects and Implications for Eastern Europe and the Former USSR." *Economic Policy* 7(14): 14–75.

Eichengreen, Barry, Mark W. Watson, and Richard S. Grossman (1985). "Bank Rate Policy under the Interwar Gold Standard: A Dynamic Probit Model." *Economic Journal* 95(379): 725–745.

Ekelund, Robert B. Jr. and Robert D. Tollison (1981). *Mercantilism as a Rent-Seeking Society: Economic Regulation in Historical Perspective.* College Station: Texas A&M University Press.

Ekelund, Robert B. Jr. and Robert D. Tollison (1997). *Politicized Economies: Monarchy, Monopoly, and Mercantilism.* College Station: Texas A&M University Press.

Elliott, Matthew and Allister Heath (2000). "The Failure of CAP Reform: A Public Choice Analysis." *Economic Affairs* 20(2): 42.

Erzberger, Matthias (1919). *The League of Nations: The Way to the World's Peace.* New York: Henry Holt and Company.

Evans, D. Morier (1859 [1969]). *The History of the Commercial Crisis, 1857-58, and the Stock Exchange Panic of 1859.* New York: Augustus M. Kelly.

Feavearyear, Albert (1963). *The Pound Sterling.* Oxford: Clarendon Press.

Federal Reserve Bank of Philadelphia (2010). *The Second Bank of the United States: A Chapter in the History of Central Banking.* Philadelphia: Federal Reserve Bank of Philadelphia.

Feldman, Gerald D. (1993). *The Great Disorder: Politics, Economics, and Society in the German Inflation, 1914-1924.* New York: Oxford University Press.

Feldstein, Martin (1992). "The Case against the EMU." *Economist.* June 13, 1992, 23–26.

Felix, David (1971). "Reparations Reconsidered with a Vengeance." *Central European History* 4(2): 171–179.

Fenstermaker, J. Van and John E. Filer (1986). "Impact of the First and Second Banks of the United Statesand the Suffolk System on New England Bank Money: 1791-1837." *Journal of Money, Credit and Banking* 18(1): 28–40.

Ferguson, Niall (2005). *Colossus: The Rise and Fall of the American Empire.* New York: Penguin Books.

Fisher, Irving (1932). *Booms and Depressions: Some First Principles.* New York: Adelphi.

Fisher, Irving (1933). "The Debt-Deflation Theory of Great Depressions." *Econometrica* **1**: 337–357.

Flandreau, Marc (1995). "An Essay on the Emergence of the International Gold Standard, 1870-80." CEPR Discussion Paper 1210.

Flandreau, Marc (1996). "The French Crime of 1873: An Essay on the Emergence of the International Gold Standard, 1870-1880." *Journal of Economic History* **56**(4): 862–897.

Frieden, Jeffry A. (2006). *Global Capitalism.* New York: W. W. Norton.

Frieden, Jeffry A. (2012) "The Modern Capitalist World Economy: A Historical Overview." In *Oxford Handbook of Capitalism.* Edited by Dennis Mueller. New York: Oxford University Press, 17–37.

Friedman, Milton (1990). "The Crime of 1873." *Journal of Political Economy* **98**(6): 1159–1194.

Friedman, Philip (1974). *The Impact of Trade Destruction on National Incomes; A Study of Europe, 1924-1938.* Gainesville: University Presses of Florida.

Fukao, Mitsuhiro (1998). "Japanese Financial Instability and Weaknesses in the Corporate Governance Structure." *Seoul Journal of Economics* **11**(4): 381–422.

Fukao, Mitsuhiro (2003). "Japan's Lost Decade and Its Financial System." *World Economy* **26**(3): 365–384.

Fukao, Mitsuhiro (2007). "Financial Crisis and the Lost Decade." *Asian Economic Policy Review* **2**(2): 273–297.

Gallagher, Thomas Michael (1982). *Paddy's Lament: Ireland 1846-1847.* New York: Harcourt Brace Jovanovich.

Gallatin, Albert (1879). *The Writings of Albert Gallatin.* 3 volumes. Philadelphia: J.B. Lippincott.

Gandal, Neil and Nathan Sussman (1997). "Asymmetric Information and Commodity Money: Tickling the Tolerance in Medieval France." *Journal of Money, Credit and Banking* **29**(4): 440–457.

Garber, Peter M. (1998). "Notes on the Role of TARGET in a Stage III Crisis." NBER Working Paper 6619.

Garnsey, Peter (1988). *Famine and Food Supply in the Graeco-Roman World: Responses to Risk and Crisis.* Cambridge and New York: Cambridge University Press.

Gatell, Frank Otto (1966). "Sober Second Thoughts on Van Buren, the Albany Regency, and the Wall Street Conspiracy." *Journal of American History* **53**(1): 19–40.

Gibney, Frank (1998). *Unlocking the Bureaucrat's Kingdom: Deregulation and the Japanese Economy*. Washington, DC: Brookings Institution Press.

Gooch, G. P. (1925). *The Later Correspondence of Lord John Russell: 1840-1878*. London: Longmans, Green.

Goodhart, C. A. E. and Dirk Schoenmaker (1995). "Institutional Separation between Supervisory and Monetary Agencies." In *The Central Bank and the Financial System*. Edited by C. A. E. Goodhart. Cambridge, MA: MIT Press, 333–413.

Goodman, John B. (1992). *Monetary Sovereignty: The Politics of Central Banking in Western Europe*. Ithaca, NY: Cornell University Press.

Goodwin, Barry K., Ashok K. Mishra, and François Ortalo-Magné (2011). "The Buck Stops Where? The Distribution of Agricultural Subsidies." NBER Working Paper 16693.

Gorton, Gary B. (2008). "The Subprime Panic." NBER Working Paper 14398.

Gourinchas, Pierre-Olivier (2010). "U.S.Monetary Policy, 'Imbalances' and the Financial Crisis." Remarks prepared for the Financial Crisis Inquiry Commission Forum, February 26–27, 2010.

Gray, Peter (1997). "Famine Relief Policy in Conmparative Perspective: Ireland, Scotland, and Northwestern Europe, 1845-1849." *Eire-Ireland* **32**(1): 86–108.

Gray, Peter (1999). *Famine, Land, and Politics: British Government and Irish Society, 1843-1850*. Dublin: Irish Academic Press.

Gregory, T. E. (1932). *The Gold Standard and Its Future*. New York: E.P. Dutton.

Gregory, T. E. (1957). " 'The Norman Conquest' Reconsidered." *Lloyds Bank Review* **46**: 1–20.

Grigg, Percy James (1948). *Prejudice and Judgment*. London: J. Cape.

Gros, Daniel (2006). "Bubbles in Real Estate, A Longer-Term Comparative Analysis of Housing Prices in Europe and the US." CEPS Working Documents Number 239.

Grossman, Richard S. (1982). "Bank Rate Policy by the Bank of England during the Gold Standard Years, 1925-1931." Unpublished A.B. honors thesis, Harvard College.

Grossman, Richard S. (1994). "The Shoe That Didn't Drop: Explaining Banking Stability during the Great Depression." *Journal of Economic History* **54**(3): 654–682.

Grossman, Richard S. (2010a). *Unsettled Account: The Evolution of Banking in the Industrialized World since 1800*. Princeton, NJ: Princeton University Press.

Grossman, Richard S. (2010b). "The Emergence of Central Banks and Banking Regulation in Comparative Perspective." In *State and Financial Systems in Europe and the USA: Historical Perspectives on Regulation and Supervision in the Nineteenth and Twentieth Centuries*. Edited by Stefano Battilossi and Jaime Reis. Burlington, VT: Ashgate, 123–138.

Grossman, Richard S. and Christopher M. Meissner (2010). "International Aspects of the Great Depression and the Crisis of 2007: Similarities, Differences, and Lessons." *Oxford Review of Economic Policy* **26**(3): 318–338.

Grubb, Farley (2008). "The Continental Dollar: How Much Was Really Issued?" *Journal of Economic History* **68**(1): 283–291.

Guinnane, Timothy W. (1994). "The Great Irish Famine and Population: The Long View." *American Economic Review* **84**(2): 303–308.

Guinnane, Timothy W. (1997a). "Ireland's Famine Wasn't Genocide." *Washington Post*. September 17, 1997, p. 19.

Guinnane, Timothy W. (1997b). *The Vanishing Irish: Households, Migration, and the Rural Economy in Ireland, 1850-1914*. Princeton, NJ: Princeton University Press.

Guinnane, Timothy W. (2004). "Financial Vergangenheitsbewältigung: The 1953 London Debt Agreement." Yale Economic Growth Center Discussion Paper 880.

Guinnane, Thmothy W. and Cormac Ó Gráda (2002). "The Workhouses and Irish Famine Mortality." In *Famine Demography: Perspectives from the Past and Present*. Edited by Tim Dyson and Cormac Ó Gráda. Oxford: Oxford University Press, 44–64.

Gylfason, Thorvaldur (1995). "The Macroeconomics of European Agriculture." Princeton Studies in International Finance Number 78.

Haggard, Stephan (1985). "The Politics of Adjustment: Lessons from the IMF's Extended Fund Facility." *International Organization* **39**(3): 505–534.

Haines, Robin F. (2004). *Charles Trevelyan and the Great Irish Famine* Dublin: Four Courts Press.

Hamada, Koichi (2004). "Policy Making in Deflationary Japan." *Japanese Economic Review* **55**(3): 221–239.

Hamada, Koichi and Asahi Noguchi (2005). "The Role of Preconceived Ideas in Macroeconomic Policy: Japan's Experiences in Two Deflationary Periods." *International Economics and Economic Policy* **2**(2–3): 101–126.

Hammond, Bray (1957). *Banks and Politics in America: From the Revolution to the Civil War*. Princeton, NJ: Princeton University Press.

Harper, Lawrence A. (1939a). "The Effect of the Navigation Acts on the Thirteen Colonies." In *The Era of the American Revolution*. Edited by Richard B. Morris. New York: Columbia University Press, 3–39.

Harper, Lawrence A. (1939b). *The English Navigation Laws: A Seventeenth-Century Experiment in Social Engineering*. New York: Columbia University Press.

Harper, Lawrence A. (1942). "Mercantilism and the American Revolution." *Canadian Historical Review* **23**(1): 1–15.

Hartcher, Peter (1998). *The Ministry: How Japan's Most Powerful Institution Endangers World Markets*. Boston: Harvard Business School Press.

Hartcher, Peter (2006). *Bubble Man: Alan Greenspan and the Missing 7 Trillion Dollars*. New York: W.W. Norton.

Harvard Business Review (2009). *Harvard Business Review on Manufacturing Excellence at Toyota*. Boston: Harvard Business School Publishing Corporation.

Hayford, Marc and Carl A. Pasurka (1992). "The Political Economy of the Fordney-McCumber and Smoot-Hawley Tariff Acts." *Explorations in Economic History* **29**(1): 30–50.

Heaton, Herbert (1937). "Heckscher on Mercantilism." *Journal of Political Economy* **45**(3): 370–393.

Heckscher, Eli F. (1935). *Mercantilism*. 2 volumes. London: George Allen & Unwin, Ltd.

Heckscher, Eli F. (1954). *An Economic History of Sweden*. Cambridge, MA: Harvard University Press.

Henderson, W. O. (1939). *The Zollverein*. Cambridge: The University Press.

Hertz, J. H. (1960). *The Pentateuch and Haftorahs: Hebrew Text, English Translation, and Commentary*. London: Soncino Press.

Hilbers, Paul, Alexander W. Hoffmaister, Angana Banerji, and Haiyan Shi (2008). "House Price Developments in Europe: A Comparison." IMF Working Paper WP/08/211.

Hill, Berkeley (2000). "Agricultural Incomes and the CAP." *Economic Affairs* **20**(2): 11.

Hill, William (1893). "The First Stages of the Tariff Policy of the United States." *Publications of the American Economic Association* **8**(6): 9–162.

Hino, Satoshi (2006). *Inside the Mind of Toyota: Management Principles for Enduring Growth*. New York: Productivity Press.

Hiwatari, Nobuhiro. (2000). "The Reorganization of Japan's Financial Bureaucracy: The Politics of Bureaucratic Structure and Blame Avoidance." In *Crisis and Change in the Japanese Financial System*. Edited by Takeo Hoshi and Hugh Patrick. Boston, Dordrecht, and London: Kluwer Academic, 109–136.

Hochschild, Adam (1989). *King Leopold's Ghost: A Story of Greed, Terror, and Heroism in Colonial Africa*. Boston: Houghton Mifflin.

Holdsworth, John Thom and Davis Rich Dewey (1910). *The First and Second Banks of the United States*. Washington, DC: Government Printing Office.

Hoshi, Takeo (2002). "The Convoy System for Insolvent Banks: How It Originally Worked and Why It Failed in the 1990s." *Japan and the World Economy* **14**(2): 155–180.

Hoshi, Takeo (2006). "Economics of the Living Dead." *Japanese Economic Review* **57**(1): 30–49.

Hoshi, Takeo and Anil Kashyap (2000). "The Japanese Banking Crisis: Where Did It Come from and How Will It End?" In *NBER Macroeconomics Annual 1999*. Edited by Ben S. Bernanke and Julio J. Rotemberg. Volume 14. Cambridge, MA, and London: MIT Press, 129–201.

Hoshi, Takeo and Anil K. Kashyap (2001). *Corporate Financing and Governance in Japan: The Road to the Future*. Cambridge, MA, and London: MIT Press.

Hoshi, Takeo and Anil Kashyap (2009). "Will the U.S. Bank Recapitalization Succeed? Eight Lessons from Japan." Chicago Booth Working Paper 09-28.

Hoshi, Takeo and Hugh Patrick (2000). "The Japanese Financial System: An Introductory Overview." In *Crisis and Change in the Japanese Financial System*. Edited by Takeo Hoshi and Hugh Patrick. Dordrecht and London: Kluwer Academic, 1–33.

Howarth, Richard (2000). "The CAP: History and Attempts at Reform." *Economic Affairs* **20**(2): 4–10.

Howson, Susan (1975). *Domestic Monetary Management in Britain, 1919-38*. Cambridge and New York: Cambridge University Press.

Hughes, Jonathan R. T. and Herman E. Krooss (1969). "Discussion." *American Economic Review* **59**(2): 382–385.

Irwin, Douglas A. (1993). "Multilateral and Bilateral Trade Policies in the World Trading System: An Historical Perspective." In *New Dimensions in Regional Integration*. Edited by Jaime de de Melo and Arvind Panagariya. New York: Cambridge University Press, 90–119.

Irwin, Douglas A. (1996). *Against the Tide: An Intellectual History of Free Trade*. Princeton, NJ: Princeton University Press.

Irwin, Douglas A. (1998a). "The Smoot-Hawley Tariff: A Quantitative Assessment." *Review of Economics and Statistics* **80**(2): 326–334.

Irwin, Douglas A. (1998b). "Changes in U.S.Tariffs: The Role of Import Prices and Commercial Policies." *American Economic Review* **88**(4): 1015–1026.

Irwin, Douglas A. (2002). *Free Trade under Fire*. Princeton, NJ: Princeton University Press.

Irwin, Douglas A. (2003). "New Estimates of the Average Tariff of the United States, 1790-1820." *Journal of Economic History* **63**(2): 506–513.

Irwin, Douglas A. (2004). "The Aftermath of Hamilton's 'Report on Manufactures.'" *Journal of Economic History* **64**(3): 800–821.

Irwin, Douglas A. (2006). "Merchandise Imports and Duties: 1790–2000." In *Historical Statistics of the United States*, Millennial Edition Online. Edited by Susan B. Carter, Scott Sigmund Gartner, Michael R. Haines, Alan L. Olmstead, Richard Sutch, and Gavin Wright. New York: Cambridge University Press, Table Ee424-430.

Irwin, Douglas A. (2011a). *Peddling Protectionism: Smoot-Hawley and the Great Depression*. Princeton, NJ: Princeton University Press.

Irwin, Douglas A. (2011b). "Anticipating the Great Depression? Gustav Cassel's Analysis of the Interwar Gold Standard." Unpublished working paper.

Irwin, Douglas A. (2012a). *Trade Policy Disaster: Lessons from the 1930s*. Cambridge, MA: MIT Press.

Irwin, Douglas A. (2012b). "The Return of the Protectionist Illusion." *Wall Street Journal*. July 2, 2012, p. A11.

Irwin, Douglas A. and Randall S. Kroszner (1996). "Log-rolling and Economic Interests in the Passage of the Smoot-Hawley

Tariff." *Carnegie-Rochester Conference Series on Public Policy* **45**: 173–200.

Israel, Jonathan I. (1989). *Dutch Primacy in World Trade, 1585-1740*. Oxford: Clarendon Press.

Israel, Jonathan I. (1997). "England's Mercantilist Response to Dutch World Trade Primacy, 1647-1674." In *Conflicts of Empires: Spain, the Low Countries and the Struggle for World Supremacy, 1585-1713*. Edited by Jonathan I. Israel. London: Hambledon Press, 305–318.

Ito, Takatoshi, Hugh T. Patrick, and David E. Weinstein (2005). *Reviving Japan's Economy*. Cambridge, MA: MIT Press.

James, Harold (2001). *The End of Globalization: Lessons from the Great Depression*. Cambridge, MA: Harvard University Press.

James, Harold (2002). "Globalization and Great Depressions." *Orbis* **46**(1): 127–136.

Janis, Irving L. (1983). *Groupthink: Psychological Studies of Policy Decisions and Fiascoes*. Boston: Houghton Mifflin.

Jones, Joseph M. (1934). *Tariff Retaliation; Repercussions of the Hawley-Smoot Bill*. Philadelphia: University of Pennsylvania Press.

Jonung, Lars and Eoin Drea (2009). "The Euro: It Can't Happen, It's a Bad Idea, It Won't last. US Economists on the EMU, 1989-2002." European Economy Economic Papers 395.

Kanaya, Akihiro and David Woo (2000). "The Japanese Banking Crisis of the 1990s: Sources and Lessons." IMF Working Paper 00/7.

Kaplan, Edward S. (1996). *American Trade Policy, 1923-1995*. Westport, CT: Greenwood Press.

Kent, Bruce (1989). *The Spoils of War: The Politics, Economics, and Diplomacy of Reparations, 1918-1932*. Oxford: Clarendon Press.

Keynes, John Maynard (1920). *The Economic Consequences of the Peace*. New York: Harcourt, Brace and Howe.

Keynes, John Maynard (1922). *A Revision of the Treaty*. London: Macmillan.

Keynes, John Maynard (1925). *The Economic Consequences of Sterling Parity*. New York: Harcourt, Brace and Company.

Keynes, John Maynard (1929). "The German Transfer Problem." *Economic Journal* **39**(153): 1–7.

Keynes, John Maynard (1932). *Essays in Persuasion*. New York: Harcourt, Brace and Company.

Keynes, John Maynard (1936). *The General Theory of Employment, Interest and Money*. New York: Harcourt, Brace.

Kindleberger, Charles P. (1968). "The Marshall Plan and the Cold War." *International Journal* **23**(3): 369–382.

Kindleberger, Charles Poor (1978). *Manias, Panics, and Crashes: A History of Financial Crises*. New York: Basic Books.

Kindleberger, Charles Poor (1986). *The World in Depression, 1929-1939*. Berkeley: University of California Press.

Kindleberger, Charles P. (1989). "Commercial Policy between the Wars." In *The Cambridge Economic History of Europe*. Vol. 8. Edited by Peter Mathias and Sidney Pollard. Cambridge Histories Online. Cambridge University Press. http://dx.doi.org/10.1017/CHOL9780521225045.

Kinealy, Christine (1994). *This Great Calamity: The Irish Famine, 1845-52*. Dublin: Gill & Macmillan.

Klovland, Jan Tore (1998). "Monetary Policy and Business Cycles in the Interwar Years: The Scandinavian Experience." *European Review of Economic History* **2**(3): 309–344.

Knodell, Jane (1998). "The Demise of Central Banking and the Domestic Exchanges: Evidence from Antebellum Ohio." *Journal of Economic History* **58**(3): 714–730.

Kohn, Meir (2005). "Government Economic Policy in Preindustrial Europe." Unpublished working paper. http://www.dartmouth.edu/~mkohn/Papers/22%20economic%20intervention.pdf. Retrieved December 13, 2012.

Krugman, Paul R. (1987). "Is Free Trade Passé?" *Journal of Economic Perspectives* **1**(2): 131–144.

Krugman, Paul R. (1999). *The Return of Depression Economics*. New York: W.W. Norton.

Krugman, Paul (2010). "The Making of a Euromess." New York Times. February 14, 2010, p. A21.

Kuczynski, R. R. (1926). "A Year of the Dawes Plan." *Foreign Affairs* **4**(2): 254–263.

Laeven, Luc and Fabian Valencia (2008). "The Use of Blanket Guarantees in Banking Crises." IMF Working Paper 08/250.

League of Nations (1933). *World Economic Survey, 1932-33*. Geneva: League of Nations.

League of Nations (1938). *Monetary Review*. Geneva: League of Nations.

Levine, Ross (2010). "An Autopsy of the U.S.Financial System: Accident, Suicide, or Negligent Homicide?" *Journal of Financial Economic Policy* **2**(3): 196–213.

Liker, Jeffrey K. (2004). *The Toyota Way: 14 Management Principles from the World's Greatest Manufacturer*. New York: McGraw-Hill.

Lindgren, Carl-Johan, G. G. Garcia, and Matthew I. Saal (1996). *Bank Soundness and Macroeconomic Policy*. Washington, DC: International Monetary Fund.

Livy (1921). *The History of Rome*. London: J.M. Dent.

Loschky, David J. (1973). "Studies of the Navigation Acts: New Economic Non-History?" *Economic History Review* **26**(4): 689–691.

Lutz, H. L. (1930). "Inter-Allied Debts, Reparations, and National Policy." *Journal of Political Economy* **38**(1): 29–61.

Maddison, Angus (2009). "Statistics on World Population, GDP and Per Capita GDP, 1-2006 AD (March 2009, vertical file, copyright Angus Maddison)." Retrieved September 2009.

Madsen, Jakob B. (2001). "Trade Barriers and the Collapse of World Trade during the Great Depression." *Southern Economic Journal* **67**(4): 848–868.

Maier, Charles S. (1975). *Recasting Bourgeois Europe: Stabilization in France, Germany, and Italy in the Decade after World War I*. Princeton, NJ: Princeton University Press.

Mallory, Walter H. (1926). *China: Land of Famine*. New York: American Geographical Society.

Mantoux, Étienne (1946). *The Carthaginian Peace; or, The Economic Consequences of Mr. Keynes*. London: G. Cumberlege.

Marks, Sally (1978). "The Myths of Reparations." *Central European History* **11**(3): 231–255.

Martins, João Nogueira (2008). "Workshop EMU@10: Achievements and Challenges." *European Economy Research Letter* **2**(1): 2–7.

März, Eduard (1984). *Austrian Banking and Financial Policy:* Creditanstalt *at a Turning Point, 1913-1923*. London: Weidenfeld and Nicolson.

McClelland, Peter D. (1969). "The Cost to America of British Imperial Policy." *American Economic Review* **59**(2): 370–381.

McClelland, Peter D. (1973). "The New Economic History and the Burdens of the Navigation Acts: A Comment." *Economic History Review* **26**(4): 679–686.

McDonald, Judith A., Anthony Patrick O'Brien, and Colleen M. Callahan (1997). "Trade Wars:Canada's Reaction to the Smoot-Hawley Tariff." *Journal of Economic History* **57**(4): 802–826.

McHugh, Roger J. (1957). "The Famine in Irish Oral Tradition." In *The Great Famine: Studies in Irish History, 1845-52*. Edited by R. Dudley Edwards and T. Desmond Williams. New York: New York University Press, 391–436.

Meissner, Christopher M. (2005). "A New World Order: Explaining The Emergence of an The Classical Gold Standard." *Journal of International Economics* **66**(2): 385–406.

Meltzer, Alan (1976). "Monetary and Other Explanations of the Start of the Great Depression." *Journal of Monetary Economics* **2**(4): 455–471.

Mencken, H.L. (2006). *On Politics: A Carnival of Buncombe*. Baltimore, MD: Johns Hopkins University Press.

Merry, Henry J. (1955). "The European Coal and Steel Community. Operations of the High Authority." *Western Political Quarterly* **8**(2): 166–185.

Milhaupt, Curtis J. and Geoffrey P. Miller (2000). "Regulatory Failure and the Collapse of Japan's Home Mortgage Industry: A Legal and Economic Analysis." *Law and Policy* **22**(3/4): 245–290.

Minford, Patrick. (1992). *The Cost of Europe*. Manchester: Manchester University Press.

Minsky, Hyman P. (1970). "Financial Instability Revisited: The Economics of Disaster." Prepared for the Steering Committee for the Fundamental Reappraisal of the Discount Mechanism Appointed by the Board of Governors of the Federal Reserve System.

Minsky, Hyman P. (1982). *Can 'It' Happen Again?* New York: M.E. Sharp.

Miron, Jeffrey A. (1986). "Financial Panics, the Seasonality of the Nominal Interest Rate, and the Founding of the Fed." *American Economic Review* **76**(1): 125-140.

Mitchel, John (2005). *The Last Conquest of Ireland (Perhaps)*. Dublin: University College Dublin Press.

Mitchell, B. R. (1978). *European Historical Statistics, 1750-1970*. New York: Columbia University Press.

Moggridge, D. E. (1972). *British Monetary Policy, 1924-1931: The Norman Conquest of $4.86*. Cambridge: Cambridge University Press.

Mokyr, Joel (1981). "Irish History with the Potato." *Irish Economic and Social History* **8**: 8–29.

Mokyr, Joel (1983). *Why Ireland Starved: A Quantitative and Analytical History of the Irish Economy*. London: George Allen and Unwin.

Mokyr, Joel and Cormac Ó Gráda (2002). "Famine Disease and Famine Mortality: Lessons from the Irish." In *Famine*

Demography: Perspectives from the Past and Present. Edited by Tim Dyson and Cormac Ó Gráda. Oxford: Oxford University Press, 19–43.

Molle, Willem (2001). *The Economics of European Integration: Theory, Practice, Policy*. Aldershot, UK, and Burlington, VT: Ashgate.

Mongelli, Francesco Paolo (2008). "European Economic and Monetary Integration, and the Optimum Currency Area Theory." Workshop EMU@10: Achievements and Challenges.

Mora, Nada (2008). "The Effect of Bank Credit on Asset Prices: Evidence from the Japanese Real Estate Boom during the 1980s." *Journal of Money, Credit and Banking* **40**(1): 57–87.

Morganthau, Henry Jr. (1947). "Our Policy on Germany." *New York Post*. November 24, 1947.

Moulton, Harold Glenn and Leo Pasvolsky (1932). *War Debts and World Prosperity*. Washington, DC: Brookings Institution.

Mullins, Claud (1921). *The Leipzig Trials: An Account of the War Criminals' Trials and a Study of German Mentality*. London: H. F. & G. Witherby.

Mundell, Robert A. (1961). "A Theory of Optimum Currency Areas." *American Economic Review* **51**(4): 657–665.

Munro, John H. (1983). "Medieval Monetary Problems: Bimetallism and Bullionism." *Journal of Economic History* **43**(1): 294–298.

Myers, Margaret G. (1970). *A Financial History of the United States*. New York: Columbia University Press.

Nakaso, Hiroshi (2001). "The Financial Crisis in Japan during the 1990s: How the Bank of Japan Responded and the Lessons Learnt." BIS Papers 6.

Nelson, Rebecca M., Paul Belkin, and Derek E. Mix (2010). "Greece's Debt Crisis: Overview, Policy Responses, and Implications." Washington, DC: Congressional Research Service Report R41167.

Nettels, Curtis P. (1952). "British Mercantilism and the Economic Development of the Thirteen Colonies." *Journal of Economic History* **12**(2): 105–114.

Nomura Fixed Income Research (2004). "CDOs in Plain English: A Summer Intern's Letter Home." http://www.vinodkothari.com/Nomura_cdo_plainenglish.pdf.

Nunn, Nathan and Nancy Qian (2011). "The Potato's Contribution to Population and Urbanization: Evidence from a Historical Experiment." *Quarterly Journal of Economics* **126** (2): 593–650.

Ó Gráda, Cormac (1989). *The Great Irish Famine*. Houndmills, Basingstoke, Hampshire: Macmillan.

Ó Gráda, Cormac (1999). *Black '47 and Beyond: The Great Irish Famine in History, Economy, and Memory*. Princeton, NJ: Princeton University Press.

Ó Gráda, Cormac (2007). "Making Famine History." *Journal of Economic Literature* **45**(1): 5–38.

Ó Gráda, Cormac (2009). *Famine: A Short History*. Princeton, NJ: Princeton University Press.

O'Brien, Anthony Patrick (1994). "The Economic Effects of the Great War." *History Today* **44**(12): 22–29.

Ogg, David (1921). *Sully's Grand Design of Henry IV. From the Memoirs of Maximilien de Béthune, duc de Sully (1559-1641)*. London: Sweet and Maxwell.

O'Neill, Thomas P. (1957). "The Organisation and Administration of Relief, 1845-52." In *The Great Famine: Studies in Irish History, 1845-52*. Edited by R. Dudley Edwards and T. Desmond Williams. New York: New York University Press, 209–259.

Oppers, Stefan Erik (1996). "Was the Worldwide Shift to Gold Inevitable? An Analysis of the End of Bimetallism." *Journal of Monetary Economics* **37**(1): 143–162.

Orlander, Jay D. and B. Graeme Fincke (2003). "Morbidity and Mortality Conference." *Journal of General Internal Medicine* **18**(8): 656–658.

O'Rourke, Kevin (1994). "The Economic Impact of the Famine in the Short and Long Run." *American Economic Review* **84**(2): 309–313.

Osono, Emi, Norihiko Shimizu, Hirotaka Takeuchi, and John Kyle Dorton (2008). *Extreme Toyota: Radical Contradictions That Drive Success at the World's Best Manufacturer*. Hoboken: John Wiley & Sons.

Packer, Frank (2000). "The Disposal of Bad Loans in Japan: The Case of the CCPC." In *Crisis and Change in the Japanese Financial System*. Edited by Takeo Hoshi and Hugh Patrick. Boston: Kluwer Academic, 137–157.

Pastor Robert (1980). *Congress and the Politics of U.S. Foreign Economic Policy, 1929-1976*. Berkeley University of California Press

Patrick, Hugh (1999). "Japan's Financial Reform." Asia Pacific Economic Papers 288.

Peek, Joe and Eric S. Rosengren (2005). "Unnatural Selection: Perverse Incentives and the Misallocation of Credit in Japan." *American Economic Review* **95**(4): 1144–1166.

Peng, Xizhe (1987). "Demographic Consequences of the Great Leap Forward in China's Provinces." *Population and Development Review* **13**(4): 639–670.

Perkins, Edwin J. (1983). "Langdon Cheves and the Panic of 1819: A Reassessment." *Journal of Economic History* **44**(2): 455–461.

Pick, Albert (1977). *Standard Catalog of World Paper Money*. Iola, WI: Krause Publications.

Polybius (1922). *The Histories*. New York: G.P. Putnam's Sons.

Porter, Eduardo (2004). "On Presidential Politics, the Fed Walks a Tight Rope." *New York Times*. January 28, 2004, p. C1.

Price, Jacob M. (1965). "Discussion of Thomas and Land Papers." *Journal of Economic History* **25**(4): 655–659.

Rajan, Raghuram. (2005). "Financial Markets, Financial Fragility, and Central Banking." *Jackson Hole Symposium*, Federal Reserve Bank of Kansas City. http://www.kansascityfed.org/publicat/sympos/2005/pdf/Rajan2005.pdf.

Ransom, Roger L. (1968). "British Policy and Colonial Growth: Some Implications of the Burden from the Navigation Acts." *Journal of Economic History* **28**(3): 427–435.

Redish, Angela (1990). "The Evolution of the Gold Standard in England." *Journal of Economic History* **50**(4): 789–805.

Redish, Angela (2000). *Bimetallism: An Economic and Historical Analysis*. Cambridge and New York: Cambridge University Press.

Reid, Joseph D., Jr. (1970). "On Navigating the Navigation Acts with Peter D. McClelland: Comment." *American Economic Review* **60**(5): 949–955.

Reid, Joseph D. Jr. (1978). "Economic Burden: Spark to the American Revolution?" *Journal of Economic History* **38**(1): 81–100.

Reid, T.R. and James L. Stanfield (1997). "The World According to Rome." *National Geographic* **192** (2): 54–83.

Rickard, Sean (2000). "The CAP: Whence It Came, Where It Should Go." *Economic Affairs* **20**(2): 27.

Ritschl, Albrecht (1996). "Sustainability of High Public Debt: What the Historical Record Shows." CEPR Discussion Paper 1357.

Robertson, D. H. (1926). "A Narrative of the General Strike of 1926." *Economic Journal* **36**(143): 375–393.

Rockoff, Hugh (1985). "New Evidence on Free Banking in the United States." *American Economic Review* **75**(4): 886–889.

Rockoff, Hugh (1990). "The 'Wizard of Oz' as a Monetary Allegory." *Journal of Political Economy* **98**(4): 739–760.

Rolnick, Arthur J. and Warren E. Weber (1983). "New Evidence on the Free Banking Era." *American Economic Review* **73**(5): 1080–1091.

Roubini, Nouriel (2012). "Greece Must Go." *Slate.com*, May 18, 2012. http://www.slate.com/articles/news_and_politics/politics/2012/05/greece_will_leave_the_eurozone_sooner_or_later_sooner_is_better_.html. Retrieved October 28, 2012.

Rosenstein-Rodan, P. N. (1945). "How Much Can Germany Pay?" *International Affairs (Royal Institute of International Affairs 1944-)* **21**(4): 469–476.

Sargent, Thomas J. (1982). "The Ends of Four Big Inflations." In *Inflation: Causes and Effects*. Edited by Robert E. Hall. Chicago: University of Chicago Press, 41–98.

Sarkees, Meredith Reid (2000). "The Correlates of War Data on War: An Update to 1997." *Conflict Management and Peace Science* **18**(1): 123–144.

Sarkees, Meredith Reid, and Frank Wayman (2010). *Resort to War: 1816-2007*. Washington, DC: CQ Press.

Sawers, Larry (1992). "The Navigation Acts Revisited." *Economic History Review* **45**(2): 262–284.

Schacht, Hjalmar (1931). *The End of Reparations*. New York: Jonathan Cape & Harrison Smith.

Schattschneider, E. E. (1935). *Politics, Pressures and the Tariff; A Study of Free Private Enterprise in Pressure Politics, as Shown in the 1929-1930 Revision of the Tariff*. New York: Prentice-Hall.

Schmoller, Gustav (1897). *The Mercantile System and its Historical Significance (1884)*. New York: Macmillan.

Schonhardt-Bailey, Cheryl, ed. (1996). *Free Trade: The Repeal of the Corn Laws*. Bristol, England: Thoemmes Press.

Schonhardt-Bailey, Cheryl (2006). *From the Corn Laws to Free Trade: Interests, Ideas, and Institutions in Historical Perspective*. Cambridge, MA: MIT Press.

Schubert, Aurel (1991). *The Credit-Anstalt Crisis of 1931*. Cambridge: Cambridge University Press.

Schuker, Stephen A. (1988). *American "Reparations" to Germany, 1919-33: Implications for the Third-World Debt Crisis*. Princeton, NJ: International Finance Section, Princeton University.

Schularick, Moritz and Alan M. Taylor (2012). "Credit Booms Gone Bust: Monetary Policy, Leverage Cycles, and Financial Crises, 1870-2008." *American Economic Review* **102**(2): 1029–1061.

Schweikart, Larry (1991). "U.S. Commercial Banking: A Historiographical Survey." *Business History Review* **65**(3): 606–661.

Scott, H. S. (1998). "When the Euro Falls Apart." *International Finance* **1**(2): 207–228.

Sharp, Alan (2008). *The Versailles Settlement: Peacemaking after the First World War, 1919-1923*. New York: Palgrave Macmillan.

Silverman, Dan P. (1982). *Reconstructing Europe after the Great War*. Cambridge, MA: Harvard University Press.

Skidelsky, Robert (1986). *John Maynard Keynes: Hopes Betrayed, 1883-1920*. New York: Viking.

Sprague, O. M. W. (1910). *History of Crises under the National Banking System*. Washington, DC: Government Printing Office.

Stanwood, Edward (1903). *American Tariff Controversies in the Nineteenth Century*. Boston: Houghton, Mifflin.

Stockton, David (2012). *Review of the Monetary Policy Committee's Forecasting Capability*. Report to the Court of Directors of the Bank of England, October 2012. http://www.bankofengland.co.uk/pub-lifcations/Documents/news/2012/cr3stockton.pdf.   Retrieved November 21, 2012.

Stowell, Ellery C. (1930). "Tariff Relations with France." *American Journal of International Law* **24**(1): 110–118.

Sussman, Nathan (1993). "Debasements, Royal Revenues, and Inflation in France during the Hundred Years' War, 1415-1422." *Journal of Economic History* **53**(1): 44–70.

Sylla, Richard (2011). "Financial Foundations: Public Credit, the National Bank, and Securities Markets." In *Founding Choices: American Economic Policy in the 1790s*. Edited by Douglas A. Irwin and Richard Sylla. Chicago: University of Chicago Press, 59–88.

Taussig, F. W. (1931 [1966]). *The Tariff History of the United States*. New York: Johnson Reprint Corp.

Taylor, John (2007). "Housing and Monetary Policy." Paper presented for Policy Panel at the Symposium on Housing, Housing Finance, and Monetary Policy sponsored by the Federal Reserve Bank of Kansas City in Jackson Hole, Wyoming. http://www.stanford.edu/~johntayl/Housing%20and%20Monetary%20Policy--Taylor--Jackson%20Hole%202007.pdf.

Taylor, John (2008). "The Financial Crisis and the Policy Responses: An Empirical Analysis of What Went Wrong." Bank of Canada Festschrift in Honour of David Dodge. http://www.stanford.edu/~johntayl/FCPR.pdf.

Taylor, John (2009). "How Government Created the Financial Crisis." *Wall Street Journal.* February 9, 2009, p. A19.

Temin, Peter (1968). "The Economic Consequences of the Bank War." *Journal of Political Economy* **76**(2): 257–274.

Teranishi, Juro (1994). "Japan: Development and Structural Change of the Financial System." In *The Financial Development of Japan, Korea, and Taiwan.* Edited by Hugh T. Patrick and Yung Chul Park. New York and Oxford: Oxford University Press, 27–80.

Tett, Gillian (2012). "A Finnish Parallel Currency Is Imaginable." *Financial Times*, October 26, 2012. http://www.ft.com/intl/cms/s/0/14 cbb94e-1ebb-11e2-b906-00144feabdc0.html#axzz2AGnfii5n.

Tett, Gillian (2009). *Fool's Gold.* New York: Free Press.

Thomas, Robert Paul (1965). "A Quantitative Approach to the Study of the Effects of British Imperial Policy upon Colonial Welfare: Some Preliminary Findings." *Journal of Economic History* **25**(4): 615–638.

Thomas, Robert Paul (1968). "British Imperial Policy and the Economic Interpretation of the American Revolution." *Journal of Economic History* **28**(3): 436–440.

Thomas, Samuel Evelyn (1934). *The Rise and Growth of Joint Stock Banking.* London: Sir I. Pitman and Sons, Ltd.

Timberlake, Richard H. (1978). *The Origins of Central Banking in the United States.* Cambridge, MA: Harvard University Press.

Trachtenberg, Marc (1980). *Reparation in World Politics: France and European Economic Diplomacy, 1916-1923.* New York: Columbia University Press.

Trevelyan, Charles E. (1848). *The Irish Crisis.* London: Longman, Brown, Green & Longmans.

Trouton, R. (1921). "Cancellation of Inter-Allied Debts." *Economic Journal* **31**(121): 38–45.

Tryon, James L. (1911). "The Rise of the Peace Movement." *Yale Law Journal* **20**(5): 358–371.

Turner, Adair (2010). "Economics, Conventional Wisdom and Public Policy." Institute for New Economic Thinking Inaugural Conference, April 2010. http://ineteconomics.org/sites/inet.civicactions.net/ files/INET%20Turner%20%20Cambridge%2020100409_0.pdf. Retrieved November 21, 2012.

Ueda, Kazuo (2000). "Causes of Japan's Banking Problems in the 1990s." In *Crisis and Change in the Japanese Financial System.* Edited by Takeo Hoshi and Hugh Patrick. Boston, Dordrecht, and London: Kluwer, 59–81.

United Kingdom. Committee on Currency and Foreign Exchanges after the War [Cunliffe Committee] (1918). *First Interim Report*. London: HMSO. Cd. 9182.

United Kingdom. Committee on Currency and Foreign Exchanges after the War [Cunliffe Committee] (1919). *Final Report*. London: HMSO. Cmd. 464.

United Kingdom. Committee on the Currency and Bank of England Note Issues [Chamberlain-Bradbury Committee] (1925). *Report*. London: HMSO. Cmd. 2393.

United States. Bureau of Labor Statistics (2008). "International Comparisons of Annual Labor Force Statistics, 10 Countries, 1960-2007." http://iwsdninternational.blogspot.com/2008/10/iws-bls-international-comparison-of.html.

Urwin, Derek W. (1991). *The Community of Europe: A History of European Integration since 1945*. London and New York: Longman.

Van Tyne, Calude H. (1951). *The Causes of the War of Independence*. New York: Peter Smith.

Vogel, Steven K. (1996). *Freer Markets, More Rules: Regulatory Reform in Advanced Industrial Countries*. Ithaca: Cornell University Press.

von Glahn, Richard (1996). "Myth and Reality of China's Seventeenth-Century Monetary Crisis." *Journal of Economic History* **56**(2): 429–454.

Walton, Gary M. (1971). "The New Economic History and the Burdens of the Navigation Acts." *Economic History Review* **24**(4): 533–542.

Walton, Gary M. (1973). "The Burdens of the Navigation Acts: A Reply." *Economic History Review* **26**(4): 687–688.

Warburg, Paul M. (1930). *The Federal Reserve System: Its Origin and Growth*. New York: Macmillan.

Webb, Steven B. (1989). *Hyperinflation and Stabilization in Weimar Germany*. New York: Oxford University Press.

Weigall, David and Peter Stirk (1992). *The Origins and Development of the European Community*. Leicester: Leicester University Press.

Wells, David A. (1900). *The Theory and Practice of Taxation*. New York: D. Appleton and Company.

Whaples, Robert (1995). "Where Is There Consensus among American Economic Historians? The Results of a Survey on Forty Propositions." *Journal of Economic History* **55**(1): 139–154.

Whaples, Robert (2006). "Do Economists Agree on Anything? Yes!" *The Economists' Voice* **3**(9): 1–6.

White, Eugene N. (2001). "Making the French Pay: The Costs and Consequences of the Napoleonic Reparations." *European Review of Economic History* 5(3): 337–365.

Williamson, Jeffrey G. (2006). "Explaining World Tariffs 1870-1938: Stolper-Samuelson, Strategic Tariffs and State Revenues." In *Eli F. Heckscher, International Trade, and Economicv History*. Edited by R. Findlay, R. Henriksson, H. Lindgren, and M. Lundahl. Cambridge, MA: MIT Press, 199–228.

Winters, Bill (2012). "Review of the Bank of England's Framework for Providing Liquidity to the Banking System." Report to the Court of Directors of the Bank of England, October 2012. http://www.bankofengland.co.uk/publications/Documents/news/2012/cr2winters.pdf. Retrieved November 21, 2012.

Woodham-Smith, Cecil (1962). *The Great Hunger: Ireland 1845-1849*. New York: Harper & Row.

World Trade Organization. (2012). "Report to the Trade Policy Review Body from the Director-General on Trade-Related Developments." Released June 29, 2012. http://www.wto.org/english/news_e/news12_e/fullreport.doc. Retrieved November 16, 2012.

Wyplosz, Charles (2006). "European Monetary Union: The Dark Sides of a Major Success." *Economic Policy* 21(46): 207–261.

Yeager, Leland B. (1966). *International Monetary Relations: Theory, History, and Policy*. New York: Harper and Row.

Yoder, Amos (1955). "The Ruhr Authority and the German Problem." *Review of Politics* 17(3): 345–358.

Youngson, A. J. (1960). *The British Economy, 1920-1957*. London: George Allen & Unwin.

INDEX